MONOPOLY AND COMPETITION
IN BANKING

The author is Assistant Professor of Business Administration at the University of California, Berke-
ey.

Publications of the
Bureau of Business and Economic Research
University of California

MONOPOLY AND COMPETITION IN BANKING

BY

DAVID A. ALHADEFF

UNIVERSITY OF CALIFORNIA PRESS

BERKELEY AND LOS ANGELES

1954

UNIVERSITY OF CALIFORNIA PRESS

BERKELEY AND LOS ANGELES

◇

CAMBRIDGE UNIVERSITY PRESS

LONDON, ENGLAND

PRINTED IN THE UNITED STATES OF AMERICA
BY THE UNIVERSITY OF CALIFORNIA PRINTING DEPARTMENT

Preface

THE MAIN PURPOSE *of this study is to examine existing banking markets from a market structure viewpoint and to observe how (or whether) banking markets and banking structures have been affected by banking concentration in the form of giant branch banks. Such an analysis is a necessary prelude to an examination of the implications of banking concentration for the monopoly problem. The major emphasis in this study is upon banking concentration in the form of branch banking. Where it has been permitted by law, branch banking has been the most obvious vehicle for concentrating banking resources over a wide geographical area. Because branch banking has grown more rapidly in California than in any other part of the country, the analysis of branch-bank concentration in this study is based upon the California experience. With minor modifications, both the analysis and the conclusions are capable of general application in this country wherever banking concentration develops under a branch organization of banking.*

This study is, I believe, unique both in its approach and in its content, since it represents an attempt to analyze the operations and economic implications of branch banking with the analytical tools developed in the field of industrial organization as well as those of general economic theory, and to base the analysis as far as possible on the statistical record. Earlier studies of branch banking have been primarily institutional in orientation and descriptive in content, and most of the published works on the subject are at least twenty years old, and many of them, much older. Much has obviously happened in this field during that long period. Furthermore, many of the analytical tools employed in this study have only been developed by students of industrial organization during the last twenty years. Since existing studies of branch banking deal adequately with the formal organization and structure of branch banks, this information will not be repeated here.

Part of the analysis, especially the chapter, "Pricing Practices and Price Policy," is based on interviews with senior loan officers of the major branch systems in California. It is natural that those involved in the day-to-day operations of a bank should take a highly particularized view of their operations and tend to put great stress on the wide diversity of their dealings. By contrast, my own approach has inclined in the opposite direction. Without any wish to neglect the diversity of conditions surrounding individual loans, the purpose of this study has constantly impelled me to seek common denominators in diversified operations. It is in the nature of a theoretical pattern to abstract from the diversities and complexities of real world situations, since the essence of economic theory is to spotlight the important variables and to show their interrelation. A theoretical analysis is not intended to be a mere mirror image of the situation it tries to explain. Analytical structures sometimes tend to be either completely rarefied or hopelessly involved. The useful theory must maximize the heuristic simplicity of the former condition while maintaining maximum contact with the microvariables of the system. In concentrating, therefore, on what have seemed to me to be the key variables in the banking picture, e.g., size of borrower, I do not mean to deny the importance of other relevant considerations. Under ordinary conditions, however, certain variables are usually more important than others in explaining basic patterns of action. A few key variables are critical in initially discerning the basic outlines of structure and behavior in banking markets. Once the basic outline has been developed, however, the skeletal structure of the analysis can be padded with numerous secondary considerations in order to approximate more closely the detail and complexity of real world structures.

Probably no sector of the economy is more heavily and exhaustively documented statistically than is banking. The novelty claimed for the statistical base of this study applies less to the raw data, which are generally readily available, than to their incorporation in a systematic framework of market analysis. To a great extent, however, this study is possible because operating ratios for branch banks have been made available for the first time. Unfortunately much critical information on bank operations is still not available, e.g., time series of interest rates for different size loans in individual banks in small towns. It is hoped that this study will stimulate much needed further research into the subject of the market performance of branch and unit banks.

The analysis of branch bank performance has been made possible by the coöperation of executive officers in the major branch banks of California. By their kind permission, I was permitted to examine operating ratios for individual branch banks. Although these figures must remain confidential, they form the basis for comparisons among individual branch banks and between branch banks and unit banks. Moreover, for every ratio employed, an average figure for branch banks as a group has been included in the tables. I am indebted, too, to Oliver P. Wheeler, Vice-President, and Gault Lynn, Supervisor of Research, Federal Reserve Bank of San Francisco, for their assistance in securing individual bank ratios and for compiling additional special figures from Federal Reserve records.

Permission has been kindly granted by the publishers to reproduce here material that first appeared in journals. Chapter iii is the major part of an article that first appeared in the Quarterly Journal of Economics, February, 1951, under the title, "The Market Structure of Commercial Banking in the United States." Chapter viii is largely based on an article that was published in the American Economic Review, June, 1952, under the title, "Monetary Policy and the Treasury Bill Market."

I am indebted, too, to my colleagues who read this manuscript and offered helpful suggestions. The manuscript was read by Professors W. L. Crum, H. S. Ellis, R. A. Gordon, and R. W. Jastram of the Departments of Economics and Business Administration, University of California, Berkeley. I am also grateful for the financial and clerical assistance provided by the Bureau of Business and Economic Research, University of California, Berkeley, and for the helpful coöperation of its Director, Professor F. V. Kidner.

My greatest debt is to my wife, Charlotte P. Alhadeff, for her invaluable help and advice at every stage. For whatever errors and inadequacies remain, I am alone responsible.

D. A. Alhadeff

January, 1954

Contents

I

Introduction

THE EVOLUTION of American banking has witnessed a long struggle between those convinced that "money will not manage itself" and those imbued with a strong determination to avoid the necessary management under the aegis of a monetary monopoly, even a government monopoly. Students of banking history seem agreed that the failure of the premature attempt to establish a central bank in this country, especially the Second Bank of the United States, was in large measure owing to partisan politics of the period. Inextricably involved in the event, however, was the considerable popular support for Jackson's antipathy to monopoly in any form, especially to a monetary monopoly, even if the "monopoly" was under government sponsorship and control and was demonstrably beneficial in the financial and economic affairs of the period.

The Free Banking Act of the State of New York (1838) was intended to democratize commercial banking, and its strong bias against monopoly and favored parties made it a model for many other states. The unhappy result under Free Banking statutes was an increase in bankruptcies and an era of wild speculation in which banking was regarded less as a public trust than as a quick and easy way to personal enrichment. The efforts of the Congress to rescue the economy from this chaotic situation by passing the National Banking Act in 1864 was a classic example of "too little and too late."

The pressures for responsible management of the money supply culminated in the passage of the Federal Reserve Act of 1913, but the underlying fear of monopoly reflected itself even in this Act which established a central bank. The central bank itself was broken into twelve regional banks,[1] and the tradition of inviolability of a dual banking structure was firmly established by the

---

[1] Other considerations not related to the monopoly issue were also involved in this decision.

stipulation that, except for national banks,[2] membership in the Federal Reserve System would be voluntary. In other ways, too, the original Reserve Act was one of limited scope. Subsequent crises, such as the Great Depression, have led to a strengthening of the central bank's control powers;[3] partly, too, these powers have grown by administrative interpretation of existing authority.

The issues of banking concentration and monopoly have once again been brought to the forefront of public discussion through the deliberations of congressional committees and the antitrust action by the Board of Governors of the Federal Reserve System against the Transamerica Corporation. In a staff report of the House Judiciary Committee of the 82d Congress on the subject of "Bank Mergers and Concentration of Banking Facilities,"[4] attention was directed to the historical increase in concentration of banking facilities. This "unrelenting trend towards mergers" is deplored in the Committee's report because, "This depletion of the ranks of the country's banks has lessened competition among banks in many communities."[5] The authors of the report recommended remedial legislation to ensure that governmental banking authorities, before approving any sort of bank merger or consolidation, "would be obliged to determine whether the effect of such merger might unduly lessen competition or tend to create a monopoly in the field of banking."[6] The problem of bank concentration is an urgent one, because, in the words of the report, "Concentration of financial resources and credit facilities are even more ominous to a competitive economy than concentration on an industry-wide basis."[7]

A similar concern about monopoly power has motivated the Federal Reserve Board in its recent suit against the Transamerica Corporation, alleging violation of the Clayton Act.[8] In large measure, the suit against Transamerica is a suit against Bank of America, since most of the assets of the former were, until very recently,

---

[2] National banks can easily shift from federal to state charters.

[3] Cf. John H. Williams' analysis of the Banking Act of 1935 in his *Postwar Monetary Plans and Other Essays* (2d ed., revised; New York: Alfred A. Knopf, 1945), pp. 112–129.

[4] *Bank Mergers and Concentration of Banking Facilities,* a staff report to Subcommittee No. 5 of the Committee on the Judiciary, H.R. 82d Cong., 2d sess. (1952).

[5] *Ibid.,* p. 46.

[6] *Ibid.,* appendix.

[7] *Ibid.,* p. viii.

[8] The Transamerica Corporation was charged, on June 24, 1948, with violation of Sec. 7 of the Clayton Act by acquiring controlling stock interest in various independent banks. At the time of such acquisition, these banks were in competition with one or more of the banks already controlled by the Transamerica Corporation.

those of the latter.[9] Indeed, the Board's counsel has repeatedly stated that, unless Bank of America is included in Transamerica, the Board's case against Transamerica on the basis of tendency to monopoly would probably collapse.[10]

The Transamerica case is not of direct concern in this study. The case does serve, however, to throw the spotlight of national attention upon the problems of banking concentration in one of the largest and economically most important states in the country. Under laws tolerant of branch banking, California has achieved probably a higher degree of state-wide concentration of banking assets than any other state in the Union. With few exceptions, branch banking is the vehicle par excellence for the development of the truly impressive kind of bank concentration such as is found in California. The four large branch bank systems in California are among the nation's largest banks. One of these banks is the largest bank in the country; two are among the nation's ten largest banks. California provides, therefore, an excellent case study of branch banking, bank concentration, and monopoly.

A study of banking and monopoly should clarify at least two critical questions. First, what is the meaning and nature of monopoly as applied to banking? As a corollary, what does it mean to "unduly lessen competition"? Second, what are the consequences of power, actual or potential, in concentrated banking markets? In an economic approach, it is not sufficient to demonstrate merely that monopoly power exists.[11] The history of industrial monopoly suits amply suggests that public policy is concerned not alone with power but with the manner in which power is used.[12]

Monopoly power and the consequences of monopoly are widely held to be inimical to the public interest. The concept of the public interest is a complex phenomenon, heavily weighted with normative elements. It is sufficient for this study to recognize that decisions affecting the public interest in economic affairs are rarely

---

[9] During the course of the proceedings, Transamerica Corporation sold all its stock holdings in Bank of America. Notwithstanding, the Board of Governors announced their intention to continue their lawsuit against Transamerica. Cf. *San Francisco Chronicle*, January 15, 1953, financial page.

[10] Statement by Leonard J. Townsend, Solicitor for the Board of Governors, Federal Reserve System, in *Hearings* before Governor R. M. Evans of the Federal Reserve, in the Matter of Transamerica Corporation, 8385. (Hereinafter, these hearings will be abbreviated Transamerica Hearings.)

[11] In the Transamerica Hearings, the Solicitor for the Board did not contend that Transamerica had necessarily abused its power but ". . . that they have the power to do that (i.e., control their banks' loans, etc.), and *power alone is the evil against which the statute is aimed.*" *Reply Brief of Counsel for the Board*, November 9, 1951, p. 32. (Italics mine.)

[12] Cf., for example, the titanium lead antitrust case.

made on the basis of economic considerations alone. This study is concerned with analytical clarification, not policy prescription. Although policy recommendations are not explicitly introduced, it is hoped that the results of this study will be of use in policy formulation by authorized bodies. Accordingly, the final chapter applies the analysis developed in this study to an examination of some of the economic features of monopoly power which are usually considered in official decisions concerning monopoly. Monopoly is held to be injurious to the consumer (borrower), because monopolized industries are alleged to extort high profits by restricting output, charging high prices, and exercising discriminatory powers among their customers. Both the House Judiciary Committee and the Board of Governors (in the Transamerica suit) have implicitly accepted the monopoly indictment as it applies to banking. It is the purpose of this study to develop the economic analysis necessary for an appraisal of this indictment.

CONCEPTUAL AND TERMINOLOGICAL MODIFICATIONS

The concept of industrial monopoly is not simple. Moreover, in applying this concept to banking, further complications arise. Generally, the service aspects of banking are stressed rather than its points of similarity with (say) a manufacturing industry. In this study, however, the banking business is examined after the fashion of a manufacturing industry. Bankers are businessmen, and like other businessmen, they are concerned with the problems of "producing" and "marketing" their "product." This study attempts to examine those functions by analytical techniques analogous to those employed in industry studies. However, certain conceptual and terminological modifications in the conventional views of an industry and of money are required. The kind of modifications which are necessary can be conveniently discussed by considering briefly a few points of comparison and of contrast between industrial markets and banking markets.

The products of industrial markets are economic goods; these goods can be used either for direct consumption or for further production. By contrast, the product of money markets (credit) is not an economic good; no one "buys" credit in order to consume it directly nor to employ it directly in the production of other goods. When a businessman buys credit (negotiates a loan), he is securing capital funds with generalized purchasing power, not direct goods.[13] Of course, credit has aspects other than its purchas-

---

[13] In a sense, of course, purchasing power inheres in all economic goods. This characteristic of goods is manifest in the case of simple barter in which one article

ing power. Conventional analysis directs attention to money as a store of value, as a medium of exchange, as a standard of value, and so on. But when we refer to money as an item of purchase and sale, common experience suggests that the buyers are not concerned with these other aspects of money, but rather with its ability to command goods and services, i.e., its power to purchase. Accordingly, the rate of interest is the price paid for money as the most generalized form of purchasing power,[14] and a banker may be regarded as a "merchant of credit."

Money markets and commodity markets can be compared in another way. In the market for commodities, goods are sold either on a cash or on a credit basis. In the particular money market in question (the customer loan market), money is not sold on a cash basis. In the case of a loan, this is clearly true. The sale takes place on D-1, and payment is not made until (say) D-90. The customer loan market for short-term business funds is of necessity a *market through time.*[15] This fundamental fact is obscured but not changed in the case of discounts. When a bank sells credit on a discount basis, the money passes from banker to borrower, and the borrower's note is given in exchange. The transaction is not completed, however, until the buyer on D-90 pays the seller (bank) the discounted principal plus the interest.

A third comparison between a commodity market and a money market is a corollary of identifying the money market as a market through time. When the ordinary producer of goods is in a position to negotiate a sale, the problem of securing payment for his goods (terms of sale) can be met in one of three ways. He can sell on a credit basis, in which case the seller meets the risk of default by the buyer by prior investigation of the buyer's character, gen-

---

has in effect the purchasing power to command other goods in exchange. However, the element of purchasing power that inheres in economic goods is just one of their delimiting characteristics: this purchasing power aspect is not the essence of their nature. Their nature is essentially defined pragmatically, i.e., why people want goods. As indicated above, goods are usually desired either for consumption or for productive purposes.

[14] Cf. Joseph A. Schumpeter, *The Theory of Economic Development* (Cambridge: Harvard University Press, 1936), p. 184.

[15] Schumpeter, for example, has stated that "Every individual loan transaction is a real exchange. At first it seems strange, perhaps, that a commodity is as it were exchanged for itself . . . [but] *the exchange of present for future is no more an exchange of like for like,* and therefore meaningless, than the exchange of something in one place for something in another place. Just as purchasing power in one place may be exchanged for that in another, *so present can also be exchanged for future purchasing power.* The analogy between loan transactions and exchange arbitrage is obvious, and may be recommended to the reader's attention." *Ibid.,* pp. 187–188. (Italics mine.)

eral financial capacity, and general credit rating.[16] If the prospective buyer cannot adequately meet these three tests, the seller can insist that the sale be on a cash basis, thereby completely eliminating the risk of default by the buyer. If, finally, the prospective buyer cannot satisfy the three tests, and is either unwilling or unable to buy on a cash basis, the seller can refuse to sell.

Since the banker sells present purchasing power and is subsequently paid with future purchasing power, the banker does not have the option of selling on a cash basis. He must sell on a credit basis to sell at all. Like the businessman, the banker also wishes to insure himself against risk of default by the buyer (borrower). Thus, he, too, subjects his prospective buyer to a credit examination along the lines of examining his character, general capacity to pay, and general credit rating. If these tests are satisfactorily met, the sale is made, so to speak, on an "open book" account.[17]

If, however, the prospective buyer cannot pass the three credit tests, the customs of his trade suggest another option to the banker. He can secure against risk of default by demanding collateral as security for payment. If the collateral does not adequately cover the risk of default, the remaining risk can be covered by raising the price of credit, i.e., raising the interest rate. Finally, if the prospective buyer is considered an unworthy risk on all counts, the banker can refuse to sell, i.e., deny the loan on any terms.

A fourth comparison between a money market and a commodity market concerns the costs of production and their relation to the price of the product. In many industries, the price of the product is computed by adding either a fixed sum or a fixed percentage to the average variable cost of production. This fixed sum or fixed percentage is the markup and includes an allowance for overhead costs. Net profit per unit is thus the difference between the price of the product and the average cost of production.

In like manner, bankers must purchase their most important "raw materials" in the form of deposits. They pay for the use of these deposits either directly or indirectly.[18] In addition to their raw materials, bankers are also concerned with labor costs which are the most important category of variable costs. The interest rate

---

[16] These tests are similar to the bankers' famous three C's: character, capacity, credit.

[17] This is the so-called "unsecured loan."

[18] On time deposits, interest is paid by the bank to the depositor. On demand deposits, the Federal Reserve prohibits interest payments by member banks. However, banks in effect pay for the use of demand deposits by deducting from the service charges on a checking account an amount that varies with the average size of the demand deposit during the month.

(which may also include a risk factor) in effect includes a markup on costs, and net profits are the difference between total revenues and total costs.

One complication worth discussing concerns the alleged "creation" of money by bankers. It used to be claimed that bankers could create money by the simple device of opening deposit accounts for their business borrowers. It has since been amply demonstrated that under a fractional reserve system, only the totality of banks can expand deposits to the full reciprocal of the reserve ratio.[19] The individual bank can normally expand to an amount about equal to its primary deposits. In certain cases, the proportion between the legal reserve ratio and residual deposits is such that even a single bank can expand its deposits to a somewhat greater amount than its primary deposits.[20]

Again, it might be possible for a very large bank, or a bank in an isolated community with few business connections with outside banks, literally to create money because of flow-back deposits.[21] In either case, this amounts to a partial reduction in the average cost of producing credit (making loans), at least in terms of the raw material costs. The banker then has the option, as would any businessman in a similar position, of maintaining his markup and thereby increasing his profits, or of passing on the reduction in his costs in the form of lower prices for his product (customer loan credit).

Enough has probably been said in these comparisons of money markets and industrial markets to indicate the kind of conceptual and terminological modifications which are necessary to apply the market structure analysis of product markets to money markets. The subsequent analysis will use both the terminology and concepts current in banking as well as those derived by analogy from product markets. The choice in each case will depend on which expression serves better to develop and to clarify a point.

---

[19] Cf. Chester A. Phillips, *Bank Credit* (New York: Macmillan, 1921), chapter 3, for the classical refutation of this claim.

[20] An example would be a legal reserve ratio of 10 per cent and a retained deposit ratio of 20 per cent. Under these assumptions, a primary deposit of $1,000 could be expanded to almost $1,100 according to the formula

$$X = \frac{C}{kr + 1 - k}$$

in which x is the total possible expansion, r is the legal reserve ratio, k is the retained deposit ratio, and C equals $1 - r$.

[21] Flow-back deposits refer to the circulation of deposits among the depositors of the same bank.

II

Defining the Market

To ESTABLISH the existence of monopoly, two approaches are suggested by economic theory. In examining market structures, Edward H. Chamberlin[1] concentrates on the number of sellers of a technologically identical product. If product differentiation is involved, an arbitrary line, usually acceptable on a common sense basis, sufficiently defines the "industry" for purposes of further analysis. By contrast with Chamberlin, Robert Triffin rejects the notion of an industry and concentrates on the individual firm, which is defined as the "frontier of the maximizing unit."[2] The collapse of the industry concept in Triffin's analysis follows from his attention to substitute products. In Triffin's analysis of market behavior, competition in terms of substitute products supersedes the narrower concept of competition in terms of technologically similar products. Chamberlin, following the Marshallian tradition, concentrates on the problems of partial equilibrium analysis, whereas Triffin, perhaps more influenced by Walras, deals in a framework of general equilibrium analysis. Despite the merits of Triffin's approach, economists engaged in empirical investigation have usually followed the Chamberlin approach, although including the influence of substitute products through obiter dicta. Even when the limitations of the partial equilibrium analysis are admitted, the alternative approach in terms of cross-elasticities of demand for all possible substitutes often presents extraordinary complications in a case study. This study attempts to combine both approaches, being primarily in the Chamberlinian tradition but including also extended references to substitute products.

[1] Edward H. Chamberlin, *The Theory of Monopolistic Competition* (5th ed.; Cambridge: Harvard University Press, 1945).
[2] Cf. Robert Triffin, *Monopolistic Competition and General Equilibrium Theory* (Cambridge: Harvard University Press, 1941).

[8]

ROLE OF COMMERCIAL BANKS

The definition of a market in Chamberlinian terms requires an earlier identification of the industry product.[3] All banks, depending on their size, are more or less multiproduct firms. In fact, textbook writers have characterized the modern bank as a "department store of finance." However, not all bank products are equally important in a market structure study. In this study, the most important product of a commercial bank *qua* commercial bank is defined by the role of the commercial banking system in a private enterprise economy. Neither economic history nor economic theory can unaided resolve this point, since the social purpose of an institution inevitably involves value judgments as to what the role should be. Both history and theory are suggestive, however.

Schumpeter has characterized credit as:

essentially the creation of purchasing power for the purpose of transferring it to the entrepreneur, but not simply the transfer of existing purchasing power. The creation of purchasing power characterises, in principle, the method by which development is carried out in a system with private property and division of labor. By credit, entrepreneurs are given access to the social stream of goods before they have acquired the normal claim to it. . . . And *this function constitutes the keystone of the modern credit structure.*[4]

In the Schumpeterian system, credit is the bankers' stock in trade, and the chief role of the commercial banking system is resource allocation through the process of credit creation.[5] Credit creation,

---

[3] In the Transamerica case, counsel for the Board of Governors largely avoided this problem (although it was touched upon) through his procedure of identifying illegal monopoly by simply adding such magnitudes as resources, loans, deposits, and the like, within the political boundaries of a five-state area. He then observed that the defendant banks' share of this total was large (about 40 per cent) and has been growing historically. Since the solicitor's case was based on purely legal grounds, he contended that his case did not require attention to the possibility of substitutes. There is, of course, no necessary economic significance to the political boundaries with which the case was concerned. Except that the solicitor was clearly aware of this fact, his procedure would be a perfect example of the danger of adding figures without theory.

[4] Joseph A. Schumpeter, *The Theory of Economic Development* (Cambridge: Harvard University Press, 1936), p. 107. (Italics mine.)

[5] Schumpeter's analysis actually deals with long-term credit, but as Schumpeter said, "It would be wholly wrong to believe that the price of short-term credits is a matter of indifference for new undertakings since it is long-term credit that they want." *Ibid.*, pp. 125–126. Investment bankers characteristically derive most of their funds from commercial banks in the form of *short-term* loans. This debt is then funded by the sale of securities. Furthermore, the purchase of new security issues by speculators is usually based on short-term collateral loans from banks. In effect, therefore, banks lend on short-term to businessmen via investment bankers and via speculators and brokers. On a similar point, the Chairman of the Board of Governors,

in turn, results from the monetization of private debt. If the concept of credit is expanded to include capital maintenance as well as net new investment, the characteristic function of the banking system is the provision of business loans.

Historically, too, the main concern of banks in this country was the granting of business loans, originally through the issue of notes

TABLE 1

MEMBER BANK LOANS AND INVESTMENTS, AS OF DECEMBER 31, 1951 [a]

		Amount in dollars (000,000)	Per cent of loans	Per cent of total loans and investments
A. Loans (gross) [b]		51,282	100.0 [c]	45.0
Loans	Commercial (including open market paper)	24,347	47.5	21.4
	Agricultural	2,140	4.2	1.9
	Loans for purchasing or carrying securities	2,402	4.9	2.2
	Real estate loans	11,334	22.1	9.9
	Consumer loans	10,059	19.6	8.9
B. Investments		62,687	100.0 [c]	55.0
Investments	United States government obligations (direct and guaranteed)	51,621	82.3	45.3
	Obligations of states and political subdivisions	7,528	12.0	6.6
	Other securities	3,538	5.6	3.1

[a] SOURCE: Federal Reserve Bulletin, March 1953, p. 254.
[b] Gross loans were derived by adding the individual loan components. Loans net of valuation reserves amounted to $49,561,000,000.
[c] Totals do not add to 100 per cent because of rounding.

rather than deposit accounts. The shift in commercial bank portfolios from a primary emphasis on business loans dates from the depression of 1920–1921. In 1921, commercial loans of all member banks were about 52 per cent of total loans and investments. As of December 31, 1951, the portfolios of all member banks in the United States are shown in table 1.

Federal Reserve System, stated that "To a considerable extent, the successful flotation of stocks during the twenties, as well as the buoyancy of the bond market, depended on loans on securities obtained at banks or from brokers, who for the most part obtained their funds from banks." *Monetary Policy and the Management of the Public Debt,* Replies to Questions and Other Material for the Use of the Subcommittee on General Credit Control and Debt Management, Joint Committee on the Economic Report (1952), 82d Cong., 2d sess., Vol. I, p. 532. (Hereinafter, this document will be abbreviated to Patman Report.)

The tremendous growth in the federal debt has overshadowed the total amount of bank-held private debt. Although the commercial banks of the country are currently serving as an important repository of the national debt, bankers still consider lending the heart of their function[6] and repeatedly assert their preference for loans over investments.[7] Despite the relative decline of the commercial loan, business loans still comprise 47.5 per cent of total loans. Moreover, the statistics understate the true importance of business loans. For example, real estate loans are 22.1 per cent of total loans, and, hence, an important part of the total loan portfolio. However, real estate loans are not a product of commercial banks *qua* commercial banks. Such loans appear in commercial bank portfolios only because many commercial banks perform a dual role by accepting savings deposits as well as demand deposits.[8] Moreover, at least some of the real estate loans are business loans made to contractors for construction purposes or made to businessmen for the acquisition of commercial property.

Brokers' loans constitute 4.9 per cent of the loan portfolio. At least some of these brokers' loans are for speculation pure and simple. At least part, however, are indirectly business loans for the purchase of *new* securities. No doubt, too, the miscellaneous category of "other loans" also includes an element of indirect business loans.

Consumer loans are not nearly so important in commercial bank portfolios as business loans proper. However, only a very small part of consumer loans are bona fide personal loans for education, health, and so on. The majority of consumer loans are for financing the purchase of consumer durable goods. Such loans are really alternatives to business loans. When a bank lends to a consumer for the purchase of an automobile, the bank is making a consumer loan. But if the sale of the automobile is financed by a bank loan

---

[6] Lending is more important to the community than investments of banks, particularly since investments are largely in government bonds. "The commercial bank is not rendering its proper service to the community if it confines itself too largely to merely holding low-risk investments in government bonds." Testimony of Jesse W. Tapp, Transamerica Hearings.

Maple T. Harl of the Federal Deposit Insurance Corporation made a similar observation. "The viewpoint of the Corporation is that one of the basic functions of banks is to meet the loan needs of individuals and business enterprises in the communities in which the banks are located, irrespective of the size of the borrower." Patman Report, Vol. II, p. 956.

[7] Roland I. Robinson stresses the comparative advantage of banks in making loans as contrasted to investments. Cf. Roland I. Robinson, *The Management of Bank Funds* (New York: McGraw-Hill, 1951), p. 94.

[8] *Ibid.*, pp. 219, 345.

to the auto dealer, the bank is making a business loan. To this extent, the distinction between consumer loans and business loans is artificial.[9]

In summary, it would appear that lending, not investing, constitutes the characteristic role of commercial banks in the economy. Moreover, business loans are the largest single component in commercial bank loan portfolios. Finally, the other loan components in the loan portfolios are often indirectly business loans or alternatives to business loans. As a matter of statistical record, therefore, it would seem to follow that the most characteristic product of commercial banks as such is the provision of business loans. As of December 31, 1951, business loans proper amounted to $24,000,-000,000. The magnitude of this figure leaves no doubt about the importance of bank loans in the normal operations of the business community.

ALTERNATIVE SOURCES OF SUPPLY

The identification of business loans as the most characteristic product of commercial banks is the first step in describing the market structure for such loans. Commercial banks, however, are not the only institutions which supply short-term business credit to the community.[10] Short-term business credit is supplied also by commercial finance companies, businesses which extend trade credit, the Reconstruction Finance Corporation, Federal Reserve Banks, and, in some cases, private individuals. It is necessary to ascertain whether potential suppliers of short-term business credit, other than commercial banks, must be formally included in the analysis, or whether they can be properly handled as obiter dicta and simply held in the back of the mind as modifying factors in whatever results are obtained in this study. The decision depends upon two questions: (1) the importance of the alternative suppliers; and (2) comparability of the product, i.e., the extent to which the business credit provided by these other suppliers is a reasonably satisfactory substitute for business credit provided by commercial banks. These questions will be considered jointly for each of the alleged alternative sources.

Private individuals.—Unfortunately, figures are almost completely lacking on the extent of business lending by private indi-

---

[9] This is not to suggest that banking markets for business loans and for consumer loans are necessarily the same. At this point, however, the problem is to establish the characteristic role of commercial banks as such. For this purpose, it is not irrelevant to note that consumer loans are often alternatives for business loans.

[10] Cf. Transamerica Hearings, p. 8503.

viduals. Thus, each investigator must assess the importance of such
lending on the basis of necessarily limited observation. In the
absence of definitive and comprehensive information, it seems
probable that, except in certain areas and under unusual circumstances, lending by private individuals is probably slight compared
to the volume of commercial bank lending. Furthermore, since
private loans have no formal, institutional existence, they cannot
be regarded as realistic alternatives for the majority of business
borrowers.

Federal Reserve Banks.—Under certain circumstances, the Federal Reserve Act grants the individual Federal Reserve Banks the
authority to make industrial loans. Between 1944 and 1951, the
volume of such loans varied from a low of $554,000 to a high of
$5,800,000.[11] As of October 31, 1951, the Federal Reserve Bank of
San Francisco had outstanding industrial loans of only $48,000.[12]
Such loans have been insignificant in the past, and a careful reading of the Federal Reserve Act suggests that such loans are not
reasonable substitutes for the typical business loans of commercial
banks. The relevant passage of the Federal Reserve Act reads as
follows:

In exceptional circumstances, when it appears to the satisfaction of a
Federal Reserve bank that an *established* industrial or commercial
business located in its district is *unable to obtain requisite financial
assistance on a reasonable basis from the usual sources,* the Federal Reserve bank . . . may make loans to . . . such business . . . for the purpose
of providing it with working capital . . .[13]

A source of supply, restricted in its lending activities as indicated
above,[14] cannot qualify as a bona fide alternative to the ordinary
business loans of commercial banks.

Reconstruction Finance Corporation.—Judged by the volume
of its loans, the Reconstruction Finance Corporation is not an
important supplier of business credit relative to commercial banks.
As of September 30, 1949, for the country as a whole, RFC loans
outstanding amounted to only $443,000,000. More important, per-
haps, RFC loans are not a substitute for *short-term* business loans
by commercial banks, since RFC loans are usually granted for fixed

---

[11] Board of Governors of the Federal Reserve System, *Federal Reserve Bulletin*
(November, 1951), p. 1385.

[12] *Ibid.,* p. 1384.

[13] The Federal Reserve Act, as amended to November 1, 1946, Sec. 13b, par. 1(a).
(Italics mine.)

[14] For further limitations upon the total potential volume of such loans, cf. *ibid.,*
Sec. 13b, par. 3(c).

capital and have a duration of from three to five years.[15] Further-more, in 1949, more than half the RFC loans in dollar volume were for more than $1,000,000, i.e., they were loans to big business and not to small business.[16] Finally, two requisite conditions for an RFC loan further restrict their substitutability for short-term business loans by banks. These conditions are (1) that the applicant shall have exhausted all private sources of funds, and (2) that the applicant have full security for the loan, so that the RFC could expect repayment even in event of failure of the business.[17] Finally, such loans are made only where "the interest of the general public rather than the individual borrower is principally served."[18] It is probably not irrelevant, too, to observe that the RFC is involved in politics.[19] For all these reasons, RFC loans are not in this study considered to be within the tolerable limits of substitutes for short-term business loans by commercial banks.

Trade credit.—Trade credit refers to the deferred payment com-monly granted by wholesalers and manufacturers to retailers and other distributors and by suppliers to processors. Trade credit is undoubtedly an important source of credit to small business.[20] The only question is whether open book credit is a bona fide substitute for commercial bank short-term credit.

In many ways, open book credit is an imperfect substitute for bank credit. In the first place, open book credit is not a substitute for all the purposes which short-term bank loans serve. A con-spicuous and important example is working capital for wage pay-ments. Second, the duration of the open book account is signifi-cantly shorter in many instances than a comparable bank loan would be. Trade credit is usually granted for 30 to 90 days, although practice differs widely. Third, the implicit rates of interest on trade credit are significantly higher than on comparable bank loans for any given borrower.[21] Finally, when trade credit is based on a bank

---

[15] Testimony of Harvey J. Gunderson, former Director, Reconstruction Finance Corporation, Subcommittee on Monetary, Credit, and Fiscal Policies of the Joint Committee on the Economic Report, 81st Cong., 1st sess. (1951), p. 147. (Hereinafter this document will be abbreviated to Douglas Hearings.)

[16] *Ibid.*, p. 151.

[17] *Ibid.*, p. 146.

[18] Dun and Bradstreet, Inc., *Dun's Review* (October, 1952), p. 120.

[19] The RFC is scheduled to be abolished as of June, 1954.

[20] Cf. Patman Report, Vol. II, p. 790.

[21] For example, the typical 30-day open book account specifies a 2 per cent discount for payment within 10 days or the full amount within the next 20 days. (Interest is usually at the rate of 6 per cent after the 30-day period.) On the assumption that a new open book credit is granted each month, either by the same seller or by different sellers—this is analogous to the renewable commercial loan—there are eighteen periods of 20 days per year, or an annual interest rate of 36 per cent, which is sig-nificantly more than that paid even by small borrowers.

loan negotiated by the credit supplying firm, trade credit is not altogether an independent source of funds to business.[22]

Despite these objections to including trade credit as a substitute for bank credit, many businessmen do so regard it. At least for many borrowers, therefore, though not for all purposes, open book credit must be regarded as a reasonably satisfactory substitute for short-term bank credit. However, trade credit need not be formally included in the analysis of banking markets except as obiter dicta. The majority of businessmen who approach a bank for credit have

TABLE 2

LOANS OUTSTANDING OF BANKS AND SMALL LOAN AND FINANCE COMPANIES

United States, Selected Years, 1939 to 1948

(millions of dollars)

Year[a]	Finance company loans				Banks
	Total	Small loan companies	Industrial banks	Industrial loan companies	
1939.............	678	448	131	99	21,662
1942.............	568	417	89	72	25,379
1945.............	585	439	76	70	28,309
1948.............	1,181	817	204	160	45,694

a SOURCES: For small loan and finance companies, Transamerica Hearings, Respondent's Exhibit No. 171. Total bank loans, *Rand McNally Bankers' Directory*, 1940, 1943, 1946, 1949.

presumably already exploited the resources of trade credit. Hence, although trade credit is a source of supply for short-term business credit, it is not usually a *competitive alternative* for the business borrower actually seeking a bank loan.

Specialized finance companies.—Specialized finance companies engage in various types of business financing, e.g., open accounts receivable financing, factoring, equipment and time sales financing, and so on. Specialized finance companies also differ greatly in size, ranging from giants like the C.I.T. Financial Corporation of New York City, and General Motors Acceptance Corporation,[23] to very small companies with only a few thousand dollars of capital. The importance of small loan and finance companies in the United States can be gauged from table 2 which shows loans outstanding in different years. Except for the dip in the early years of the 1940's,

---

[22] With the possible exception of the case where the credit-granting firm is in a different banking market from the recipient of trade credit.

[23] In 1950, C.I.T.'s capital was $241,242,373 and General Motors Acceptance Corporation had capital amounting to $237,015,405. Cf. Theodore H. Silbert, "Financing and Factoring Accounts Receivable," *Harvard Business Review*, XXX (January-February, 1952): 50.

small loan and finance companies have shown steady growth. For the country as a whole, however, such finance companies provided only a very small amount of the total volume of bank loans. Small loan companies in California also have grown, both in volume of business and in numbers of lenders. Between the years 1939 and 1948, loans outstanding varied between a low of $24,000,000 and a high in 1948 of $97,000,000. Between 1940 and 1948, the number of small loan companies in California ranged from 248 to 480, with a mean number of 336 firms.[24] For purposes of comparison, during the same period, Bank of America *alone* had a mean number of 498 branch offices in California. During the same period, loans of Bank of America alone ranged from a low of $778,000,000 to a high in 1948 of $2,800,000,000. In California, too, the small loan and finance companies are a very small part of the total credit resources in the state.

It has been held that many businessmen whose credit standing would entitle them to bank loans nevertheless continue to use commercial finance companies.[25] Hence, it is worth investigating to what extent loans by finance companies are really substitutes for business loans by commercial banks.[26] Whether finance company credit is a reasonably satisfactory substitute for bank business loans depends at least in part upon whether the finance companies are themselves an *independent* source of supply. This depends chiefly on the source of finance company funds. When finance companies are organized as sole proprietorships or partnerships, the prospective size of their capital funds is presumptively limited, except, possibly, for some of the very old finance company partnerships. Finance companies organized under a corporate charter are technically in a position to tap a broad source of capital funds, but this legal opportunity is often a fiction, since the corporate form is often adopted for tax and business purposes rather than to get larger capital. In practice, finance companies normally rely heavily upon banks for their loanable funds. Small finance companies may use two or three banks, and very large companies (like Commercial Credit Corporation or C.I.T.) may use anywhere from ten to thirty or forty banks as a source for their funds. Finance companies usually borrow from banks on their own paper,[27] and the size of

---

[24] Transamerica Hearings, Respondent's exhibit no. 171.

[25] Cf., for example, testimony of Neil Jacoby, *ibid.*, p. 9030.

[26] This inquiry is worth making independently of the present context, since it is a convenient way to emphasize several points of interest about both finance companies and commercial banks.

[27] In a few minor instances some finance companies rediscount their transactions with banks, usually at 6 per cent or more, to reimburse the banks for the extra labor in handling the papers involved.

their loans varies anywhere from one to three or four times the size of their capital. In other words, from a banking market structure point of view, at least part of the credit made available to business borrowers by finance companies constitutes a secondary supply of credit on the market.[28] The "secondary supply" of business credit comes on to the market, not with a great time lag, but almost immediately after the bank grants the credit to the finance company. Thus, the lending bank is in a position to regulate the supply of funds to finance companies, and, indeed, even to put pressure on their allocation by the finance companies.[29] To this extent, finance company funds are not an independent source of supply on the credit market.

It is not uncommon, too, for banks to take a detailed interest in the activities of their finance company clients. They can require not only the financial statement of the finance company, but also information on their loans, e.g., distribution of their loans with special reference to the totals loaned to any of the finance company customers, and the industry represented by the particular loans. Such information is mostly examined to ensure proper diversification by the finance company. However legitimate the purpose, the importance of this supervisory and withholding power of the banks over the finance companies can hardly be ignored in a market structure analysis. On the other hand, the extent to which the finance company must submit to bank supervision is clearly a function of the size of the finance company. In other words, for the

[28] Whether to treat this secondary supply of credit as an independent supply is analogous though not identical to the problem faced by the courts in the Aluminum Company antitrust case. The issue in the aluminum case concerned Alcoa's share of the market. Its share was only 64 per cent if secondary ingots could be considered an independent source of supply, whereas its share would be regarded as 90 per cent if secondary ingots were disregarded. Judge Learned Hand decided that Alcoa's share was 90 per cent since Alcoa was responsible for the bulk of the secondary ingot supply and could, therefore, take account of the prospective competition from this secondary supply in determining its price and production policies. Edward Mason has criticized this decision (in oral discussion of the case) not only because the Court explicitly ignored competition from substitute metals, but also because the secondary aluminum only hits the market with a fifteen-year lag (approximately) and, therefore, could hardly be considered in the profit-maximizing decisions at any moment of time. In the banking case, however, this would not hold.

[29] Raymond Rodgers has observed that, relative to sales-finance companies, factors have not achieved the same preferred borrowing position because, *"There is also a tendency on the part of the banks to view factors as competitors who should be kept in bounds!"* Raymond Rodgers, "Factors, Bank Financing of Accounts Receivable, Commercial Paper," in Herbert V. Prochnow, ed., *American Financial Institutions* (New York: Prentice-Hall, 1951), pp. 204–205. (Italics mine.) Curiously enough, according to Professor Rodgers, "the factor is in far less direct competition with banks than many other agencies, especially the sales-finance company." *Loc. cit.*

finance company as for the ordinary business borrower at a bank, much depends on the number of alternative sources of supply actually available to the finance company.

Finance company loans do not constitute an alternative source of supply for a large group of borrowers when finance company loans are secured by accounts receivable (which is very common). Many borrowers who could qualify for credit at a bank with some other security do not have accounts receivable. This condition particularly characterizes many retail firms. In other instances, finance company credit is available only for very restricted purposes.[30]

The substitutability to the business borrower between finance company credit and bank loans is further compromised by the price differences between the two services. In part, the price differences are a reflection of cost differences. When finance companies are heavily dependent upon banks for their loanable funds, the cost of funds to a finance company is likely to be higher than for a bank. The banks must cover their costs and seek to make a profit on finance company loans. Thus, the cost of finance company funds must start from a base which already includes the full cost of funds to the bank.[31] Partly, the price differences are owing to the fact that banks can get greater leverage on their equity capital than finance companies. For an individual bank, the important source of loanable funds is not equity capital but demand and time deposits. Although a finance company can borrow bank funds and thus increase its own supply of loanable funds, the ratio of borrowed to equity capital is generally far greater for a bank than for a finance company. The greater leverage in banks than in finance companies means that the same rate of interest on loans by both lenders would, *ceteris paribus,* yield a higher net rate of return on capital to banks than to finance companies. Partly, of course, the price differences reflect the greater risks assumed by finance companies on loans which banks would reject outright.

Large borrowers encounter no shortage of alternative sources of supply, since large borrowers are not restricted to their local areas in securing credit. For certain weak borrowers, however, finance

---

[30] For example, one of the largest finance companies, General Motors Acceptance Corporation, deals only in auto-financing and the financing of its own appliances. Cf. Silbert, *op. cit.,* p. 52.

[31] Since cost of funds is not always the only nor even the most important cost of making a loan, this cost discrepancy could conceivably be compensated by a possible greater efficiency in the granting of certain kinds of credit in which finance companies specialize. Since at least some California banks, especially Bank of America, have entered the finance company territory, even this possibility is likely to be illusory.

company loans may be the only available source of supply, since their credit standing may fall below the minimum limit acceptable to banks.[32] However, for all the reasons indicated, finance company loans are only highly imperfect substitutes for bank business loans. Furthermore, finance companies are not an important part of the short-term business loan market in California. Because of the small influence of finance companies, their impact on the structure of California banking markets is ignored for the remainder of this analysis.

Summary.—Trade credit is the only important example of alternative sources of supply for short-term bank business loans which can meet at least some of the tests of a reasonable substitute. At best, however, even trade credit is a highly imperfect substitute for bank loans, and, under most conditions, does not constitute a competitive alternative source of supply. Hence, the market for bank loans can be examined by itself.

---

[32] Raymond Rodgers states that banks will not, for example, make accounts receivable loans to a firm with a poor financial condition, unless they are already lending to it when the unsatisfactory situation develops. Cf. Rodgers, *op. cit.*, p. 211.

III

The Market Structure of Unit Banking

In an article published in 1938, L. V. Chandler pointed to the impressive degree of monopolistic competition in banking.[1] The groundwork there established can be elaborated profitably to focus more sharply on those features of banking market structures which are relevant in considerations of policy alternatives. At the same time, the sketch of unit banking markets in this chapter provides the necessary framework for the more detailed investigation of the effects of concentration in the rest of the study.

Under a unit system of banking, America necessarily has many more independently owned banks than exist in branch-banking countries like England or Canada. Mere numbers, however, are no guarantee of competition. The thousands of unit banks are not equal in size and economic strength. Banking in the United States is a highly concentrated business. The movement toward concentration of banking in larger units dates from 1924 and seems to have accompanied a similar concentration in the industrial sector. The movement took two forms: (1) mergers of existing banks, and (2) conversion of unit banks into branch banks. As a result of these combinations and mergers, in 1935, approximately 3 per cent of the banks had 70 per cent of all deposits; in 1941, 1.08 per cent of the banks had almost 62 per cent of total deposits; and in 1947, 1.34 per cent of banks had 52.11 per cent of deposits.[2] These statistics on concentration are suggestive in their implications about the

[1] See Lester V. Chandler, "Monopolistic Elements in Commercial Banking," *Journal of Political Economy*, XLVI (February, 1938).

[2] The percentages were computed from data in the following sources: For 1935, *Federal Reserve Bulletin*, August 1937, p. 793; for 1941, Board of Governors, of the Federal Reserve System, *Banking and Monetary Statistics* (Washington, D.C.: National Capital Press, 1943), pp. 43, 45; for 1947, FDIC, *Annual Report for 1947*, pp. 140–141.

kind of markets in which banks do business. The existence of concentration no more proves monopoly influence, however, than does the mere existence of several thousand banks assure competition among them. The banking market structure must be examined more closely.

In attempting to define the market structure of commercial banks, it is convenient to proceed through the following steps: (1) setting of the stage—a factual discussion of fundamental features of a banking market; (2) an analysis of banks' prices, profits, and costs;[3] and (3) formal models of banking markets which emerge from the analysis of (1) and (2).

SOME DEFINING FEATURES OF A BANKING MARKET

Alternative sources of supply.—In considering the meaning of competition in banking, the existence of alternative sources of supply for a prospective borrower is of obvious importance. As a first approximation, alternative sources can be counted as they exist objectively in any given market area. If a prospective borrower wants to negotiate a loan and is dissatisfied with the price or terms of sale offered by one bank, or is denied a loan by a bank, is there another bank in his community to which he can turn? In a limited sense, the "natural" market area of a bank is the city in which it is situated. All but the largest borrowers will normally borrow funds from banks in their respective cities or towns.

As a first approximation, therefore, the number of banks in a community is a rough index of alternative sources of supply. In 1926, 34 per cent of the banks were in cities (or towns) having only one bank; in 1936, 51.9 per cent; and in 1949, 52.8 per cent of the banks were in one-bank cities. In other words, in the latter two years, more than one-half of the banks in the country faced no competition from other banks in the same city. Furthermore, in the latter two periods, this situation held in 75 per cent of the cities in the country in which there were any banks at all. The complement of this picture is that by 1949 only about 6 per cent of the banks faced ten or more competitors in their own cities, and this situation held for only four-tenths of 1 per cent of all cities having banks.[4]

---

[3] The reader may have noticed that step (1) is reminiscent of the "market conditions" approach and step (2) of the "market standards" approach to workable competition. Cf. Corwin Edwards, *Maintaining Competition* (New York: McGraw-Hill, 1949), pp. 9–10. In this study, these two approaches are employed heuristically, not normatively.

[4] Data for 1936 were taken from Chandler, *op. cit.*, p. 7. Percentages for 1926 and 1949 were computed from data in *Rand McNally Bankers' Directory* (Chicago: Rand McNally and Company), January, 1926, pp. 33–1489, and January, 1949, pp. 1515–1750. The Rand McNally definition of "bank" includes all unit commercial

Relation of bankers and borrowers.—In those cities which have, say, two, three, or four banks, the existence of objective alternative sources is by no means equivalent to the existence of *real* alternatives for a particular borrower. The discrepancy is ultimately explained by the elements of monopolistic competition which bind borrowers to bankers with whom they have historically done business. The banker-customer relationship develops by a process of mutually selective discrimination in which personal considerations are often of paramount importance.

In addition to selective discrimination founded on personal considerations, the requirements of a sound portfolio policy also compel the banker to prefer certain kinds of paper (and, hence, certain borrowers) to others. The main problem facing a banker is often stated as the "dilemma between liquidity and profits." This dilemma confronts every banker in the composition of his portfolio. A bank can enhance its profit—and not irrelevantly, its loss-prospects—by heavy and not too conservative lending, but at the risk of endangering liquidity. Conversely, a conservative and cautious lending policy insures liquidity but reacts negatively on profits. Diversification of the portfolio is a common rule in striking a balance between liquidity and profitability. Banking manuals advocate diversification by type of loan and investment, by amount invested in any single enterprise, and by geographical location. In a large city, there is maximum scope for diversifying the type of loans made and for securing a large number of borrowers. Diversity by geographical location is also possible by lending to borrowers from all parts of the country through the open market. In the extreme case of a country bank, the opportunities for diversification are practically limited to real estate and small local loans. But whether the city is large or small, a banker is under constant pressure to discriminate among loan applicants and to select those loans dictated by the needs of sound portfolio composition.

Size of borrower.—Monopolistic competition in banking[5] and the

---

banks and trust companies which perform commercial banking services, members of chain and group systems, banking offices of branch banking systems (but not more than one banking office in each city), and savings banks.

[5] The spirit of monopolistic competition seems to dominate the banking mentality quite completely. Official spokesmen have publicly declared that, "The competition between banks is in quality of service; . . . there is seldom a question of price; . . . there is no real problem of cheaper banking for us to solve." Hearings before the Committee on Banking and Currency, HR, 71st Cong., 2d sess., *Branch, Chain, and Group Banking*, Vol. II, pp. 1785–1786. (Hereinafter, this document will be cited as Branch Bank Hearings.) Or again, that, "Banks have no bargains to offer, no cut rates." American Institute of Banking, *Bank Management* (revised ed., New York: American Institute of Banking, 1933), p. 256. Competition has shifted from the price sphere to competition in service.

discrimination it breeds are both involved with the distinction between large and small borrowers. This distinction, it will be shown later, plays a significant role in conditioning the type of market structure in which banks operate. The point at issue is quite simple: large borrowers have alternative sources of supply; small borrowers do not. The reasons for this difference were well expressed in the testimony of Governor Young before a congressional committee:

> For instance, let us take a small community in South Dakota: A farmer who has to borrow $1,000 or $2,000 is known to the local banker and not known to anyone else. He cannot go to New York, Vermont, or Maine and present his note. No one knows him. Therefore, he has to pay the legal rate or contract rate . . . [of, say] 10 per cent. That is the rate he would probably have to pay to the local bank unless he was well enough known so he could go to a nearby town with a very desirable piece of paper and drive a bargain, say, for 8 per cent.[6]

By contrast, the large borrower's credit rating does not depend on his being known to the local banker. The resources of his business and his borrowing history are known and are sufficiently impressive so that the large borrower need not depend on his personal acquaintance with a banker to secure accommodation. Indeed, notes of the very largest borrowers can be sold on the open market in a completely impersonal fashion. Borrowers with wide connections and alternative sources in all parts of the country are given the most favorable rates possible when they borrow funds. For borrowers with the option of going to the open market, bankers will sometimes grant loans at rates *less* than those prevailing on the open market.

Fundamentally, there seems little doubt that different interest rates to different borrowers, as well as the availability of funds, originate in the difference in alternative sources available. Some bankers have rationalized the difference in rates by explaining that large borrowers bring a lot of business to a bank. In order to secure this volume, a banker finds it worth while to attract the customer with price concessions. No doubt business volume provided by a customer is important. Generally, however, lower rates are granted because the borrower has alternative sources of supply.

Not only is the small borrower confronted with discrimination in the rates he must pay; often he is refused a loan altogether by his home banker. In a survey conducted by the National Industrial Conference Board, small borrowers complained of the "unwilling-

---

[6] Cf. Branch Bank Hearings, *op. cit.*, Vol. I, p. 709.

ness to grant loans if other banks, for any reason whatsoever or no explained reason, have refused loans."[7] The resulting impasse is often acute, and led one student to comment that "The unit banker . . . has found it possible to establish a type of petty local monopoly in some instances as vicious in its incidence on a small scale as anything which ever disturbed the reflections of our ardent legislative champions of freedom."[8]

Problem of entry.—A projected bank in our country must first secure a charter. Hence, the question of entry in banking is intimately connected with the laws and statutes regulating the issuance of charters and is by no means exclusively a corollary of any particular market structure. The legal issue is particularly complicated in the United States because of the existence of forty-nine chartering jurisdictions, each operating under its own set of rules. The chartering issue is actually much more than a legal one—it is also political and has been so since the early days of the nation.

It has sometimes been said that the banking industry as a whole, as a supplier of short-term commercial credit, has entered the declining phase. One segment, however, is still young and growing— or rather would grow if legal barriers were lifted. For the segment in question, branch banks,[9] entry is decidedly difficult. Only a few states permit state-wide branch banking, and even in such states, entry is not always easy. Again the issue often turns on political considerations and, sometimes, even on personalities.[10]

The powerful opposition to branch banks in certain quarters has found expression in *laws which are intended to protect unit banks from the competition of branch banks.*[11] A case in point is the

---

[7] National Industrial Conference Board, Inc., *The Availability of Bank Credit* (New York: National Industrial Conference Board, 1932), p. 119.

[8] Joseph Stagg Lawrence, *Banking Concentration in the United States* (New York: Bankers' Publishing Company, 1930), p. 213.

[9] "Branches" here refers to offices outside the metropolitan area of the parent bank.

[10] A conspicuous example of blocked entry is that of the large California branch banking organization which was not permitted to open new offices in the city of Los Angeles at a time when that city was experiencing rapid growth and while other banks were being issued permits to open new offices. The bank in question maintained that it was politically victimized by its banking competitors, charging that the latter put pressure on the California Superintendent of Banks (who issued permits for new banks) to deny permits to the plaintiff bank. Whatever the merits or demerits of this case, there can be no doubt that entry into banking was made decidedly difficult for the bank in question by the attitude of the chartering official. For a detailed discussion of this case, see Branch Bank Hearings, *op. cit.*, Vol. II, p. 1506 ff.

[11] Cf. Ray B. Westerfield, *Historical Survey of Branch Banking in the United States* (New York: American Economists Council for the Study of Branch Banking, 1939), pp. 26 ff. The kind of "competition" eliminated will be discussed later. As will be seen, branch bank competition is also far from pure.

McFadden-Pepper Act of 1927, which permitted national banks to establish branches in the metropolitan area of the parent bank, provided state laws similarly privileged state-chartered institutions. This law explicitly forbade the establishment of branches in towns of less than 25,000 population. Only one branch would be authorized in towns of 50,000 population and not more than two branches in towns of 100,000 population. Where population exceeded 100,000, branches could be established only with the approval of the Comptroller of the Currency. If possible political overtones are ignored,[12] then the purely economic effect of such a law has tended to preserve *competitors* rather than *competition*.[13]

Independence of action.—The unrelenting official concern lest branch banks compromise banking "competition" is in striking contrast to official acquiescence in the most flagrant "restraints of trade" practiced commonly by most bankers, branch as well as unit. The marvel is the complete frankness with which collusive agreements are accomplished. Such agreements are not described as collusion by bankers. They are called "mutual assistance," "elimination of unhealthy competition," "necessary coördination of activity," and so on. And there can be no doubt that the losses experienced under a competitive regime have often been converted into profits once agreement has been secured among erstwhile competitors.[14]

It is well known that the clearinghouse is often one of the most effective means by which bankers can join in agreements on a local and regional basis. Clearinghouse agreements have gradually been extended until they cover nearly every phase of bank activity. It is common knowledge, for example, that clearinghouses may regulate the maximum rate of interest to be paid on time deposits. They also have eliminated competition among banks in the matter of service charges. Banking hours, today taken for granted, are another item that became generally standardized under the clearinghouse

---

[12] In an actual policy decision, political considerations cannot be ignored. In analysis, however, clarity of thinking is aided by distinguishing between economic and political aspects of a case.

[13] This intent of the McFadden-Pepper Act is similar to Adelman's interpretation of the Justice Department's approach in the A and P case. See M. A. Adelman, "The A and P Case: A study in Applied Economic Theory," *Quarterly Journal of Economics*, Vol. LXIII (May, 1949), especially p. 256. Ironically, in the banking case, the law has not even succeeded in preserving competitors since it is in small communities where branch banks are excluded that a serious number of bank failures have occurred.

[14] "The effects [of restricting competition] have been to increase profits, to eliminate dangerous kinds of competition, to give impetus to improving service, and to maintain the respect and confidence of the public." *Bank Management, op. cit.*, p. 465.

imprimatur. Advertising is still another feature of the banking business under clearinghouse supervision. As a result of clearinghouse activity, a code of ethics has been evolved with regard to securing new business. Bankers seem agreed that, in soliciting new business, there should be *"nothing in the spirit of the bank's approach that can be interpreted as a bid for any considerable portion of the business of the other banks."*[15] It would be difficult to conceive a more gentle approach to "competition." Indeed, about the only matter not regulated by clearinghouses (though some have considered it) is the rates of interest at which banks should lend. The reason for this conspicuous omission is the feeling among bankers that such control would virtually eliminate the surviving vestigial remnants of individual initiative in bank management, and, furthermore, it would "smack of monopoly control and invite restrictive legislation."[16]

The independence of the unit banker in matters of loan and general business policy is compromised not only by clearinghouse agreements but also by the nature of the correspondent relationship. The correspondent system has remained an important part of banking organization despite the advent of the Federal Reserve System. A correspondent bank provides various services for its bank customers. It holds funds on deposit for them, it invests funds for them, it grants them loans, and it gives them advice on matters of loan and general bank policy. By this relationship, the discretion of the local banker is at times considerably restricted. For example, when a bank requests a loan from its correspondent, the correspondent will first make a thorough examination of the bank. Furthermore, it will require certain types of collateral from the bank, thereby practically forcing the local bank to purchase securities of business concerns outside its community. In this and other ways, ". . . the large city banks have had a very profound influence upon the thought of small bankers as well as upon the policies and practices followed by them."[17]

PRICES, PROFITS, COSTS

An analytical treatment of the commercial loan market must include information on prices, profits, and costs, as well as the primarily institutional description already presented. To be meaningful,

---

[15] *Ibid.*, p. 24. (Italics mine.)

[16] *Ibid.*, p. 465.

[17] John M. Chapman, *Concentration of Banking* (New York: Columbia University Press, 1934), p. 270. For a good discussion of these aspects of the correspondent relationship, see chapter iv.

statistics on prices, earnings, and costs must be set within a useful frame of reference. The discussion of the previous section has suggested the importance for market structure of alternative sources of supply. Although the number of banks within a given city[18] is not always a true measure of alternatives available to borrowers, such a breakdown of banks can serve as a useful first approximation toward the theoretical models.

Prices.—Available statistics show that, on the average, customer loan rates in small towns are higher than in large cities.[19] It can be inferred from this fact that a purely competitive link does not exist between banks in large and small cities; otherwise, only one uniform price (allowing for risk differences) would prevail in all banks, regardless of location. This deductive evidence is reinforced by empirical knowledge that small banks do not engage in intercity competition because most small borrowers are tied to their local banks.

The higher rates in small-town banks are sometimes explained by reference to their higher operating costs. Table 3 shows the relation between expenses and assets for different size banks (and, by our assumptions, for banks in different size cities). The assets of a bank are overwhelmingly its loans and investments. During the years covered by the table, expenses were almost invariably higher for small banks than they were for large banks. It would appear, therefore, that if a common rate could be enforced in large- and small-city banks by competition between them, many small-town banks would be forced out of business because they are the marginal producers in the banking business. In order to decide whether higher costs are a *sufficient* explanation for the higher rates in small-town banks, profit figures must also be examined.

Profits.—Unfortunately, "profitability" of a bank is not an unambiguous concept. Does profitability refer to the rate of return on assets or to the rate of return on capital? Part of the difficulty inherent in this problem reflects the unresolved confusion between accounting terminology and the concepts of economic theory.[20] Re-

---

[18] Unfortunately the data are rarely available by number of banks within a given size city but rather in terms of size of bank. An approximation to the desired categories is provided by the size-of-bank statistics. The justification is as follows: Size of bank is highly correlated with size of city; size of city is highly correlated with number of banks in each size city; therefore, size of bank is a good approximation to number of banks in each size city.

[19] Cf. chart printed in W. W. Riefler, *Money Rates and Money Markets in the United States* (New York: Harper & Brothers, 1930), p. 64.

[20] Cf. the comment of Arthur S. Dewing, *Financial Policy of Corporations* (4th ed., New York: Ronald Press, 1941), Vol. I, p. 654, note c.

turn on capital as a measure of profitability is not entirely satisfactory because it is largely arbitrary. The rate of return on assets measures the economic earning power of an institution; rate of return on capital is a function also of the capital structure. The distinction between equity capital and borrowed capital is reasonably clear in the case of a manufacturing corporation, but the distinction also holds for a bank. A bank's power to produce (i.e.,

TABLE 3

TOTAL EXPENSES AS PERCENTAGES OF TOTAL ASSETS BY YEARS

Size of banks by deposits[a]	1941	1942	1943	1945	1947
$100,000 or less	....	1.08	....	....	....
$100,000–$250,000	....	1.02	....	....	....
$250,000 or less	3.4	....	2.20	....	....
$250,000–$500,000	3.0	0.95	1.75	....	....
$500,000 or less	....	....	....	1.85	1.98
$500,000–$1,000,000	2.7	0.90	1.59	1.49	1.61
$1,000,000–$2,000,000	2.5	0.88	1.46	1.36	1.49
$2,000,000–$5,000,000	2.3	0.84	1.40	1.27	1.46
$5,000,000–$10,000,000	2.2	0.78	1.35	1.26	1.49
$10,000,000–$50,000,000	1.9	0.72	1.25	1.20	1.47
More than $50,000,000	1.4	0.63	0.83	....	....
$50,000,000–$100,000,000	....	....	....	1.08	1.42
More than $100,000,000	....	....	....	0.82	1.14

[a] SOURCES: The data for 1941 are from *Banking and Monetary Statistics*, p. 275. The figures refer to member banks, and "Total Expenses" includes salaries and wages, interest on time deposits, and other current expenses.
    The data for the other years were derived from the corresponding *Annual Report of the FDIC*, 94, 100, 138, and 142, respectively, for the years indicated. In the FDIC, "Total Expenses" includes total current operating expenses (excluding taxes). FDIC data are compiled only for insured commercial banks rather than all member banks.

loans and investments) is determined not so much by its equity capital as by the amount of its deposits. These deposits in a very real sense are borrowed capital from the viewpoint of the bank, which is required to pay interest on them (explicitly or implicitly). The capital-deposit ratio is thus a good guide to the capital structure of a bank.

There would be no serious problem if these two measures of profitability happened to give consistent results. Unfortunately they do not. Table 4 compares the profitability of large and small banks (and, by assumption, for banks in different size cities) by taking profits as a percentage of assets. Small-city banks are by this measure definitely more profitable than banks in large cities. It should be stressed that these figures are net, not gross. That small-city banks should be more profitable than large-city banks is not surprising in view of the higher rates generally charged by small-city banks. That they should make larger net profits even after deducting their higher operating costs is truly striking. It raises serious doubts whether the higher rates in small-city banks are sufficiently explained by reference to higher operating costs and inadequate intercity competition. The implications for the banking structure in small towns will be discussed presently.

If profitability of banks is measured by rates of return on capital (and surplus), the situation as between large-city and small-city

TABLE 4

NET CURRENT OPERATING EARNINGS PER $100 OF TOTAL ASSETS
BY YEARS

Size of banks by deposits[a]	1941	1942	1943	1944	1945	1947
$100,000 or less.............	....	1.08	....	....	....	....
$100,000–$250,000...........	....	1.02	....	....	....	....
$250,000 or less.............	1.4	....	0.86	....	....	....
$250,000–$500,000...........	1.2	0.95	0.85	....	....	....
$500,000 or less.............	....	....	....	0.83	0.77	1.11
$500,000–$1,000,000.........	1.1	0.90	0.80	0.77	0.74	0.98
$1,000,000–$2,000,000........	1.0	0.88	0.78	0.72	0.72	0.96
$2,000,000–$5,000,000........	0.9	0.84	0.75	0.67	0.65	0.90
$5,000,000–$10,000,000.......	0.8	0.78	0.71	0.63	0.61	0.85
$10,000,000–$50,000,000......	0.8	0.72	0.69	0.60	0.58	0.75
More than $50,000,000........	0.6	0.63	0.71	....	....	....
$50,000,000–$100,000,000..,,.	....	....	....	0.58	0.57	0.67
More than $100,000,000......	....	....	....	0.66	0.64	0.66

   [a] SOURCES: The data for 1941 are from *Banking and Monetary Statistics*, p. 275, and cover all member banks. The data for 1942–1947 are from the corresponding years of the *Annual Report of the FDIC*, 94, 100, 49, 138, 142, respectively, for the year in question. The FDIC figures cover only insured commercial banks.
   All figures are averages of individual bank ratios.

banks is inconclusive. During the years covered by table 5, small banks were sometimes more and sometimes less profitable than large banks; in other years, the pattern is not consistent. So far as a tendency can be discovered, small-city banks are less profitable than large-city banks. Small-city banks are less profitable because their higher operating costs are a function of their high capital-deposit ratios. The effect of this high capital-deposit ratio is to overcome the higher prices charged and thus to lower net profits.

Operating costs of banks in large and small cities.—Operating costs are higher in small-city banks because in small cities there are, quite naturally, fewer deposits than in large cities. Since deposits are the raw materials from which bankers make loans and investments, the total volume of loans and investments (or "output") is smaller in small-city banks than in large-city banks. However, the

unit cost of handling a loan or investment becomes smaller as the
number of loans increases. In other words, banking costs initially
fall as output (loans) increases. But if output is arbitrarily limited
by the amount of capital (deposits) which can be borrowed, then
output is arrested while the bank is still within the range of decreasing costs. Thus a basic reason for higher operating costs in small-
city banks is that such banks have available less loanable funds than
large-city banks.[21]

TABLE 5

NET CURRENT OPERATING EARNINGS PER $100 OF TOTAL CAPITAL
ACCOUNTS BY YEARS

Size of banks by deposits[a]	1941	1942	1943	1944	1945	1947
$250,000 or less	9.76	7.96	6.30	....	.....	.....
$250,000–$500,000	11.00	9.12	8.50	....	.....	.....
$500,000 or less	....	....	....	8.01	7.71	11.30
$500,000–$1,000,000	10.89	9.57	9.53	9.73	10.14	13.67
$1,000,000–$2,000,000	10.19	9.48	10.00	10.35	11.48	14.99
$2,000,000–$5,000,000	9.58	9.36	10.00	10.16	11.06	14.77
$5,000,000–$10,000,000	....	9.04	9.74	9.99	10.87	14.13
$10,000,000–$50,000,000	9.59	9.54	10.43	10.11	10.61	12.46
More than $50,000,000	8.35	9.50	11.34	....	.....	.....
$50,000,000–$100,000,000	....	....	....	11.55	11.60	11.47
More than $100,000,000	....	....	....	11.27	11.58	10.02

[a] SOURCES: *Annual Reports of the FDIC:* for 1941–1953, 37; 1944, 49; 1945, 138; and 1947, 142. Figures
are for all insured commercial banks operating throughout the year.

This inability of small-city banks to secure large amounts of
deposits also helps to explain the discrepancy in profitability when
measured against asset figures as compared to capital figures. Partly,
of course, the discrepancy is accounted for in terms of the composition of the respective banks' portfolios. In 1944, for example,
assets of small-city banks were heavily invested in (higher-yielding)
long-term government securities, whereas assets of large-city banks
were more heavily concentrated in (lower-yielding) short-term government issues.[22] Partly, however, the higher earnings on assets are
probably the result of the higher rates charged, which are more
than sufficient to compensate for the higher operating costs. When
these earnings are translated into a ratio to capital, the small-city

[21] Cf. Riefler, *op. cit., p.* 110. Cf. also E. A. Goldenweiser, *Federal Reserve System in
Operation* (New York: McGraw-Hill, 1925), p. 45, who emphasizes "the relatively
greater cost of conducting the banking business in country districts where the volume
of operations is smaller and overhead expenses per dollar loaned are correspondingly
larger."

[22] Cf. *Annual Report of the FDIC,* December 31, 1944, p. 49.

banks appear to be less profitable because they have higher capital-deposit ratios than the large-city banks.[23]

The information just presented on banking prices, profits, and costs may be regarded as building blocks for the models about to be attempted. The situation in terms of prices and costs is reasonably unambiguous. As for profits, the following analysis will proceed on the assumption that the profitability of small-city banks is less than, or at most equal to, that of large-city banks. In other words, the measure of profitability to be employed is the rate of return on capital. The rationalization for this selection can be more conveniently presented at a later stage in the analysis.

BANKING MARKET STRUCTURE IN SMALL TOWNS AND LARGE CITIES

In small towns.—Since the earnings of small-city banks are assumed to be less than or equal to those in large cities, the higher prices (rates) in small towns are not sufficiently explained by lack of intercity competition. In this case, the lack of such intercity competition is merely permissive of higher prices in small towns; the higher prices are forced by the higher operating costs, that is, if the small-town banks are to remain in business.

In those small towns which have only one bank, that one bank is in a position of local monopoly. Since it is a sole seller in its market, it exploits by itself whatever demand curve for loanable funds exists. Presumably, too, its demand curve is roughly tangent to its cost curve somewhere in the falling range of that cost curve.[24] The reason such a "monopolist" does not try beyond limits to increase his profits is that in such a one-bank town at least some of the borrowers are likely to have access to banking facilities in a near-by town, so there is potential and possibly even some actual competition. Furthermore, for this one bank to make high profits would probably attract new bankers into the town. A new entry would mean that the first banker would have to share his demand curve, and so his profit prospects in the long run are not thereby enhanced. Finally, there is a strong notion in rural areas of the "customary" or "just" price,[25] and this attitude cannot be too

---

[23] Cf. Board of Governors of the Federal Reserve System, *Banking Studies* (Baltimore: Waverly Press, 1941), p. 104

[24] This follows from the hypothesis that its profits are not above the average and that operating costs are higher than in large-city banks.

[25] "In small communities having only one bank, . . . it is no uncommon occurrence to find country banks lending their funds season after season and year after year at the same rate, regardless of general financial conditions. If the bank lends at all, it lends at the rate which custom dictates." From a quotation in Gaines T. Cartinhour, *Branch, Groups and Chain Banking* (New York: Macmillan, 1931), p. 16.

flagrantly violated by the sole seller without consequences adverse in the end to profits.

In those small towns which have (say), two, three, or four banks, the situation is one of monopolistic competition, including both oligopoly and differentiated product. Again, under the hypothesis that small-town bankers are not earning "excess" profits, the prevalence of rates higher than those in large cities is permitted by lack of intercity competition. Furthermore, each of the oligopolists in the small town is operating on the falling range of his cost curve. This is borne out by the existence of operating costs higher than those in large cities. If any one of the oligopolists could expand his output (loans), his operating costs would fall just as they do in larger cities where banks have larger output. Thus the equilibrium achieved by a group of oligopolists under conditions of falling costs can be interpreted as a recognition of their mutual dependence, reinforced by conditions of product differentiation to be found in the market. *Ceteris paribus,* a falling cost curve would otherwise lead to local monopoly. Such bankers have probably preferred to share the market rather than engage in cutthroat competition which, at least in the short run, might involve them all in serious losses.

The oligopolistic rationale[26] to stabilize prices at a level that permits all bankers to get along is abetted by the other aspect of monopolistic competition that ties many borrowers to the bank with which they have historically done business. This feature of monopolistic competition introduces an independent element of stability in the market relationships. The limited control over their demand curves thus secured by each banker strengthens the stabilization achieved under an oligopolistic rationale. Each banker well recognizes that it would be very difficult to try to out-compete his rivals since price[27] is by no means the only consideration when many borrowers negotiate loans.

---

[26] This "oligopolistic rationale" is sometimes cemented with a little collusion. "[In country towns and rural communities] there seem to be many cases in which informal agreements exist between banks that money shall not be loaned for less than 6%, 8%, or 10%, as the case may be." *Bank Management, op. cit.,* pp. 465–466. Whether there is overt collusion or just a recognition of mutual dependence is fairly indifferent from an economic standpoint since the same result is approximated in either case.

[27] The "price" referred to in the text is a brief expression for the pattern of rates at which different classes of applicants can borrow. The stabilization thus refers to the pattern of rates and not to any given rate. In many cases, however, the pattern is practically reduced to a single rate because of the general homogeneity of borrowers in a small community.

The earlier decision to concentrate on the rate of return on capital as the relevant measure of profitability now becomes clear. Profitability as a rate of return on capital is an important consideration in entry. If profits in small-town banks are greater than "normal," the presumption is that new entrants would be attracted into the town. In line with the above analysis, the entry of new bankers might well have the effect of raising the level of rates, because a larger number of oligopolists are now sharing the market, and each is thus forced to a higher point on his cost curve. Whatever would happen to prices, it seems very probable that the "excess" profits (which might be inferred from the use of rate of return on assets as a measure of profitability) would vanish.[28] In fact, however, bank failures have drastically reduced the number of small-town banks.[29] The situation has not been one of a rush into small towns by new entrants; the problem is rather the number of small towns left bankless by widespread bank failures.[30]

In large cities.—In analyzing the market structure of large cities, it is convenient to discuss the banking structure in New York City as the prototype of large-city markets; the market structure of small-city banks has already been analyzed; the remaining cities are ranged in their market structure somewhere between the two extremes.

No American city surpasses New York City in the number of its banks. In 1947, for example, New York City had 136 banks (of all kinds) with total assets of $37,743,659,000. As indicated earlier, however, the total number of banks is a fallible clue to the nature of competition among them. The five largest banks in the city held assets of $16,810,666,000 or about 43 per cent of the total; the ten largest held assets of $22,845,887,000, or about 60 per cent of total bank assets in New York City.[31] In other cities, asset concentration is even higher than in New York City.

New York City has the lowest customer loan rates in the country; the highest rates are in the small towns; the intermediate-sized towns have rates between these two extremes. It is also highly significant that New York City has the most *sensitive* customer loan

---

[28] Cf. Edward H. Chamberlin, *The Theory of Monopolistic Competition* (5th ed.; Cambridge: Harvard University Press, 1945), especially pp. 104–105.

[29] During 1921–1935, more than 70 per cent of the bank failures were in towns with a population of 2,500 or less. Cf. *Federal Reserve Bulletin*, May, 1948, p. 506.

[30] Shirley D. Southworth and John M. Chapman, *Banking Facilities for Bankless Towns* (New York: American Economists Council for the Study of Branch Banking, 1941).

[31] These figures were computed from *Rand McNally Bankers' Directory* (Chicago: Rand McNally and Company, 1947).

rates.[32] In particular, New York City customer loan rates follow the open market rates more closely than do the customer loan rates elsewhere. What is to be made of these facts?

In the first place, the low level of rates in New York City reflects the lower costs in that city. Some of the country's largest banks are in New York City, and it was shown earlier that operating costs (and losses) fall as the size of the bank increases. Thus, all other things being equal, large-city banks can afford to charge lower rates whereas comparable uniformly low rates in small towns would drive many small-town banks into bankruptcy. Lower costs, however, are not a sufficient explanation for more sensitive prices. Sensitivity of prices generally reflects the type of market structure in which a firm operates. All other things being equal, a monopolistic seller will tend to have rigid prices; on the other hand, a pure competitor tends to have more flexible prices. The rather rigid rates in small towns are owing to the influence of monopolistic competition: an oligopolistic rationale, the force of custom, and a differentiated product. The high degree of concentration in New York and other large cities would at first glance suggest the presence of oligopoly, but an oligopolistic determination of prices does not seem probable in view of the considerable sensitivity of customer loan rates corresponding to changes in open market rates. The sensitivity of price suggests rather a fairly high degree of competition.

The earmarks of oligopoly are not inconsistent with competitive behavior. New York City is the financial center of the country, just as many other large cities are financial centers in their own areas. As a result, borrowers at New York City banks are not limited to local residents, but include also borrowers from other areas. These large borrowers typically maintain banking connections with a few, and sometimes several, banks in different cities or within the same city. The banks themselves urge their largest customers to keep open their credit lines with other banks although doing business with any one or a group of them. National banks are prohibited from lending more than 10 per cent of their capital and surplus to any single borrower. Furthermore, few banks would wish to have their resources too heavily invested in any single commercial firm; prudent financial management demands diversification of the bank portfolio. The result is that banks in large cities often deal with borrowers of established credit ratings and with

---

[32] See Hardy's comments on the greater sensitivity of New York City customer loan rates as compared to other cities. Charles O. Hardy, *Credit Policies of the Federal Reserve System* (Washington, D.C.: Brookings Institution, 1932), pp. 301–302.

established banking connections in several banks. Borrowers thus provided with alternative sources of supply are in a position to demand a competitive price for the funds they need. In dealing with such large borrowers, the banks in a large city recognize that the cross-elasticity of demand for their loans approaches infinity. Such banks are competing not only with other banks in the same city, but often with other banks in different cities.

Even the smaller borrowers in large cities are not so tightly restricted as are their counterparts in smaller towns. Commercial borrowers in large cities frequently have credit ratings from agencies which specialize in such matters. Consequently such a borrower can operate in a somewhat more impersonal market. If the terms or price offered by one banker are not suitable, he can (though with greater difficulty than the large borrower) go to another bank. It might be argued that such a borrower even in a small town would have alternative sources, and to an extent he has, but he is still likely to pay somewhat more than a similar borrower in a large city.[33] Because of higher operating costs, the banks in small towns cannot in many cases afford to grant the price he could get in a large city.

Still another factor makes New York City rates lower and more flexible than the rates in small-town banks. The largest banks in New York City are the bankers of the open market. Should there be, for example, a credit stringency, it is felt first in the open money market and somewhat later in the market for customers' loans. Since the large New York banks are intimately connected with the open money market, they are the first ones among commercial banks to feel a change in credit conditions. If the money situation has become tight, the bankers are forced to raise rates or to deny loans in order to protect their tightened reserve position. When the money situation is eased and excess reserves threaten, competitive action will tend to lower rates. Finally in the case of the largest borrowers, the large New York City banks directly compete for their business with the open market.

The crux of the distinction between the market structure in large and small cities is that competition is a function of alternative sources of supply, but alternative sources are only to a slight extent a function of the objective number of alternatives (as measured by the number of banks in a community). Alternative sources of supply are far more significantly related to the size and financial standing of the borrower. Statistics compiled by the Board of

[33] Cf. table 6, below.

Governors of the Federal Reserve System in 1942 would certainly seem to support this position. In table 6, Group A banks are those having more than $10,000,000 of commercial loans outstanding; Group B banks are other banks in cities with more than 100,000 population; and Group C banks are those in cities with less than 100,000 population. Because of the high correlation between size of bank and size of city,[34] these groupings correspond roughly to "large," "medium-size," and "small" cities.

The first thing to be observed about this table is that for borrowers of any given size class, rates charged are somewhat lower

TABLE 6

AVERAGE INTEREST RATES ON COMMERCIAL LOANS AT MEMBER BANKS, BY CLASS OF
BANK AND SIZE OF BORROWER, APRIL 16–MAY 15, 1942

(per cent per annum)

Size of borrowers by assets[a]	All banks	Group A banks	Group B banks	Group C banks
Less than $50,000.........	5.5	4.7	5.1	5.8
$50,000 to $500,000.......	4.5	4.1	4.6	5.0
$500,000 to $5,000,000....	3.1	2.9	3.5	3.8
More than $5,000,000.....	1.8	1.8	1.8	2.4

[a] SOURCE: *Federal Reserve Bulletin*, November, 1942, p. 1091.

in the largest cities than in the smallest cities. Thus borrowers in any given size group pay roughly one point more in small than in large cities. Significantly, it is somewhat more than one point difference for the smallest borrowers, and somewhat less than one point difference for the largest borrowers. All groups of borrowers in medium-size cities are without exception ranged somewhere in between.

The difference between cities for any particular size group of borrowers is admittedly of minor importance when contrasted with the difference among different size borrowers within any one group of cities. This disparity does not invalidate the stress in this chapter on the market structure in different size cities. The assumption throughout (sometimes implicit) has been that, predominantly, large borrowers (in terms of total volume of loans even if not in number) tend to operate through large cities, and small borrowers are similarly preponderant in small cities. This assumption, though not invariably true, is a legitimate simplification, and explains why average rates to *all* borrowers are lower in big cities and higher

[34] Cf. n. 18, above.

in small cities, despite the fact that the importance of the size of borrower cuts across groupings of cities by size.[35]

The "market area" in which any given banker operates is thus not only a spatial market but is also defined by the particular class of borrower he serves. Toward the small borrower, a banker may be in the position of a monopolist whereas at the same time, with some large borrower, the banker is in a keenly competitive situation. The spatial market is not, however, completely eliminated in this analysis, and to this extent the matter of actual numbers of bankers within a locality is important. Table 6 shows that *for any given size borrower,* a higher rate is charged in the small town, where there is less competition, than in a large city. In other words, the cross-elasticity of demand of a banker in either the large or small city is influenced by the number of *objective* alternatives facing a borrower.

---

[35] The Federal Reserve study made a similar point in referring to "the greater importance in large cities of large loans [and large borrowers]." *Federal Reserve Bulletin,* July, 1947, p. 810. Or again, "Reflecting their greater size and loan capacity, large banks lend primarily to large business operations . . . Since banks are generally prohibited by law from lending to any one borrower in excess of a specified proportion of capital, the medium- and small-size banks lent principally to medium and small business enterprises . . . Loans to large borrowers by the large banks were concentrated in the heavy manufacturing industries, while a large proportion of the loans of small banks went to small retailers." *Federal Reserve Bulletin,* March, 1947, p. 253.

IV

Concentration in California Banking

IN 1948, there were 210 commercial banks in California. Forty of these banks operated a total of 905 branches, making a total of 1,115 banking offices.[1] Of the forty banks operating branches, four account for more than 50 per cent of the banking business done in the state. Indeed, for the purposes of this study, only four of the branch banks in California are bona fide branch banks since only these four banks have branch offices outside the head-office city. In this study, one-city banks are treated as unit banks, irrespective of the number of their branch offices.[2] The four important intercity branch systems in California are, in order of their size, Bank of America National Trust and Savings Association, Security–First National Bank, American Trust Company, and the Anglo-California National Bank. Bank of America's 526 branches blanket the entire state; American Trust, with 82 branches, operates primarily in fourteen counties of northern California; Security–First National, with 132 branches, has its head office in Los Angeles and primarily serves central and southern California; Anglo Bank, with 30 branches, operates primarily in San Francisco and central and northern California. The analysis of concentration in California will be limited to these four large branch systems. For brevity, they will sometimes be designated the "Big Four."

California banks differ vastly in economic size. More significantly, perhaps, not all borrowers have equal access to bank credit.[3]

---

[1] *Monthly Review*, Federal Reserve Bank of San Francisco, April, 1949.

[2] Although official statistics classify any bank with more than one banking office as a branch bank, one-city branch banks lack most of the distinguishing economic characteristics of intercity branch systems. Accordingly, for purposes of market analysis, the former are regarded as unit banks.

[3] As the Comptroller of the Currency has stated: "It is undoubtedly true that giant corporations with large resources, which have been long established and which have a certain dominance in their markets, have a better access to bank credit than the smaller and younger enterprise, *even if there is comparable soundness*." Patman Report, II, 933. (Italics mine.)

For very large borrowers, who either have or could readily secure interstate banking connections, the credit market of the country is truly a national market. Westerfield's contention that "the credit market of the U.S. is a national market"[4] holds strictly only for very large borrowers, and only much more tenuously for small and medium-size borrowers. As will be shown, neither credit availability nor rates and terms present any serious problems for large borrowers. The market structure problem is relevant, however, for medium-size and small borrowers,[5] who must operate in narrower markets. Other things being equal, the extent of local banking concentration could affect materially the kind of credit market in which such borrowers must operate.

CONCENTRATION OF MARKETS AND ALTERNATIVE SOURCES OF SUPPLY

Industrial markets in this country are widely characterized by a high degree of concentration and a correspondingly small number of objective alternative sources of supply. This is but another way of saying that large segments of American industry are oligopolistic in structure. In a study of a selected group of eighteen industries, the proportion of value product supplied by the first eight firms in 1935 ranged between 82.2 per cent and 100 per cent.[6] On the one hand, these figures overstate the degree of effective market concentration (i.e., in terms of alternative sources) since they do not take into account substitute products. On the other hand, where the national market is effectively segmented (e.g., by freight barriers), the effective concentration in local areas may be even higher for certain industries than is indicated by the concentration ratios.

The problem of determining effective market concentration because of substitute products and segmented markets is also encountered in measuring banking concentration. Effective substitutes for commercial bank loans could render commercial bank concentration ratios meaningless in terms of alternative sources, whereas even very low concentration figures might not begin to convey a sense of the limited alternatives available, especially to small bor-

---

[4] Testimony of Ray B. Westerfield, *Transamerica Hearings*, p. 9318.

[5] These terms will be defined at a later point.

[6] This high degree of concentration is characteristic of, among others, cigarettes, typewriters and parts, motor vehicles, rubber tires and tubes, agricultural implements, tin cans and other tinware, railroad cars, aluminum products, and the like. Cf. Joe S. Bain, "Relation of Profit Rate to Industry Concentration: American Manufacturing, 1936–1940," *Quarterly Journal of Economics*, LXV (August, 1951): 312.

rowers. In trying to assess the extent of effective banking concentration, the influence of possible substitute products can be ignored in line with the decision in chapter ii. The consequences of segmented markets for effective concentration is critical to the analysis and must be carefuly explored. The following discussion of concentration is broken down into the different segments which comprise the total banking market for short-term funds.

In industrial markets, concentration is measured in several different ways, including value added, employment, sales, and the like of the top (say) four firms. Although it is not always indifferent which of these measures is used,[7] for general descriptive purposes any of them is generally adequate. Similarly, in banking, a good impression of concentration can be derived from the use of either deposit or loan figures. Deposit figures show the concentration in terms of potential capacity;[8] the loan figures show the concentration in terms of that kind of output of most immediate concern in this study.[9]

Very large borrowers.—The analysis of unit bank market structures (chapter iii) has shown that banking markets are basically segmented by size of borrower. The largest borrowers operate on a national market, and the relevant concentration ratios must, therefore, be computed on a national basis. Table 7 measures this national concentration by showing the per cent of deposits and loans in the entire country which is held by the ten largest banks in the country as well as the per cent held by the Big Four branch banks of California. It is clear from table 7 that, if the banking market be taken as a national market, the degree of concentration in banking is significantly less than in many industrial markets. Furthermore, whereas concentration in industrial markets has probably increased since 1938, the trend in banking (as measured by deposits) would appear to be in the opposite direction, at any rate since the beginning of the Second World War.[10] Admittedly, the concentration in terms of the California Big Four has increased.

[7] For example, an assets measure of concentration may show higher concentration than (say) employment, because large firms usually have highly capitalistic structures, i.e., they have more capital per worker or more capital per dollar of output than smaller firms.

[8] Although capital and surplus provide part of a bank's lending power, the amount so provided is normally very small compared to the lending power based on deposits.

[9] A necessary qualification to the loan figures is that "loans" include all kinds of loans and not just business loans in the narrow sense. This same qualification also applies to all other loan figures employed in later tables.

[10] Part of the reason, no doubt, is the enormous increase in total deposits which accompanied the sharp increase in the national debt; government bonds were purchased by both large and small banks.

Indeed, in the postwar period, loan concentration of the Big Four increased in spite of the fact that their deposit concentration was comparatively stable. Notwithstanding, the absolute concentration figures are, relatively speaking, very low and present no monopolistic threat to the class of very large borrowers who operate on a national market.

TABLE 7

CONCENTRATION IN NATIONAL BANKING MARKETS, 1938–1950

(per cent of national totals)

Year[a]	Deposits[a]		Loans[a]	
	Ten largest banks	Big Four	Ten largest banks	Big Four
1938	20.8	4.0	17.0	5.1
1939	22.8	4.0	16.8	5.2
1940	24.8	3.9	16.3	5.6
1941	23.1	3.6	17.8	5.2
1942	26.7	3.8	17.3	5.4
1943	22.5	4.4	21.5	5.3
1944	21.8	4.6	22.9	5.0
1945	21.1	4.7	25.6	4.9
1946	17.1	5.1	23.1	5.4
1947	18.4	5.2	23.3	7.1
1948	17.7	5.4	22.0	7.7
1949	17.5	5.3	19.3	7.5
1950	18.7	5.5	22.6	7.3

[a] SOURCES: The figures for the Big Four are computed from data in *Rand McNally Bankers' Directory*, 1939–1951. The figures for the ten largest banks are computed from Moody's *Investors Service*, "Banks, Insurance, Real Estate, Investment Trusts," 1939–1951.

Intermediate-size borrowers.—The kind of concentration faced by intermediate-size and small borrowers is strikingly different from that faced by the very large borrowers. Whereas the very large borrowers operate on a national market, the intermediate-size borrowers are defined so that the limits of their relevant spatial market areas are roughly coterminous with the California state boundaries.[11] The small borrowers are even more sharply limited to their immediate local area and possibly adjacent communities. Thus,

[11] There is, of course, no intention to suggest that the political boundaries of the state have any necessary economic significance except so far as legal provisions have economic implications. The state boundaries are here selected as a matter of statistical convenience, but so far as medium-size borrowers can operate only within a roughly similar geographical area, a rough approximation to the relevant market for such borrowers is adequately described by the state borders. In California in particular, medium-size borrowers are more nearly confined to the state borders than would be true in a state of different geographical size.

the borrowers *potentially* affected by the concentration of banking in California are the intermediate-size and small borrowers.
It will be shown that even these two classes of borrowers are not
uniformly affected by the concentration, nor even always in the
same direction.

Tables 8 and 9 give some idea of the degree of concentration
faced by intermediate-size borrowers in California. Table 8 shows

TABLE 8

CONCENTRATION OF CALIFORNIA DEPOSITS BY THE BIG FOUR BRANCH BANKS, 1938–1950
(per cent of state totals)

Year[a]	Bank of America	Security Bank	American Trust	Anglo Bank	Total Big Four
1938	34.0	14.4	6.6	5.1	60.1
1939	34.0	13.8	6.9	4.8	59.5
1940	34.4	13.5	6.8	4.3	59.0
1941	34.7	12.8	7.0	4.3	58.8
1942	37.0	12.2	6.9	3.8	59.9
1943	38.3	12.8	6.8	3.8	61.7
1944	40.0	12.5	7.3	3.5	63.3
1945	39.3	12.5	7.2	3.6	62.6
1946	40.3	12.7	7.2	3.5	63.7
1947	40.8	12.6	7.2	3.3	63.8
1948	41.7	12.5	7.1	3.4	64.7
1949	42.5	12.2	7.0	3.5	65.2
1950	43.6	11.7	7.1	4.3	66.7

[a] SOURCE: Computed from figures in Rand McNally *Bankers' Directory*, 1939–1951.

the concentration of capacity in terms of deposits (both demand
and time) for each of the four large branch banks in California
as a per cent of the total deposits in the state.[12] Two facts are particularly striking in table 8. By 1950, the Big Four branch banks
held 66.7 per cent of the state's total deposits. Moreover, two-
thirds of the Big Four holdings were concentrated in one bank,
Bank of America. It is also interesting that Bank of America's share
of the market increased impressively, whereas Security Bank's and
Anglo Bank's shares of the market fell somewhat between the beginning and end of the period. The share of American Trust also

[12] In the Transamerica Hearings, Counsel for the Board of Governors held that
Bank of America figures should really be expanded to include the other bank holdings of Transamerica. Whether Bank of America was, in effect, an integral part of
the Transamerica system is not at issue in this study. In any case, the concentration
ratios for Bank of America are not significantly affected if recomputed as part of the
Transamerica holdings.

rose somewhat, but for the period as a whole, its share was comparatively stable.

Table 9 shows the loans of each of the Big Four as a per cent of the state total.[13] In comparing the concentration in terms of deposits with that in terms of loans, concentration by the Big Four on a loan basis is invariably higher than on a deposit basis. In 1950, for example, the Big Four transacted 74.9 per cent of the

TABLE 9

CONCENTRATION OF LOANS BY THE BIG FOUR BRANCH BANKS IN CALIFORNIA, 1938–1950
(per cent of state totals)

Year[a]	Bank of America	Security Bank	American Trust	Anglo Bank	Total Big Four
1938	36.2	13.9	7.3	5.3	62.7
1939	38.9	13.6	7.3	3.8	63.6
1940	39.7	12.7	8.1	3.6	63.6
1941	40.7	12.4	7.7	3.7	64.5
1942	42.7	12.2	7.9	3.3	66.1
1943	42.9	12.0	8.5	3.0	66.4
1944	44.9	10.6	9.5	2.9	67.9
1945	42.2	10.1	8.0	2.5	62.8
1946	47.5	9.2	8.7	2.8	68.2
1947	54.6	8.1	5.3	3.0	71.0
1948	54.7	8.5	7.4	3.2	73.8
1949	54.9	8.2	7.4	3.7	74.2
1950	55.8	7.2	7.8	4.1	74.9

[a] SOURCE: Computed from figures in Rand McNally *Bankers' Directory*, 1939–1951.

loan business but held only 66.7 per cent of the state's deposits. As with deposits, loan concentration of the Big Four increased significantly between the beginning and end of the period. This fact is particularly worth noting, since only Bank of America significantly increased its share of loans between 1938 and 1950. Security Bank's share was cut almost in half by 1950, and Anglo Bank's share also declined. In the period as a whole, American Trust's share was comparatively stable. The loan shares of both Anglo and Security were somewhat below their deposit shares; by contrast, both Bank of America and American Trust held a higher percentage of loans than of deposits.

A comparison between banking concentration in California and in the country as a whole reveals that the concentration in Cali-

[13] The loan percentages are actually based on the loan totals of each bank and not just those loans made to firms and individuals domiciled in California.

fornia is significantly higher than in the national credit market.[14] Furthermore, whereas concentration in the national market by the country's ten largest banks has been declining since 1940, concentration in California has conspicuously increased. Thus, although the concentration of California banking is negligible for very large borrowers, this cannot be said for intermediate-size borrowers. Within the California state boundaries, concentration

TABLE 10

NUMBER OF BANKS IN DIFFERENT SIZE CALIFORNIA CITIES AND TOWNS, 1950

Size of town[a] (population)	Number of banks									
	1	2	3	4	5	6	7	8	10	13
Under 1,000	44	..	..	1	..	..	..	..	..	..
1,001–2,500	99	11	1	..	..	..	..	..	..	..
2,501–5,000	57	24	1	..	..	..	..	..	..	..
5,001–10,000	36	24	5	..	..	..	..	..	..	..
10,001–25,000	17	42	14	2	1	..	..	..	..	..
25,001–50,000	..	4	6	6	..	..	..	..	..	..
50,001–75,000	..	1	..	4	1	..	..	..	..	..
75,001–100,000	..	..	3	2	..	..	..	..	..	..
100,001–200,000	..	..	..	1	..	1	1	..	..	..
200,001–300,000	..	..	..	..	..	..	..	..	1	..
300,001–400,000	..	..	..	..	..	..	1	1	..	..
Los Angeles	..	..	..	..	..	..	..	..	..	1[b]
San Francisco	..	..	..	..	..	..	..	..	1[b]	..
Totals	253	106	30	16	2	1	2	1	2	1

[a] SOURCE: Computed from *Rand McNally Bankers' Directory*, 1951.
[b] Number of competing banks only; excludes foreign banks. There are sixteen banks in Los Angeles and seventeen in San Francisco.

ratios of banking approximate the high concentration found in many manufacturing industries.

Small borowers.—Small borrowers are typically limited in market scope to the banks in their respective cities, and, possibly, to the banks in adjacent communities. Accordingly, the relevant concentration of banking markets for small borrowers is measured in terms of the number of alternative sources available to borrowers within each city and town. Table 10 shows this information for different size cities in California. In this table, a branch bank is listed only once for any city in which it appears although it may have multiple offices in that city.

[14] The reader's attention is directed to the fact that the country's *ten* largest banks have a lower share of the national market than California's Big Four banks have in California.

Small borrowers in California cities, including Los Angeles and San Francisco, face distinctly oligopolistic markets. Indeed, in about 85 per cent of the cities, small borrowers face either monopolistic or duopolistic markets, qualified only to the extent that access is possible to *different* banks in near-by cities. As might be expected, the objective number of alternative sources available to small borrowers increases as size of city increases. However, the number of cities with more than five banks is very small. Most startling of all, perhaps, is the very low number of banks in Los Angeles and San Francisco. Los Angeles, in particular, had a population of almost two million people in the 1950 census, but had only thirteen competing banks. In contrast, New York City had ten times as many banks as Los Angeles. Even when allowance is made for the greater population of the former, New York City still had proportionately more than three times as many banks as Los Angeles.[15] New York City is the financial capital of the world, and might be expected to have a very large number of banks. It should be noted, however, that New York City has a large number of unit banks in addition to the large number of branch offices of giant intracity branch systems.

The small number of banks in California's leading cities illustrates again the adverse effects of concentration on the number of alternative sources available to intermediate-size borrowers. The kind of market faced by such borrowers is necessarily conditioned by the market structure in the largest cities in California where the major banks are situated. In California's major cities, banking markets are distinctly oligopolistic. At least in terms of numbers of banks, comparable markets in New York City have a more nearly competitive structure.

On the basis of table 10, the conclusion seems justified that California's small borrowers face heavily concentrated banking markets and are, perhaps, even worse off than intermediate size borrowers. The situation confronting small borrowers in California is put in perspective by comparing their position with that faced by small borrowers in other parts of the country where concentration (as measured by the usual kind of official statistics) is allegedly less intense.[16] Table 11 compares the market structure in terms of alternative sources of supply for small borrowers in all

---

[15] No suggestion is intended that number of banks should be proportional to population. The figures in the text are merely for purposes of rough comparison.

[16] As far as the concentration problem is concerned, the reader is reminded that the only realistic alternative to branch banking is unit banking, which predominates in the country as a whole.

parts of the United States and in California cities. The comparisons in the table will probably be surprising to most readers. Although the percentage figure of one-bank cities is high in California, it is substantially higher in the entire country.[17] Correspondingly, a higher percentage of California cities has a larger number of rival banking institutions than have the corresponding categories of all cities in the country. California even leads the

TABLE 11

NUMBER OF CITIES WITH DIFFERENT NUMBER OF BANKS, UNITED
STATES, 1949, AND CALIFORNIA, 1950

Number of banks in city [a]	United States (1949)		California (1950)	
	Number of cities in each class	Per cent	Number of cities in each class	Per cent
1	7,885	75.5	253	61.3
2	1,900	18.2	106	25.6
3	369	3.5	30	7.3
4	134	1.3	16	3.9
5	53	0.5	2	0.48
6	23	0.2	1	0.24
7	19	0.2	2	0.48
8	13	0.1	1	0.24
9	10	0.1	0	0.0
10 or more	41	0.4	3	0.73
Totals	10,447	100.0 [b]	414	100.0 [b]

a SOURCE: *Rand McNally Bankers' Directory*, 1950 and 1951.
b Totals do not add exactly to 100 per cent because of rounding.

national average in the per cent of its cities having more than ten banks. Thus, although the small borrowers in California cities unquestionably face heavy concentration in the markets in which they must operate, the position of small borrowers is even less favorable in the country as a whole.

CONCENTRATION AND BANKING MARKETS

The concentration of banking in California affects not only the number of alternative sources available to different size borrowers, but is reflected also in the market situations of banks operating in the state. To the extent that banking competition is a function of the number of independently owned banks,[18] the high concen-

[17] Under branch banking, California has no real problem of bankless towns.
[18] Cf. p. 37 which shows *some* influence of numbers of objective alternative sources of supply.

tration of banking in California will influence the kind of market conditions faced by each of the Big Four in different California communities. It has been shown that banking markets are effectively separated into three major categories, depending upon the size of the borrower.[19] In the large-borrower loan market, the Big Four face a competitive market situation, because large borrowers operate on a national credit market. Since the intermediate-size and small borrowers are limited to local market areas, the concen-

TABLE 12

BANKING OFFICES OF THE BIG FOUR BRANCH BANKS AS A PER CENT OF
THE STATE TOTAL, 1938–1950

Year[a]	Bank of America	Security Bank	American Trust	Anglo Bank	Big Four	Unit banks
1938	44.9	11.1	5.9	1.8	63.7	36.3
1939	45.3	10.8	5.8	1.8	63.7	36.3
1940	45.8	10.8	5.8	1.9	65.3	34.7
1941	46.0	10.8	5.9	2.0	64.7	35.3
1942	46.3	10.7	5.8	2.0	64.8	35.2
1943	45.5	10.6	6.0	2.0	64.1	35.9
1944	44.9	10.4	5.8	1.9	63.0	37.0
1945	43.9	10.7	5.7	2.0	62.3	37.7
1946	45.6	11.0	6.2	2.2	65.0	35.0
1947	45.8	11.1	6.7	2.3	65.9	34.1
1948	45.6	11.1	7.1	2.3	66.1	33.9
1949	45.8	11.2	7.1	2.5	66.6	33.4
1950	44.0	11.0	6.9	2.5	64.4	35.6

[a] SOURCE: Computed from figures in *Rand McNally Bankers' Directory*, 1939–1951.

tration of banking in California could materially affect the market position of the Big Four in local markets. Accordingly, the discussion of the effects of concentration on the banking markets faced by the Big Four will be limited to the markets for intermediate-size and small borrowers.

In the state.—For the state as a whole, table 12 gives a general idea of concentration of the Big Four in terms of banking offices.

[19] It may perhaps labor the obvious to observe that the effectiveness of the separation of the three markets will obviously vary for individual borrowers in particular circumstances. Although the separation of markets by size categories seems clearly established, mobility among the market categories may exist for particular borrowers, depending on other circumstances. In emphasizing the separation of market by size of borrower, I do not mean to suggest that size of borrower is literally the only consideration affecting market behavior, but rather that it is the single most important factor. In general, the effects of size of borrower will be decisive in determining the market in which the borrower must operate. Almost any generalization, however, must allow for individual exceptions, and that applies in this case, too.

As might be expected, banking offices, like deposits and loans, show
a very heavy concentration. By the end of the period, the Big Four
held about 65 per cent of all banking offices in the state. Bank of
America alone had 44 per cent of the state's banking offices. In
1950, California had 1,195 banking offices,[20] but because of the
very high concentration, the large number of banking offices is
not synonymous with the number of *independent* sources of supply.
It is a legitimate simplification to proceed on the assumption that,
predominantly, size of borrower (in terms of total volume of loans
even if not of number) is related to size of city.[21] It is revealing,
therefore, to break down the competitive situation of the Big Four
by size of city.

In metropolitan areas.—As mentioned earlier, the market situation faced by the intermediate-size borrowers depends essentially
upon the kinds of banking markets that exist in the metropolitan
centers of the state, since the important banks of the state are all
represented in the metropolitan centers. In practice, most intermediate-size borrowers probably deal directly with banks in metropolitan centers. Even when their loans are negotiated in small
towns or cities, their competitive position is largely determined
by the fact that they have access to the banking markets of the
metropolitan centers.

There are eight important metropolitan areas in California, including San Francisco, Los Angeles, San Diego, Fresno, San Jose,
Sacramento, Bakersfield, Stockton. These cities are not necessarily
the largest cities in the state in terms of resident population, but
they are the most important economic centers. In 1947, the eight
areas combined had a population of almost eight million or about
80 per cent of the state's total population. Table 13 shows the distribution of bank deposits of individuals, partnerships, and corporations for each of the Big Four banks in these eight centers. The
dominance of the Big Four in these eight areas is unmistakable.
Together they held 63.5 per cent of all deposits in these areas. Moreover, Bank of America by itself held more deposits than all the
unit banks[22] combined. In the loan market for intermediate-size
borrowers, the Big Four operate in an oligopolistic structure in
which one firm is clearly dominant.

In different size cities.—The banking market for small borrowers is fragmented into the numerous submarkets situated in dif-

---

[20] *Rand McNally Bankers' Directory* (Chicago: Rand McNally and Company, 1951).
[21] Cf. chapter iii, n. 35.
[22] As used in this study, the term "unit banks" includes all banks except the Big
Four branch banks.

ferent California cities and towns. The market situation of the Big
Four must be considered separately for each of these submarkets.
Table 14 gives this information for the year 1950. The table reveals, as might be expected, that the absolute number of each
bank's branches which face no competition within their respective
communities varies directly with size of branch bank.[23] The per
cent of each bank's offices located in one-bank towns differs strikingly, however. The percentages for each bank are: Bank of America, 48.7; Security–First National, 15.4; American Trust, 9.5; and
Anglo-California, 21.1. In deriving these percentages, the figure

TABLE 13

DISTRIBUTION OF BANK DEPOSITS OF INDIVIDUALS, PARTNERSHIPS, AND CORPORATIONS,
CALIFORNIA BANKS IN EIGHT METROPOLITAN AREAS, 1947

Banks[a]	Deposits (000,000)	Total of eight areas (per cent)
Bank of America	3,762	38.1
Security–First National	1,408	14.3
American Trust	778	7.9
Anglo-California	320	3.2
All other banks	3,588	36.5

[a] SOURCE: Transamerica Hearings, Respondent's Exhibit 124.

for the total number of branches for each bank was obtained by
considering multiple offices of the same bank in a given city as one
"branch."[24] In assessing market structures, totals based on this com-
putation are clearly preferable to the absolute total of banking
offices of a branch system.

The apparent monopoly position of the Big Four banks in many
small-borrower markets is qualified to the extent that even small
borrowers can establish banking connections in near-by communities. Many of the one-bank towns in California are only a few
minutes to a half-hour by automobile from a bank in another community. Of course, the borrower may discover upon reaching the
near-by community that it, too, is dominated by the same branch
bank situated in his own town. Where banking connections in
near-by towns are possible to a small borrower, however, and where
the near-by bank is the branch of another bank or is a unit bank,

[23] There were no cases of multiple offices of the same bank in an otherwise one-bank
town. Where multiple offices of the same bank existed in other cities, the multiple
offices were lumped together as one bank.

[24] In this section, the word "branch" refers to *all* the branch offices of a single branch
bank within each city.

even the nominally sole bank occupant of a town faces a potential competitor, and the relevant market area is greater than the geographical limits of the town in which the bank is situated.

As for Bank of America, 248 of its "branch"[25] banks, or 82.7 per cent of its "branches," operate in either monopolistic or duopolistic small-borrower markets. Fully 60 per cent of Security's "branches" and the "branches" of American Trust face only one rival or no competition in the small-borrower market, and even 52.6 per cent

TABLE 14

NUMBER OF BANKS IN DIFFERENT BANK-CITY CATEGORIES, CALIFORNIA, 1950

Number of banks[a] in city	Number of banks in cities of each class			
	Bank of America	Security Bank	American Trust	Anglo California
1	146	8	4	4
2	102	24	21	6
3	29	11	6	3
4	14	6	7	3
5	2	..	1	..
6	1	..	1	1
7	2	1	..	..
8	1	..	1	1
9	..	..	..	..
10	2	1	1	1
11	..	..	..	..
12	..	..	..	..
13	1	1	..	..

[a] SOURCE: Computed from *Rand McNally Bankers' Directory*, 1951.

of Anglo's "branches" operate in similar markets. Only a very small number of "branches" in each bank face more than three other competitors in the same city. In other words, more than half of the "branches" of the Big Four operate in either monopolistic or duopolistic small-borrower markets, and most of the rest of their "branches" are in a very strong oligopolistic position. In the very largest cities of the state, the Big Four banks may face as many as nine or twelve rival banks. But their effective concentration in the small-borrower market of large cities is even greater than implied by these figures, since at least some of the branches of the Big Four in large cities will face some small borrowers as sole sellers.

The potential monopolistic power of the Big Four in the small-borrower market would seem to be very great on the basis of the

[25] See n. 24, above.

previous table. The actual monopoly power of the Big Four will depend additionally upon the competition of possible substitute forms of credit provided by nonbank suppliers and by the conditions of entry into these markets. Both of these matters are further considered later in this study. Before leaving this section, however, it is well to put the intense concentration in the California small-borrowers' market in a broader perspective. For public policy, it

TABLE 15

NUMBER OF BANKS IN DIFFERENT BANK-CITY CATEGORIES, UNITED STATES, 1949, AND CALIFORNIA, 1950

Number of banks in city[a]	United States (1949)		California (1950)	
	Number of banks in cities of each class	Per cent	Number of banks in cities of each class	Per cent
1	7,885	52.8	253	36.0
2	3,800	25.5	212	30.2
3	1,107	7.4	90	12.8
4	536	3.5	64	9.1
5	265	1.8	10	1.4
6	138	0.9	6	0.85
7	133	0.9	14	2.0
8	104	0.7	8	1.11
9	90	0.6	0	0.0
10 or more	860	5.8	52	7.4
Totals	14,918	100.0[b]	709	100.0[b]

[a] SOURCE: Computed from *Rand McNally Bankers' Directory*, 1950 and 1951.
[b] Totals do not add to 100 because of rounding.

is relevant to ascertain not only what the existing concentration may be, but how it compares with the most realistic alternative conditions, viz., unit banking. In other words, it is desirable to compare the concentration in the California small-borrowers' markets under branch banking with the situation in the rest of the country where the banking organization is still predominantly unit banking.

Table 15 compares the number of banks in different bank-city categories in the United States with the number of banks in corresponding California cities. This table gives perspective to the highly concentrated position of the Big Four in the small-borrowers' market, not only in relation to small-borrower markets in other parts of the country but even to the small-borrower markets in California itself. The table reveals that in almost every category,

small-borrower banking markets in California are *less* concentrated
than in the rest of the country, despite the giant branch banks in
California. The number of banks[26] holding a monopoly position,
for example, is strikingly less in California than in the United
States as a whole. In spite of the very high degree of concentration
of banking resources in California, a higher proportion of banks
and branches in California face rival banks in their local communities than is true in the country as a whole. Surprisingly, this is true
even of the percentage of banks which face ten or more rivals in
one city. Although it is undoubtedly true that banking concentration in the small-borrower markets is intense in California, it is
far from obvious that the situation would be significantly changed
if unit banks were to replace the existing branch banks in the state.

Paradoxically, perhaps, the high concentration of banking resources in California is in large part responsible for the high proportion of banks facing rivals in their local markets. Although
California concentration is a function of branch banking, there
can be little doubt that, in turn, branch banking is largely responsible for the proportionately greater number of banking offices
in towns having banks, and, correspondingly, for the proportionately smaller number of one-bank towns. This fact is particularly
worth stressing, since branches are often established in communities which could not support a unit bank. The result is that California has no real problem of bankless towns.

SUMMARY

The concentration statistics in this chapter are highly unorthodox.
Conventional concentration statistics in the field of banking are
usually computed on a legalistic or political-jurisdiction base;
hence, the common practice of showing concentration of banking
resources on a state-wide basis. Statistics computed in this manner
may conceivably serve legalistic or political purposes. For economic
analysis, such statistics are meaningless, or worse. It is only by
chance that statistics thus computed may sometimes find a place
in economic investigations. To compute concentration statistics
meaningful for economic analysis, it is first necessary to have a
theory of the structure of banking markets. The sketch of banking
markets presented in chapter iii suggested a convenient threefold
breakdown of borrower-loan markets by size of borrower, viz.,
large borrowers, intermediate-size borrowers, and small borrowers.
Given this basic division of markets, concentration was examined

---

[26] "Banks" here refers to "branches." Cf. n. 24.

from the point of view of the borrower and then from the position of the Big Four branch banks.

The investigation revealed that concentration of banking resources within the political boundaries of California has no perceptible effect on the alternative sources of supply available to large borrowers. Large borrowers operate in a reasonably competitive national market, and even the very high degree of banking concentration in California is not very impressive in that context. The concentration of banking resources in California does, however, affect the intermediate-size borrowers, because such borrowers are, roughly speaking, confined to bank sources within their own states. As a result of the concentration, intermediate-size borrowers in California face far more limited alternative sources of supply than in other parts of the country. Whereas such borrowers face only loosely oligopolistic markets or even approximations to competitive markets in many other parts of the country, the intermediate-size borrowers in California are confronted with distinctly oligopolistic markets. In about 85 per cent of California's cities and towns, the small borrowers face either monopolistic or duopolistic markets. The surprising fact is that small borrowers in California face monopolistic markets in 61 per cent of California's cities and towns, but in the country as a whole, small borrowers face this situation in 75 per cent of the nation's cities and towns.

In the large-borrower loan market, the Big Four branch banks face a competitive market situation because they are part of a national market in which such borrowers operate. The concentration of banking resources in California gives the Big Four a much stronger position in the intermediate-size borrower loan markets. In these markets they constitute an oligopolistic market in which one of the Big Four holds a distinctly dominant position. The Big Four concentration within the state affects also their market position in the small-borrower markets. More than half of the Big Four "branches" operate in either monopolistic or duopolistic small-borrower markets, and most of the rest of their "branches" are in a very strong oligopolistic position. In small-borrower loan markets in California as a whole, however, a higher proportion of all the banks and "branches" in the state faces rival banks in their local communities than is true in comparable markets throughout the United States.

When concentration is computed on an economic base rather than a legal or political-jurisdiction base, both the extent of the concentration and its effects are considerably different from what might be expected on the basis of conventional calculations. As stated earlier, the addition of figures without a theoretical analysis to guide the computations can lead to seriously misleading conclusions. Throughout the balance of this study, therefore, every effort will be made to mold the analysis within the division of markets identified in chapter iii. Unfortunately, available statistics are not often broken down into the economic categories identified in this study. In some cases, such as in this chapter on concentration, it is possible to put available figures on the economic basis pertinent in this study. In other cases, that kind of breakdown cannot be made, or the figures do not exist in any form. Where it seems desirable but not possible to present statistics in terms of the different banking markets, the interpretations at least will follow that division.

V

Measures of Output Performance

THE CONCENTRATION of California banking described in the previous chapter leaves no doubt that the *structure* of banking markets in California—with the possible exception of the banking market for the largest borrowers—falls considerably short of the requirements of purely competitive markets. The number of banks in an area is at least one clue to market structures, and there are fewer independent banks in California relative to the size of the market to be served than in most other areas of the country. The critical question is whether this concentration has resulted in less competitive *results* than might be expected with a larger number of independent banks. In any list of operating results, comparative levels of output are an important consideration. It can be shown as a theoretical proposition that firms in noncompetitive markets are likely to produce a smaller output than firms operating in competitive markets. The discussion in this chapter will investigate two important questions in connection with output: (1) Do branch banks have an inherent superiority in their ability to produce? and (2) Has the high degree of bank concentration in California resulted in a restriction of loan output?[1]

PRODUCTION CAPACITY AND LOCAL LOAN MARKETS

BANK RESOURCES AND UTILIZED CAPACITY

The "load factor" in banking.—The banking "load factor" provides an index of the efficiency of different banks in utilizing resources in a directly productive (i.e., earning) manner. The load factor is an expression usually applied to hydroelectric generating plants to describe the ratio of used capacity to total capacity. In

---

[1] It has been alleged that one of the factors which have tended to restrict credit availability is "the decline in the number of banks through failure and consolidations." Testimony of C. S. Young, President, Federal Reserve Bank of Chicago, Patman Report, Part 2, p. 809.

TABLE 16

Loans and Investments as a Per Cent of Total Assets, by Size and Kind of Bank, California, 1938–1950

Unit banks[a] (by size)	1938	1939	1940	1941	1942	1943	1944	1945	1946	1947	1948	1949	1950
Smallest.......	69.8	73.2	61.9	62.0	56.6	62.7	66.8	68.8	71.0	69.4	69.7	67.4	68.0
2...............	69.8	65.6	69.4	64.6	61.2	61.7	70.6	72.2	74.5	75.5	75.1	75.5	75.4
3...............	71.2	70.8	63.2	61.8	63.6	65.0	73.4	76.1	78.3	79.5	79.2	78.5	78.8
4...............	68.6	70.0	66.8	64.5	62.4	67.3	73.8	74.2	76.4	75.9	76.5	76.6	75.9
5...............	73.3	68.9	64.9	65.5	66.9	72.2	74.6	77.8	79.4	79.1	78.1	78.5	81.9
6...............	70.6	68.8	67.8	65.0	....	72.0	74.8	77.3	77.2	75.3	73.9	75.4	77.0
7...............	69.5	70.0	67.2	66.4	....	....	....	....	....	....	....	....	....
8...............	69.9	70.0	....	....	....	....	....	....	....	....	....	....	....
Unit bank averages......	70.5	69.5	65.8	63.9	61.5	65.1	71.5	74.0	76.2	76.7	76.3	75.9	76.6
Branch bank averages...	76.8	76.4	73.0	72.7	72.6	75.8	79.0	80.0	80.5	79.0	77.7	78.7	80.7

For sources and notes to table, see Appendix.

[a] Federal Reserve size groupings of banks changed considerably during the period. For example, the smallest category of banks in 1938 was described as "Under $250,000," but in 1950, the smallest category was "Under $2,000,000." Hence, in these tables, absolute size groupings were ignored, and banks were ranked by size from smallest to largest in each year.

banking, total assets are a rough gauge of "capacity," and the ratio of loans and investments to total assets is analogous for banks to the load factor in hydroelectric plants. The load factor for different size banks in California (table 16) shows no clear tendency to vary with size of unit bank, except that the smallest unit banks almost invariably have the lowest load factors. In at least half the years of the study period, the second smallest banks had the second lowest ratios. Although there is no pattern of variation by size of bank, there is a wide range in the load factor among different unit banks. The absolute difference between the lowest and the highest load factor in any year ranged from 4.6 to 13.9 percentage points. The mean of these differences for the period as a whole is 8.1 percentage points. These differences are not inconsiderable, but they are not related to size of unit bank.

By contrast with the unit banks, the load factor tends to vary directly with size of branch bank. This pattern of variation is most sharply defined at the extremes of the different size branch banks. There is a mild blurring of the pattern between the two middle-size branch banks during the early part of the period. Generally, however, the load factors of the top three banks are reasonably close together. For all branch banks, the annual absolute difference in the range of the load factor varied between 1.7 and 10.1 percentage points. The mean of the absolute differences, however, is only about 5.4 percentage points. Moreover, these percentage points represent differences among larger figures than for the unit banks.

The load factor for the average of branch banks is higher in every year than the load factor of the largest unit banks. Furthermore, in almost every year, even the branch banks with the lowest load factor among all branch banks still had a higher load factor than the largest category of unit banks. Similarly, the load factor for the average of branch banks was higher in every year than that for the average of the unit banks. In almost every year, too, even the lowest ranking branch bank had a higher load factor than the unit bank average.

To summarize, the load factor is not related to size of unit bank, except that the smallest unit banks had the lowest load factors. Branch banks as a group have a larger productive potential with given resources than unit banks. Furthermore, although the smallest of the branch banks is smaller in size than some of the large unit banks in California, the former generally has a higher load factor than the largest category of unit banks. These facts suggest that the load factor is a function of bank organization, whether branch or unit. Large branch banks have a productive capacity advantage over smaller branch banks, which suggests that the load factor is a function not only of branch organization but also of size of branch bank.

Reasons for different load factors.—Many factors account for the different load factors in different unit banks and between branch banks and unit banks. One important element that potentially affects the load factor is the ratio of time deposits to total deposits. Although there is no strong pattern among unit banks between size of bank and ratio of time deposits to total deposits, the smallest category of unit banks tends to have comparatively low time deposit ratios.[2] Similarly, it will be recalled, although the load factor is not related to size of unit bank, the smallest unit banks almost invariably have the lowest load factors. With the exception of American Trust Company, time deposit ratios of branch banks tend to vary directly with size of bank. Among branch banks, the load factor also tends to vary directly with size of bank. The load factor pattern between branch and unit banks is also duplicated in the time deposit ratios. In every year, the average time deposits of branch banks were higher than the largest unit banks, and higher than the average of unit banks. Finally, in almost every year, even the branch bank with the lowest time deposit ratios had a higher ratio than the largest unit banks.

This pattern of association between load factors and time deposit ratios is not fortuitous. The ratio of time deposits to total deposits can affect the load factor in either or both of two ways. First, time deposits in member banks of the Federal Reserve System are subject to much lower reserve requirements than demand deposits.[3] Other things being equal, for given cash assets (or reserves), a bank with a high ratio of time deposits to total deposits can "produce" more loans and investments than a bank with a low ratio. This factor is only a potential factor and could be dissipated in excess reserves. In practice, however, this potential factor is characteristically utilized in extensions of credit. A high ratio of time deposits also facilitates a high load factor because time deposits imply less pressure for liquidity than demand deposits. Legally, time deposits are not subject to demand payment. Although banks rarely insist

[2] See Appendix table A.

[3] For example, as of June 1, 1952, reserve requirements on demand deposits were 24, 20, and 14 per cent, respectively, in central reserve city banks, reserve city banks, and country banks. At the same time, reserve requirements on time deposits of all member banks were only 6 per cent.

on this legal provision, time deposits are somewhat more stable than demand deposits.[4] Accordingly, less vault cash need be tied up for a given amount of time deposits than for a comparable amount of demand deposits. The vault cash thus released is available for further credit expansion and serves to raise the load factor in banks with high ratios of time deposits to total deposits.

The statistical record suggests, and the preceding analysis explains, why the time deposit ratio is at least one factor influencing the load factor among banks. The time deposit ratio cannot, however, be the only determining factor. In the first place, although the largest unit banks had the lowest time deposit ratios in all but four years of the study period, they were far from having the lowest load factors. Second, although the second smallest branch bank invariably had the highest ratio of time deposits among the branch banks, its load factor was invariably lower than that of some other branch bank. Third, although the average ratio of time deposits of branch banks was usually below at least one category of unit banks, the average branch bank load factor was typically higher than for any category of unit banks. Finally, although the average time deposit ratios for unit banks and branch banks were very similar between 1941 and 1946. the load factors differed substantially, relative to other years studied.

Fundamentally, the explanation for a high load factor is directly related to a bank's economizing of reserves. Time deposit ratios affect load factors by economizing reserves. In many cases, however, the economy of reserves implied by a high time deposit ratio is counteracted by other considerations which increase the liquidity of a bank. For example, large banks have a large number of depositors, and the action of no single depositor is likely to be unstabilizing. In a small bank, however, the erratic movement of a few large accounts can place severe pressure on the bank's reserves and on its liquidity. The result is that small banks need more liquidity than large banks. Similarly, the loan markets served by small banks are often limited, and small banks are not nearly so efficient nor so knowledgeable as larger banks about investing surplus funds on the open market. Moreover, small banks must carry correspondent balances with large banks in metropolitan centers. At any moment of time, at least part of these funds may be idle. By contrast with small banks, large banks rarely carry surplus cash even momentarily. Excess reserves of large banks are

---

[4] With the possible exception of "abnormal" periods. Cf. Albert G. Hart, *Money, Debt and Economic Activity* (New York: Prentice-Hall, 1948), pp. 40–41.

loaned on the federal funds market even on an overnight basis. All these factors result in greater liquidity in many of the smaller unit banks than is found in the largest unit banks. The high liquidity requirements implied by the very low time deposit ratios in the largest unit banks (and the high reserves ratios most of them must legally carry) is thus counterbalanced by all the factors which increase the liquidity of unit banks with higher time deposit ratios. Thus, although the largest unit banks have the lowest time deposit ratios among the unit banks, their load factors are often comparatively high.

In branch banks, interbranch mobility of funds further reduces the low liquidity requirements implied by a high time deposit ratio. Internal mobility of funds permits a high turnover of resources. Slack demand in one area can be compensated by shifting resources to other areas where demand for funds is greater. Small banks, and especially rural banks, may hold excess reserves if the demand for funds is slack in their local areas. Accordingly, branch banks have a higher average load factor than the average of unit banks even when the time deposit ratios of the two categories are very similar. Branch banks emerge with a higher load factor than unit banks even in those cases where branch banks have lower time deposit ratios than particular categories of unit banks. The leverage from mobility of funds operates even among branch banks themselves, with the greatest leverage secured by the largest branch system with banking offices all over the state.

In summary, a high load factor is a function both of size of bank and of bank structure, but the latter is clearly the more important. Bank size and structure, in turn, directly and indirectly bear upon the economy of reserves by influencing the composition of deposits and the various factors which determine the liquidity position of a bank. In the net interplay of these factors, branch banks emerge with a clear superiority in load factor over unit banks. Quite specifically, this conclusion means that, with given resources, branch banks have an inherent superiority over unit banks in their ability to produce all kinds of bank credit.

MAJOR COMPONENTS OF BANK CREDIT

Loan ratios.—The load factor tends to vary directly with size of branch bank, and, other things being equal, is larger for branch banks than for unit banks. The load factor, however, includes both loans and investments. Investments are undoubtedly an important "product" of commercial banks, but the discussion in chapter ii makes it clear that loans, not investments, must be considered as the primary form of output of commercial banks. It is relevant, therefore, to examine the percentage of total resources which commercial banks of different size and organization devote to loan production. Table 17 shows loans as a percentage of total assets of different size banks. In the prewar period (1938–1941), most unit banks were devoting a significant proportion of their resources to loan production, usually more than 40 per cent of total assets. This ratio fell to less than half that per cent during the war years, and, although the ratio increased during the postwar period, it never again reached the general levels of the prewar period. The largest unit banks had the lowest loan ratios among unit banks throughout the entire period. Generally, however, no clear pattern of variation emerges between the loan ratio and size of unit bank.

The loan ratio for the average of branch banks was invariably much higher than the loan ratio of the largest unit banks. In almost every year, too, the average loan ratio of the branch banks was higher than the average of unit banks. However, in all but four years of the study period (viz., 1943, 1944, 1948, 1949), at least one and usually more than one category of unit banks had larger loan ratios than the average of branch banks. The branch banks themselves exhibited no stable pattern of variation by size of bank. American Trust and Bank of America had the highest loan ratios among branch banks during the early and latter years of the study period, respectively. Anglo Bank and Security–First National held bottom place during the first and last parts of the study period, respectively. In general, the range of variation among branch banks was comparable to that among unit banks.

Although several unit bank categories had higher loan ratios than the branch bank average in most years, the highest of the branch banks was (except in the early years) also higher than any of the unit banks. On the other hand, the lowest of the branch banks was quite often surpassed by some of the unit banks, as, indeed, it was often surpassed by the average of unit banks.

Investment ratios.—The investment ratio pattern is to a certain extent, but by no means completely, the counterpart of the loan pattern.[5] In the prewar period, all banks devoted considerably less of their productive capacity to investments than to loans. However,

---

[5] Since loans and investments do not constitute the total assets of a bank, the proportion of productive capacity devoted by different banks to investments (securities) is examined separately. Appendix table B, shows a breakdown of investments between U. S. government securities and all other securities. For the years 1938 through 1941, these two categories are listed jointly.

TABLE 17

Loans as a Per Cent of Total Assets, by Size and Kind of Bank, California, 1938–1950

Unit banks[a] (by size)	1938	1939	1940	1941	1942	1943	1944	1945	1946	1947	1948	1949	1950
Smallest	50.7	53.8	43.0	41.0	27.7	19.4	12.3	13.5	12.0	20.4	25.1	25.5	33.0
2	43.1	44.6	42.3	40.4	30.4	19.8	12.9	10.7	14.5	20.2	26.8	29.3	29.6
3	41.7	43.8	39.6	39.8	32.3	17.0	15.3	12.9	15.4	20.9	25.2	27.0	31.2
4	44.5	45.7	44.6	43.9	36.7	20.7	16.2	14.8	17.2	24.3	28.3	29.9	29.4
5	40.7	41.5	33.4	29.8	25.0	22.8	18.0	16.9	21.2	29.7	32.9	31.1	36.4
6	40.3	41.1	46.0	45.7	....	14.7	11.9	10.3	11.1	16.7	19.8	20.4	20.1
7	41.8	43.1	26.2	25.7	....	....	....	....	....	....	....	....	....
8	31.4	28.6	....	....	....	....	....	....	....	....	....	....	....
Unit bank average	42.0	42.9	40.9	32.5	30.6	19.0	13.9	12.4	15.2	21.2	26.3	27.3	30.3
Branch bank average	42.2	41.3	38.0	39.4	35.5	24.0	19.2	16.8	18.3	27.4	34.0	35.9	35.6

For sources and notes to table, see Appendix.
[a] See notes to table 16.

the largest unit banks were devoting more of their productive capacity to securities than was any other size bank. In fact, while all but the largest unit banks were making more loans than investments between 1938–1941, the largest unit banks reversed this pattern and made more investments than loans. As the country moved into the Second World War, all banks significantly increased their holdings of government securities. Again, however, the largest unit banks held proportionately more government securities than any other unit banks. After the war, the percentage of bonds to total assets declined in all banks, but the largest unit banks still tended to have the highest ratios of government securities to total assets. The smallest unit banks held least securities before the war and tended to hold least government securities even during the war and postwar periods. The ranking of the intermediate-size bank categories was scrambled, but their percentages were also fairly close together in most years. During both the war and postwar periods, the largest unit banks tended to hold very low percentages of "other securities" compared to those held by the rest of the unit banks, although in some instances, other unit banks held as low or lower percentages. With the exception of the largest unit banks, no ranking pattern is descernible between percentage of "other securities" and size of bank.

In the prewar period, the branch banks as a group held somewhat lower percentages of securities than the largest unit banks. Since the latter had the highest ratios among unit banks, the average holdings of branch banks were nevertheless considerably higher than those of many unit banks. During the war period, too, the average holdings of government securities by branch banks were proportionately less than for the largest unit banks, and the same pattern has continued to the present. Again, however, the largest unit banks tended to hold proportionately more government securities than the rest of the unit banks. Although branch banks held proportionately less government bonds than the largest unit banks, both during and after the war, they held a higher percentage of "other securities" than the largest unit banks and usually fell in a roughly intermediate position in the range of the unit banks. On the other hand, the largest unit banks also tended to have the lowest holdings of "other securities" among the unit banks.

Size of branch bank seemed to have no decisive influence on percentage holdings of securities by branch banks. Security–First National Bank and Anglo Bank held the highest proportions of government bonds both during and after the war. Usually, Security

Bank had the highest ratio. On the other hand, Bank of America, the largest of the branch banks, usually had the lowest ratio of government bonds. The situation was just reversed in holdings of "other securities"; Bank of America usually held a higher percentage than its rivals. Anglo Bank and Security Bank held the smallest percentages of "other securities."

In very rough terms, therefore, the pattern on investment ratios is the counterpart of the pattern on loan ratios, although loans and investments do not comprise the total of bank assets.

LOAD FACTORS AND LOAN RATIOS

As of December 31, 1951, 82.3 per cent of all member bank investments were in United States government obligations. Twelve per cent were in obligations of states and political subdivisions and a miscellaneous 5.6 per cent were in other securities.[6] The 5.6 per cent of member bank investments in other securities amounted only to 3.1 per cent of total loans and investments of member banks.[7] In other words, only a very small percentage of banking resources is made available to businessmen in the form of corporate ("other") securities. Overwhelmingly, member bank investments take the form of United States government securities. In the main, therefore, bank investments are made in a national market. By contrast, although loans, too, can be made in a national market, the majority of loans, even of the largest banks in California, are probably made in local market areas.[8]

Irrespective of whether a bank makes loans or investments, the greater part of its output is based on its deposits. Whereas deposits can be garnered in a national market, most primary deposits probably are gathered in the local market areas of the banks involved. This fact, obviously true for the small banks, holds, in all probability, for the very largest banks as well.[9] Whereas loans return deposits primarily to local areas, investments distribute them to a national market. The load factor has already been identified as a

---

[6] See table 1, chapter ii.

[7] *Loc. cit.*

[8] Even the largest branch banks pride themselves on being "retail banks" (Security) or "the little fellow's bank" (Bank of America).

Similarly, the Chairman of the Board of Governors of the Federal Reserve System has observed that "The lending rather than the investing phase of the credit-granting function ... is the phase most directly concerned with the community in which a banking office is situated." Patman Report, Part I, p. 574, n. 4.

[9] The very large banks in money market centers are possible exceptions. Such banks handle not only the deposits of national concerns but act also as correspondents for smaller banks in all parts of the country.

gauge of the utilized capacity[10] of different banks. The loan ratio shows the per cent of a bank's resources that is returned to the areas which initially produced the deposits. Hence, a comparison of the loan ratio with the load factor shows the per cent of a bank's resources made available to local borrowers as compared with the per cent of its utilized capacity.

In unit banks, the load factor is not related to size of bank, and this is also true for loan ratios. Although there are no loan ratio patterns among unit banks by size of bank, the penultimate size unit bank had the highest loan ratios (among unit banks) in many years when it did not have the highest load factor. By contrast, although the largest unit banks had comparatively high load factors, their loan ratio was invariably lowest among the unit banks. Although productive capacity is high in the largest unit banks, there is no reason for assuming that the per cent of their resources made available to local borrowers will be correspondingly high. In part, no doubt, the failure of the load factor pattern to be matched by a similar loan ratio pattern is because of the demands of portfolio diversification in different banks.

Load factors and loan ratios among branch banks are not highly related. Although branch bank load factors tend to vary directly with size of branch bank, a corresponding pattern for loan ratios is considerably less pronounced. American Trust, third largest of the branch banks in Califorina, was often first in the per cent of its resources made available to local borrowers. By contrast, Security–First National, the second largest branch bank in California, was often the lowest in the per cent of its resources made available in loans to local borrowers.

The most interesting comparison, perhaps, is between branch banks and unit banks. Bank of America usually had a higher load factor than any other California bank, branch or unit, and also devoted a larger percentage of its resources to satisfying the demands of local borrowers. This fact is not surprising, if for no other reason, because a large branch system through its widespread branch offices is in intimate contact with numerous local loan markets in all parts of the state. On the other hand, although the average load factor for all branch banks was almost invariably higher than that of unit banks of any size and invariably higher than the average of unit banks, at least some of the unit banks often surpassed the branch banks as a group in the per cent of resources devoted to local areas. Moreover, in most years, the loan ratio of an

---

[10] Clearly, no bank can operate at 100 per cent capacity.

individual branch bank was surpassed by the average of unit banks. The mobility of funds within a branch bank system is alleged to permit such banks to secure portfolio diversification more heavily among loans than would be true for unit banks, which must resort instead to open market investments to secure diversification. In practice, however, the diversification potential within the loan portfolio of branch banks is not always so fully exploited as in some unit banks. As a group, branch banks do make a higher percentage of loans than unit banks as a group. On the other hand, although it is presumed that both branch banks and unit banks secure the overwhelming amount of their deposits in local areas, at least some unit banks return more of these resources in loans to local markets than do some of the branch banks.

No value judgment automatically attaches to these conclusions. During the war years, for example, the comparatively low loan ratios of the largest unit banks reflected their comparatively heavy purchase of United States government securities. Again, a comparatively low loan performance by an individual branch bank may simply reflect a particular point of view about sound portfolio policy. The matching of loans with deposit-gathering areas has obvious implications for the allocation of resources. Even under a regime of pure competition, however, there is no presumption that this matching would necessarily result in an "optimal" allocation. The pertinent fact is the explicit statistical refutation of the widely held view that the potential ability of branch banks to make a higher percentage of local loans than unit banks is tantamount to proof that all branch banks in fact always do so.

EFFECTS OF CONCENTRATION ON LOAN PRODUCTION

This section considers whether the concentration of banking resources in California under the Big Four branch banks has resulted in restriction of loan output. For purposes of this examination, the Big Four branch banks are compared, individually and collectively, with the unit banks in the state. Although many large banks undoubtedly make loans to firms outside California, it is assumed that most of the loan business of California banks is with California firms and individuals. Accordingly, the Big Four loan output is compared with that for the unit banks in the state, since both are confronted with a roughly similar economic environment. It seems particularly desirable to restrict the comparison to California banks since California has experienced in the last two decades a rate of growth and development considerably greater than that in other parts of the country. In this comparison, all California banks except the Big Four branch banks are considered unit banks, although the latter category includes some intracity branch systems.

AN INDEX OF LOAN OUTPUT

Table 18 shows the loan index of different banks on a 1939 base. The final column, showing an index of total income payments in

TABLE 18

LOAN INDEX OF BRANCH AND UNIT BANKS IN CALIFORNIA, 1938–1950

(1939 = 100)

Year[a]	Bank of America	Security Bank	American Trust	Anglo Bank	Average Big Four		Unit banks	California income payments
					"Unweighted"	"Weighted"		
1938.......	91	100	98	135	106	96	100	94.6
1939.......	100	100	100	100	100	100	100	100.0
1940.......	112	101	120	104	102	110	109	111.1
1941.......	121	107	123	112	116	117	113	139.6
1942.......	128	105	126	100	115	121	109	185.2
1943.......	112	90	118	79	100	106	94	246.6
1944.......	122	84	139	79	106	114	96	272.2
1945.......	135	93	135	81	111	122	126	275.0
1946.......	175	97	168	104	136	152	123	300.8
1947.......	307	131	160	169	192	244	175	317.9
1948.......	371	168	272	225	259	309	192	336.9
1949.......	404	173	290	275	286	333	204	336.9
1950.......	415	158	310	309	298	341	201	.....

[a] SOURCES: California income payments are provided by the *California Yearbook*. All other figures were computed from data in *Rand McNally Bankers' Directory*, appropriate years. "Average of Big Four" computed from percentage figures of the individual branch banks. For explanation of "weighted" and "unweighted" series, see text, p. 68.

California, has been included to give a general idea of the growth of the state.[11] The index of income payments illustrates the impressive growth of the state betwen 1938 and 1950. In almost all years, the state's economic activity was expanding much more rapidly than loans. By itself, this fact is not proof of restriction of loan output, and for at least two reasons. First, the index of income payments is not a perfect indicator of the economic growth of the state because it includes items like transfer payments. California has a high percentage of aged people, and transfer payments are not insignificant. Second, there is no necessary reason for loans to

[11] No index is presented for loans of all California banks. Such an index would not be very enlightening when compared to loan changes of the Big Four, because the latter are a large percentage of the former.

expand at the same rate as general economic activity. Ever since 1921, business loans at all banks have expanded less rapidly than has general economic activity. Furthermore, during the Second World War loan expansion by banks was relatively retarded all over the country although national income rose very sharply.

The rate of loan expansion among individual branch banks has varied considerably. Bank of America conspicuously led the group with more than 300 per cent expansion. Both American Trust and Anglo expanded by more than 200 per cent, whereas Security's loans increased only slightly more than one-half. An examination of individual years reveals equally striking differences. Between 1943 and 1944, for example, both Bank of America and American Trust were expanding their loans whereas Anglo's loans were constant, and those of Security Bank actually declined. Even with the qualifications to the use of California income payments as an index of state growth, the discrepancy between the rates of growth of the individual branch banks and of the state as a whole is very marked in most years. By the end of 1950, however, the loan index of at least three of the Big Four approximated that of state income payments—Bank of America's loan index markedly surpassed the state—and only Security Bank's loans lagged conspicuously behind.

The average loan index of the Big Four branch banks is shown in two ways, "weighted" and "unweighted." The "unweighted" series is an average of the individual branch bank loan indices in each year. This series is not strictly comparable to the loan series for the unit banks, because the latter series is an average computed from the actual loan figures for the unit banks in each year. This noncomparability is overcome by the "weighted" series for the Big Four, which is computed on the same basis as the loan index of the unit banks. The "weighted" series for the Big Four inevitably reflects the dominating position of Bank of America. For this reason, both the "weighted" and "unweighted" series have been computed.

The "unweighted" loan index for the Big Four shows that after 1939, they outpaced the unit banks in all but two years. The Big Four loans ran moderately ahead of the unit bank loans during the prewar and war years and pulled strongly ahead in the postwar period. In the period as a whole, whereas the unit banks had only doubled their loans, loans of the Big Four had been tripled. Moreover, the comparative performance of branch and unit banks accords with that already described, even when the unit bank series is matched with the "weighted" average of Big Four loans. On this basis, then, there is no evidence of restriction of output by the Big Four as a group.

A somewhat different picture results when the loan index of the unit banks is compared with the individual branch bank loan indices. Bank of America and American Trust Company surpassed the unit banks in practically every year of the study period. By contrast, Security Bank almost invariably lagged behind the unit banks, and this was also true of Anglo Bank for about half of the period. In other words, the loan performance of the individual branch banks was unequal—some surpassed the performance of the units, whereas others lagged behind it.

A conspicuously high loan index of Bank of America relative to any individual bank may be partly due to an aggressive loan policy, but at least in part it can be a function of flow-back deposits. Given its basic reserves, a bank's ability to extend credit is a function primarily of the legal reserve ratios. However, a given legal reserve requirement does not automatically imply the same lending ability by two banks of a given size. A reserve requirement of (say) 20 per cent against demand deposits legally permits the individual bank to expand its deposits to the reciprocal of the reserve ratio. In practice, however, most banks cannot create money; they can only lend money they already have.[12] If the ordinary bank were to lend beyond this limit, it would threaten its liquidity by risking a probable severe drain of reserves to other banks.

Under exceptional circumstances, the ordinary limits would not hold. For example, a monopoly bank in an isolated area (i.e., in a self-contained community having no important business transactions with other areas) or a very large bank in a given trade area might approximate the lending potential of the banking system. In either case, the enhanced lending capacity is a function of flow-back deposits. Large branch bank systems have a large number of depositors over a widespread area, and flow-backs are a function of business transactions among these depositors. In 1950, the four branch bank systems discussed in this study held 66.7 per cent of all deposits in California. Bank of America alone held 43.6 per cent of the total deposits in the state.[13] Since California's boundaries are not necessarily the appropriate boundaries for the determination of flow-back possibilities, the figures presented are merely suggestive of the kind of considerations involved. Although flow-backs are only a potential factor increasing the loans of large branch banks, in practice, most banks do not normally carry excess reserves.

[12] Cf. Chester Phillips, *Bank Credit* (New York: Macmillan, 1921), chapter 3.
[13] See table 8, chapter iv.

So far as Bank of America's high loan index relative to any individual bank is related to its flow-back deposits, its loans are partly made at the expense of other banks in the state. The normal circulation of deposits among the banks of an area is the mechanism by which these banks accomplish a multiple expansion of deposits on a fractional reserve basis. When one branch bank in an area is very large, however, flow-back deposits preclude the normal circulation of deposits (and reserves) among the other banks. To this extent, even a very high loan index in Bank of America is no necessary evidence of "superior" performance in loan output relative to smaller branch banks or to individual unit banks. When flow-back deposits are taken into account, an apparently superior loan performance may mean only that a very large bank has made the loans which other banks might otherwise have made.[14]

LOAN OUTPUT AND BANK GROWTH

An index of loan expansion based on absolute loan figures is potentially misleading because it takes no account of the possibility of different rates of growth of the resources of different banks. Accordingly, it would be possible, for example, for a high loan index for branch banks to conceal any evidence of restriction of ouput, even if such evidence existed. One way to get around this complication is to construct a loan index showing loans as a ratio to deposits. Deposits are a good measure of the growth of a bank, and a loan-deposit index would show loan change independently of (possible) differing rates of growth of the resources of various banks. A loan-deposit index also reveals whether a bank's loan growth has kept pace with its deposit growth. An examination of the loan-deposit index of different banks should thus reveal not only how the individual bank's loans have kept pace with the growth of the resources of the bank but also how its relative loan change compares with other banks.

Table 19 gives this information for the different categories already identified in table 18. The impressions gained from the table of loan indices are considerably modified by the indices of loan-deposit figures. On the basis of the loan index, it appeared that the greatest loan growth was in Bank of America. However, its loan expansion was much less impressive when loans are considered relative to growth of bank. Indeed, compared to its size, loan growth in Anglo Bank was fully as great as that in Bank of America during

---

[14] It should be noticed that the effect of flow-back deposits is concealed by a loan/ assets measure of loan performance.

most years, and Anglo actually ended the period with a higher index. Similarly, although the absolute loan output of American Trust grew more than 200 per cent during the period, its loans actually failed to keep pace with its growth by 1950. The record of Security Bank is the most striking. The absolute loan growth in Security Bank was not impressive, but it was positive. Compared to

TABLE 19

LOAN-DEPOSIT INDEX OF BRANCH AND UNIT BANKS IN CALIFORNIA, 1938–1950

(1939 = 100)

Year[a]	Bank of America	Security Bank	American Trust	Anglo Bank	Average Big Four		Unit banks
					"Un-weighted"	"Weighted"	
1938.......	93.9	99.1	103.9	130.0	106.7	98.2	104.1
1939.......	100.0	100.0	100.0	100.0	100.0	100.0	100.0
1940.......	96.6	93.6	106.3	101.2	99.4	97.8	93.2
1941.......	101.4	98.1	102.4	107.0	102.2	101.7	93.9
1942.......	91.9	92.4	97.4	96.2	94.5	93.7	83.1
1943.......	53.4	52.1	64.4	53.9	56.0	55.1	52.9
1944.......	46.2	40.5	56.8	46.9	47.6	46.6	45.5
1945.......	41.7	37.0	46.3	38.8	41.0	41.6	49.1
1946.......	46.4	33.6	50.9	45.2	44.0	45.1	43.5
1947.......	84.6	47.4	50.0	80.8	65.7	75.0	64.2
1948.......	97.0	58.8	83.0	99.7	82.1	90.2	74.9
1949......,	100.8	61.1	88.9	116.6	91.9	94.8	73.1
1950.......	98.8	55.4	90.6	104.7	87.4	93.0	73.7

   [a] SOURCES: See notes to table 18.

its own growth, however, Security Bank's loans drastically failed to keep pace.[15]

During the last three years of the study period, the Big Four loan output (unweighted series) definitely pulled ahead of the unit banks. During the war years, however, the unit bank loan-deposit ratios roughly matched those of the Big Four. The individual branch banks did not always match the unit banks, however. In most years, Security Bank's loan-deposit ratio was less than that for the unit banks. Moreover, although Anglo Bank's loan index failed to equal that for the unit banks in half the years of the study period, Anglo Bank outperformed the unit banks relative to its own growth in all but one year. In the postwar years especially, Anglo Bank's loan-deposit ratio pulled far ahead of the unit banks, and, indeed, generally outperformed the loan-deposit ratio of any of the indi-

[15] This is related to Security Bank's loan policy.

vidual branch banks as well. Both Bank of America and American Trust Company outperformed the unit banks in almost every year.

For the Big Four taken together, the loan-deposit ratio was lower at the end of the period than in the base year. Although the Big Four loan-deposit ratio had fallen from its prewar base year, the fact that it substantially exceeded the unit bank ratios suggests that, far from restricting output, the branch banks as a group have been quicker than their unit bank rivals to meet the postwar demands for business and other loans. Again, there is no substantial difference in the results described, irrespective of whether unit banks are compared with the "weighted" or "unweighted" series for the Big Four. If the unit bank performance is taken as a guide, there is again no evidence of loan output restriction by the Big Four as a group, even when allowance is made for their more rapid growth in the state. At least one branch bank, however, has not recovered the position it held relative to the unit banks during the prewar years.

COMPARATIVE LEVELS OF OUTPUT

The comparative output performance of the Big Four and of the unit banks is an important consideration in any policy decisions involving banking concentration. It is important, therefore, to ensure that necessary statistical manipulation of the original data should not inadvertently yield misleading results. With this caution in mind, one final comparison is indicated. The indices of both tables 18 and 19 were computed on a fixed base, viz., 1939. Probably most students would agree that 1939 is a reasonable base year, since it was the last "normal" year before the outbreak of world war. It is always possible, however, that even an eminently "normal" year for an entire industry may be decidedly abnormal for some particular firm in the industry.[16] Accordingly, table 20 shows the loan-deposit index for all banks, using the loan-deposit ratio of all California banks in each year as the base. If the loan expansion of a bank keeps pace not only with its own growth (as measured by its deposits) but keeps pace also with the total loan-deposit change for all banks in the state, the bank's index will be 100 per cent in every year. Ratios more or less than 100 per cent indicate performance which is either better or worse than for the state as a whole.

---

[16] Specifically, there is reason to suspect that 1939 was a year of abnormally low loans for Anglo Bank. If this is true, the loan index for all subsequent years is correspondingly exaggerated.

Table 20 solves the problem of a fixed base year, but employs base data which are not ideal, since the figures for all banks in the state are to a considerable extent the figures for the Big Four. It seems worth accepting this deficiency in this calculation in order to avoid the danger of an ill-chosen base period. Since the previous tables do not employ figures for all banks as a base, the possibility of misleading inferences is reduced.

TABLE 20

LOAN-DEPOSIT INDEX OF BRANCH AND UNIT BANKS IN CALIFORNIA, 1938–1950, ON AN ANNUAL BASE

(Annual Loan/Deposit Ratios for all Banks in California = 100)

Year[a]	Bank of America	Security Bank	American Trust	Anglo Bank	Average of Big Four		Unit banks
					"Un-weighted"	"Weighted"	
1938.......	106.4	96.1	109.9	103.7	104.0	104.1	93.6
1939.......	114.9	98.1	106.5	79.8	99.8	107.2	90.9
1940.......	115.3	93.5	118.4	85.0	103.1	109.2	86.9
1941.......	117.3	97.0	109.8	85.9	102.5	110.0	85.9
1942.......	116.7	100.2	114.6	84.8	104.1	111.1	83.5
1943.......	111.9	93.2	125.0	78.4	102.1	107.6	87.7
1944.......	113.4	85.1	129.4	80.1	102.0	107.0	88.6
1945.......	107.3	81.2	110.4	69.3	92.1	100.0	100.0
1946.......	118.0	74.0	120.1	79.9	98.0	107.2	87.6
1947.......	134.0	64.1	73.4	88.8	90.1	110.9	80.4
1948.......	131.2	67.9	104.1	93.7	99.2	113.9	80.3
1949.......	129.4	67.0	105.7	103.9	101.5	113.5	74.3
1950.......	128.1	61.4	108.9	94.2	98.2	112.6	75.6

[a] SOURCES: See notes to table 18.

Although Bank of America's loan output may not always have kept pace with its own growth, it has performed far better than the state as a whole. In most years, this is also true for American Trust. On the other hand, both Anglo Bank and Security Bank normally compared less favorably in this regard. Taken as a group, the Big Four loan production ("unweighted" series) usually kept pace with the state. In most years, they either slightly outperformed or slightly underperformed the state. In terms of the "weighted" series, the Big Four outperformed the state in every year. By comparison, the unit banks fell far below the state performance in every year but one. Similarly, the unit banks also fell far below the performance of the Big Four. However, the loan performance of the unit banks in many years exceeded that of Security Bank, and, during the war years, the comparative loan output of the unit banks was also greater than that of Anglo Bank.

The loan performance of the Big Four relative to the state reflects in large measure Big Four domination of the state totals. Hence, there is undeniably an element of tautology in comparing the Big Four to the state. On the other hand, if comparing the unit banks to the state figures is but an indirect way of comparing them with the Big Four, then the defect of the table in using state bank totals is not so serious after all, since ultimately the desired comparison is between the Big Four branch banks and the unit banks. If unit bank performance is taken as the criterion of public policy, the Big Four as a group have not restricted loan output but have, indeed, exceeded the state standard. Again, this conclusion is based mainly on the performance of three of the Big Four branch banks. One of the branch banks has steadily lost ground during the latter years of the war and the postwar period.

SUMMARY

This chapter has investigated the effects of banking concentration in California on comparative levels of loan output. To gain perspective, it was necessary also to inquire into the comparative production potential of branch and unit banks. The measure employed for this test was the load factor. The investigation revealed that both as a function of their size and also of their branch structure, branch banks have an inherent superiority in their ability to produce. In other words, with given resources, a branch bank is able to produce a larger amount of credit (both loans and investments) than a unit bank.

The mere fact that a branch bank can potentially produce a proportionately larger total output than unit banks provides no assurance that branch banks will actually devote a proportionately larger share of their portfolios than unit banks to the production of loan output. The majority of bank investments are made in United States government securities and, to a considerably less extent, in the securities of states and local political subdivisions. Only a very small part of the total investment portfolio of banks is in corporate securities. The possible restriction of output under concentrated banking thus concerns business borrowers more in terms of loan output than total output.

The record shows that branch banks as a group devoted a larger proportion of their resources to loans than did unit banks as a group. This also held true in comparison with the unit banks most nearly comparable in size to the branch banks, i.e., the largest unit bank category. Moreover, branch banks as a group expanded their loans more rapidly than unit banks as a group. The superior loan performance of branch banks as a group was maintained even when their loan output was measured in terms of the growth of their own resources. Finally, the superior loan performance of branch banks as a group was not a function of selecting any particular year as a base period. For the branch banks as a group, the record provides no serious evidence of restriction of output despite the intensive concentration of banking resources in California.

The record does show, however, that the performance of branch banks as a group was not matched by each of the branch banks taken individually. In different years, at least some branch banks devoted a smaller percentage of their resources to loan output than did the unit banks. The loan output of at least one branch bank was quite regularly surpassed by that of the unit banks, especially when measured against the growth of its own resources. Moreover, in many years, at least some individual unit bank categories out-performed individual branch banks. On the other hand, the largest branch bank surpassed any of the unit banks in its loan output during most of the years of the study period.

Throughout this chapter, the possibility of restriction of loan output by the Big Four has been examined by comparing Big Four loan output with that of the unit banks. *Taken as a group,* Big Four loan performance compares favorably with that of the unit banks by the various criteria employed. On the other hand, in various years, the loan output of *individual branch banks* has fallen below the standard of the unit banks in terms of the various cri-teria employed to measure loan growth. When the unit banks are the standard for comparison, it is possible to make categorical state-ments about whether or not the Big Four individually or collec-tively have restricted loan output.

Although definite conclusions can be reached about the actual performance of the branch and unit banks, it is only possible to speculate whether banking concentration in California has *on bal-ance* resulted in a smaller absolute level of loan output than an exclusively unit banking structure would have produced. The question of possible restriction of loan output in this more basic sense has not been answered in this chapter—and is unanswerable. The results of a comparison of actual branch bank loan perform-ance with the actual performance of unit banks is insufficient basis for attempting to answer the broader question of restriction of loan output. It is as important to recognize the limitations of statisical data as it is to extract the greatest possible amount of information from them. In this case, it would be fallacious to assume that results of a comparative survey of actual branch and unit bank loan performance could be projected for an exclusively unit banking structure. That kind of projection would require knowledge or an assumption as to exactly what the alternative would be. It is not sufficient to posit unit instead of branch banking. It is necessary also to speculate on the size distribution of the unit banks which might replace existing branch organizations because loan output differs among unit banks. It cannot be easily assumed that an exclusively unit bank structure would be simply a replica of existing banks with the difference that all branch offices be converted into unit banks. Branch offices can exist where unit banks cannot profitably operate. In some instances, unit banks have historically been absorbed by branch banks in order to save them from bankruptcy.

To repeat, whether the performance of branch banks as a group would on balance outweigh the performance of unit banks as a group is unknown. The fact that some unit banks might outperform at least some branch banks in loan production cannot determine whether unit banks would on balance outperform branch banks. So far as certain very large business loans can be handled only by giant banks, the local unit banks might be unable to produce this output at all. Or, again, at least some unit banks might have to look more heavily than do branch banks to open market investments for portfolio diversification, with a consequent reduction of loan output. In short, although unit banks outperform some individual branch banks, they fail to match the performance of others. Whether a dissolution of *all* existing branch systems in California would on balance result in larger loan output than at present must remain a moot point.

Finally, it is important to recognize that a comparatively small loan output by an individual branch or unit bank is not presumptive evidence of output restriction deliberately framed to raise prices in local loan markets. The proportions of loans and other output are a function not only of market structures but also of portfolio policy and, indeed, of general business policy. What may appear on the surface as evidence of monopolistic restriction of output may be nothing more than a different judgment on sound bank management—and such judgment has basically no connection with concentration.

VI

Comparative Cost Patterns

AN EXAMINATION of unit costs of the different banks constitutes an essential and integral part of this study. It seems most useful to investigate separately both unit bank and branch bank costs before undertaking a comparative cost analysis of branch and unit banks.

UNIT BANK COSTS

UNIT COSTS IN DIFFERENT SIZE UNIT BANKS

Table 21 shows unit costs of production for different size unit banks and for an average of branch banks between 1938 and 1950.[1] The output of a bank consists primarily of its loans and investments. Therefore, total expenses/loans and investments constitutes the average cost (ATUC) of production per $100 of output. Table 21 reveals a pretty clear pattern in which unit costs vary inversely with size of bank. There is a mild erraticism of ranking in the intermediate-size categories. In precisely these categories, however, the absolute figures are very close together, so that the mild erraticism of ranking does not negate the generalization about costs and size of bank. Unit costs of the smallest-size banks are usually almost twice as large as unit costs of the largest category of banks in each year.

The pattern of cost variation in different size banks depends upon the pattern of variation of the component elements of unit cost. From data publicly available, unit costs can be broken into unit wage and salary costs, unit interest costs on time deposits, and unit costs of "all other expenses."[2] Table 22 shows wage and salary costs for different size banks. The table shows a reasonably clear-cut pattern in which wage costs vary inversely with size of bank, al-

---

[1] 1938 was selected as the opening date because it is the first year in which operating ratios comparable to the rest of the period are available.

[2] These breakdowns are not ideal for our purposes, but they are the best available.

TABLE 21

Total Expenses as a Per Cent of Loans and Investments, by Size and Kind of Bank, California, 1938–1950

Unit banks[a] (by size)	1938	1939	1940	1941	1942	1943	1944	1945	1946	1947	1948	1949	1950
Smallest	6.33	3.40	5.76	5.96	4.87	3.64	2.14	2.33	2.11	3.68	3.63	4.30	4.38
2	5.06	5.45	4.28	4.59	3.87	3.03	1.92	1.68	1.82	2.09	2.48	2.64	2.89
3	4.15	4.31	4.13	4.08	3.61	2.50	1.97	1.62	1.68	1.85	2.19	2.24	2.56
4	4.17	4.11	3.88	3.95	3.57	2.48	1.81	1.70	1.80	2.15	2.37	2.73	2.82
5	3.61	3.83	3.90	3.49	2.57	2.14	1.73	1.55	1.56	1.90	2.15	2.34	2.55
6	4.01	4.03	3.91	3.71	....	1.64	1.55	1.37	1.45	1.69	1.99	2.03	1.99
7	3.81	3.62	2.49	2.36	....	....	....	....	....	....	....	....	....
8	2.91	2.59	....	....	....	....	....	....	....	....	....	....	....
Unit bank average	4.16	4.13	4.21	4.20	3.80	2.58	1.93	1.70	1.79	2.06	2.52	2.65	2.84
Branch bank average	3.18	3.15	2.92	2.76	2.62	1.86	1.50	1.42	1.62	1.96	2.16	2.21	2.29

For sources and notes to table, see Appendix.
[a] See notes to table 16.

TABLE 22

Wages and Salaries as a Per Cent of Loans and Investments, by Size and Kind of Bank, California, 1938–1950

Unit banks[a] (by size)	1938	1939	1940	1941	1942	1943	1944	1945	1946	1947	1948	1949	1950
Smallest	3.22	1.60	2.99	3.17	2.31	1.89	1.01	1.16	1.16	1.84	1.92	2.17	2.30
2	2.53	2.79	1.89	2.07	1.80	1.45	.92	.78	.89	1.04	1.23	1.29	1.42
3	2.01	1.92	1.91	2.01	1.63	1.24	.94	.74	.79	.92	1.04	1.08	1.22
4	1.91	1.90	1.74	1.82	1.47	1.13	.77	.73	.82	.97	1.07	1.23	1.28
5	1.61	1.68	1.80	1.60	1.14	.97	.74	.65	.71	.86	.99	1.10	1.23
6	1.85	1.83	1.52	1.60	....	.81	.75	.70	.74	.92	1.05	1.13	1.02
7	1.48	1.39	1.15	1.13	....	....	....	....	....	....	....	....	....
8	1.29	1.14	....	....	....	....	....	....	....	....	....	....	....
Unit bank average	1.95	1.90	1.93	1.99	1.78	1.28	.91	.78	.84	1.00	1.15	1.29	1.39
Branch bank average	1.39	1.36	1.28	1.28	1.16	.89	.73	.63	.79	.94	1.02	1.06	1.07

For sources and notes to table, see Appendix.
[a] See notes to table 16.

TABLE 23

Interest on Time Deposits as a Per Cent of Loans and Investments, by Size and Kind of Bank, California, 1938–1950

Unit banks[a] (by size)	1938	1939	1940	1941	1942	1943	1944	1945	1946	1947	1948	1949	1950
Smallest	1.28	0.57	1.10	1.13	0.96	0.59	0.47	0.42	0.27	0.32	0.32	0.44	0.41
2	0.92	1.08	1.26	1.20	0.81	0.61	0.35	0.37	0.37	0.41	0.52	0.56	0.59
3	1.22	1.21	1.07	1.01	0.87	0.44	0.41	0.37	0.36	0.40	0.51	0.54	0.60
4	1.10	1.07	1.12	1.08	0.85	0.55	0.38	0.39	0.42	0.49	0.58	0.63	0.62
5	1.19	1.17	1.16	1.04	0.42	0.50	0.41	0.39	0.38	0.45	0.53	0.50	0.56
6	1.27	1.34	1.22	0.99	....	0.27	0.25	0.25	0.24	0.29	0.31	0.30	0.29
7	1.26	1.08	0.66	0.53	....	....	....	....	....	....	....	....	....
8	0.84	0.70	....	....	....	....	....	....	....	....	....	....	....
Unit bank average	1.14	1.11	1.11	1.06	0.84	0.52	0.39	0.37	0.36	0.41	0.50	0.53	0.56
Branch bank average	1.05	0.97	0.81	0.75	0.61	0.35	0.32	0.33	0.36	0.44	0.48	0.50	0.59

For sources and notes to table, see Appendix.
[a] See notes to table 16.

though there is a mild erraticism in the ranking of some of the mid-categories. Again, the disarrangement of the ranking pattern in the midcategories does not seriously impair the general pattern, since the absolute figures in those categories are quite similar. The absolute range between lowest and highest wage costs is approximately 1 per cent, i.e., one dollar per $100 of output.

Table 23 shows unit interest costs on time and savings deposits. The figures in this table represent the effective rather than the nominal interest rates paid on time deposits. In most cases, the effective rate is less than the nominal rate because of the methods of computing interest on time deposits. For example, the interest-earning period for the depositor may not begin till January 1, although money may be deposited in the account for a couple of months before that date.[3] For cost purposes, the effective interest rate is clearly preferable to the nominal rate. In almost all years, interest cost varies inversely with size among the larger-size bank categories, and, in every year but one, the largest category of banks has the lowest unit interest costs. Among the smaller unit banks, interest costs tend to rise initially and then to drop off, or remain fairly stable. In general then, with the exception of the smallest banks, unit interest costs are either fairly stable initially, and then vary inversely with size, or show some erraticisms in the smaller categories although tending to diminish as size of bank increases.

Table 24 shows unit costs on all other expenses, hereinafter called unit miscellaneous costs. This component includes, among other things, most of the fixed costs, including overhead and depreciation on buildings and equipment, as well as lawsuits and court costs, advertising outlays, office supplies, and the like. The smallest category of banks has the highest unit miscellaneous costs, and the largest category of banks has the lowest miscellaneous costs. The intermediate-size categories show a mixed pattern in ranking. In some years, the absolute figures in the intermediate categories are similar, but in many other years, they are not. Generally, unit miscellaneous costs decline in the early stages; in the midcategories, there is no ranking pattern and the figures are often close together; for the largest banks, unit miscellaneous costs again begin to fall.

This survey of the components of unit cost has shown that large banks have lower unit costs than smaller banks because a similar

---

[3] For example, in 1938, Security Bank paid interest at rates varying from 1/4 per cent to 2 per cent, depending on the amount and length of time for which deposits were accepted. Security–First National Bank, *Annual Report*, 1938. Some banks paid no interest at all on very small savings accounts. See Anglo-California Bank, *Annual Report*, January, 1940, p. 6.

TABLE 24

ALL OTHER EXPENSES AS A PER CENT OF LOANS AND INVESTMENTS, BY SIZE AND KIND OF BANK, CALIFORNIA, 1938–1950

Unit banks[a] (by size)	1938	1939	1940	1941	1942	1943	1944	1945	1946	1947	1948	1949	1950
Smallest	1.83	1.15	1.56	1.66	1.60	1.06	0.66	0.77	0.73	1.51	1.40	1.70	1.67
2	0.91	1.50	1.04	1.30	1.26	0.98	0.65	0.53	0.55	0.64	0.73	0.79	0.88
3	1.02	1.09	1.03	1.06	1.11	0.83	0.61	0.51	0.53	0.53	0.64	0.62	0.74
4	1.26	1.07	0.94	1.05	1.26	0.80	0.66	0.58	0.56	0.69	0.72	0.87	0.92
5	0.81	0.89	0.73	0.86	0.87	0.69	0.58	0.51	0.47	0.58	0.63	0.75	0.77
6	0.89	0.84	1.01	1.13	....	0.57	0.52	0.45	0.47	0.52	0.65	0.63	0.66
7	1.07	1.06	0.70	0.72	....	....	....	....	....	....	....	....	....
8	0.79	0.69	....	....	....	....	....	....	....	....	....	....	....
Unit bank average	1.03	1.06	1.04	1.15	1.20	0.86	0.63	0.54	0.54	0.64	0.73	0.83	0.89
Branch bank average	0.73	0.72	0.63	0.74	0.82	0.62	0.49	0.43	0.42	0.59	0.65	0.66	0.64

For sources and notes to table, see Appendix.
[a] See notes to table 16.

pattern holds for each of the component elements of unit cost. In each case, the pattern is typically defined most sharply at the extremes of the size categories. Significantly, too, the pattern for unit costs tends to blur in the midcategories because of the closeness of the figures. As a general proposition, unit costs decline as size of bank increases, but unit costs are comparatively stable for a size variation of banks of several million dollars of deposits. The actual range varies in different years, partly because the over-all size of banks has increased over time.

In the prewar period, unit costs show no great variation for banks ranging between $500,000 and $50,000,000 deposits. During the war and postwar periods, the range of fairly constant costs is somewhere between $2,000,000 and $50,000,000 deposits, or even somewhat more.[4] If unit costs for different size banks were plotted on a scatter diagram with unit costs on the ordinate, and size of bank (or level of output)[5] on the abscissa, a curve drawn by least squares would decline fairly sharply in the early ranges, remain fairly constant over a wide intermediate range, and then decline again in the range of the largest banks. Although it would not be technically precise to call such a curve an envelope cost curve, it would nevertheless convey a sense of the general pattern of variation of unit costs as size of bank (plant) increases, i.e., of returns to scale. If the unit costs of branch banks are temporarily ignored, the largest unit banks in California have not yet reached the point of decreasing returns to scale. Whether this conclusion still holds with reference to branch banks will be considered later.

PROPORTIONS AND COSTS

Edward H. Chamberlin has pointed out that the kind of returns to scale (whether increasing, decreasing, or constant) is a function of size of firm and of the varying proportions in which the factors of production are combined. Contrary to a widely held opinion, returns to scale are not a function of divisibility of the factors. Divisibility affects only the smoothness of the envelope curve.[6] It is interesting in this connection to compare the proportions in which the components of expenses are used in different size banks. Here, again, the analysis is intended to be suggestive, not technically precise. There are no perfect analogues in banking for

[4] Cf. table 21 above for cost pattern, and Appendix table L for dollar breakdown of size categories.

[5] Volume of output generally increases as size of bank increases.

[6] Cf. Edward H. Chamberlin, "Proportionality, Divisibility and Economies of Scale," *Quarterly Journal of Economics,* Vol. LXII, No. 2 (February, 1948)

physical factors of production in manufacturing enterprises. In this context, therefore, the components of expenses are analogous to the percentage cost data in the manufacturing census based on the dollar cost figures of the factors of production. Moreover, the classification of the components of expenses must be related to available statistical breakdowns, viz., the wages and salary bill, the bill for interest on time deposits, and the bill for miscellaneous expenses.

The wages and salary expense of different banks is not related to size of bank. Indeed, in many years, the ratios for wages and salary expense are identical for different size banks,[7] or at least are very similar.[8] The situation is roughly the same for interest on time deposits, except that in the postwar period, interest on time deposits was a conspicuously smaller percentage of total expenses for the smallest category of banks than for any of the other size banks.[9] Generally, no meaningful distinctions emerge from a ranking of the size categories of banks by the percentage of interest on time deposits over total expenses. Finally, miscellaneous expenses are in roughly the same proportions in all size categories.[10] The only exception to this generalization is in the postwar years when the smallest category of banks tends to have somewhat higher ratios than the other size categories. In general, however, the various components of expenses bear the same proportions in all size banks. Large banks do not economize on any one component as against any of the other components, or, at least, of those components which have been identified.[11]

---

[7] Appendix table C.

[8] This conclusion is independently corroborated by a breakdown of wages and salaries/total expenses for member banks in the Twelfth Federal Reserve District, classified by loans as a percentage of total assets. In 1950, for example, the following table shows banks classified according to loans/total assets and wages and salaries/total expenses.

Loans/Total Assets (averages in per cent)	Wages and Salaries/Total Expenses (in per cent)
8.6	52
14.8	51
24.8	50
34.9	49
46.7	49

In other words, wages and salaries/total expenses was constant despite a tremendous variation in the ratio of loans/assets. Cf. Federal Reserve Bank of San Francisco, *Operating Ratios of Member Banks, Twelfth Federal Reserve District*, 1950.

[9] Appendix table D.

[10] Appendix table E.

[11] It is worth mentioning in this connection that although the components of cost are not so finely broken down as might be wished, the two components which are reasonably satisfactorily broken down, viz., interest expense and wage expense, comprise about 75 per cent of total expense.

The fact of approximately constant proportions as size of plant (bank) increases is not characteristic of many manufacturing enterprises. Indeed, for manufacturing industries, the range of decreasing costs on the envelope curve is owing to the fact that there are no ideal proportions independent of scale. As far as unit banks alone are concerned,[12] it is a curious fact that, consistent with (roughly) constant proportions of the components of expenses[13] at all sizes of plant (bank), there are initially increasing returns to scale (decreasing costs), then a wide range of fairly constant returns to scale (constant costs), and, finally, a range of further increasing returns to scale (decreasing costs). It follows, therefore, that *all* the components of cost (previous exceptions mentioned) are economized in the early range, that there are no significant economies of *all* the components in the middle range, and, finally, that *all* components are economized again at the range of the very large banks. In other words, the economies of scale are related to size of bank, but not to the proportions of the components of expenses.

Labor economies.—Since the components of expenses have all been described in percentages based on dollar figures, further investigation is required into the composition of the individual expense components. The wages and salary bill, for example, is a function of the volume of employment and of the wage rate. The volume of employment depends on the number of employees and the hours worked, and working hours are generally uniform among different banks. The wage rate (except for top-level executives) appears also to be fairly uniform among all banks, irrespective of size of bank, because, within each community, all banks draw their labor force from a common labor pool. Presumably, too, the labor market for bank employees is competitive. If, therefore, large banks "economize" on the wages and salary cost (i.e., wages and salaries/loans and investments) relative to small banks, it must be owing to an economy of actual labor. Small banks use proportionately (i.e., relative to output—loans and investments) more labor than large banks.

The "economy" of labor of large banks as compared with small banks is partly a function of the "size mix" of different size banks. The size mix refers to loans broken down by size of loan. It follows from their respective sizes that large banks predominantly make

---

[12] Branch banks are considered later.

[13] Of course, the miscellaneous component of expenses is itself a composite of a variety of cost items.

large loans and small banks predominantly make small loans.[14] A given volume of loans is more expensive for the bank to transact if there is a large number of small loans instead of a small number of large loans. For example, it takes no longer (and often a shorter time) to transact a large loan than a small loan. Similarly, the credit check of a large borrower is likely to be less expensive than for a small borrower. Therefore, mere size of bank, and the size of loan that naturally predominates in different size banks, is an important determinant of labor economies, and *ceteris paribus,* makes for lower unit costs.

Large banks economize labor for still another reason. The metropolitan bank provides a large number of financial and other services for its customers. These numerous functions are most exhaustively provided by the largest banks.[15] Smaller banks may provide some of these services only imperfectly or not at all. By virtue of the volume of business done in the different aspects of banking, large banks can afford to hire expert talent and to give its personnel in various fields an opportunity to specialize in their limited areas. Specialization breeds expertise, and expertise enhances efficiency. In the banking functions of business lending and securities investment, the bankers in large institutions are probably more knowledgeable in their respective fields than their small-bank counterparts. In short, specialization in large banks is conducive to greater efficiency of labor and, *ceteris paribus,* to lower unit costs for reasons analogous to those long ago identified by Adam Smith in his *Wealth of Nations.*

Partly, wage costs are higher in small unit banks than in large unit banks because of the different "loan mix" in different size banks. The loan mix refers to the composition of the loan portfolio by kind of loan. In large unit banks, such loans as consumer loans or installment credit loans are relatively unimportant, whereas they may bulk large in the portfolios of small unit banks. These are high cost loans, especially in terms of the amount of labor they involve.

Interest economies.—The bill for interest on time deposits de-

---

[14] An intensive study of member banks in 1946 by the Federal Reserve revealed that "the proportion of loans to small business was higher in the smaller banks—more than 90%—than in the larger banks." Patman Report, Vol. II, p. 790. Or, again, "A substantial proportion of the commercial banking business is itself small business, and small manufacturing, trade, service, utility, and construction firms comprise the principal, if not the only, market for the loans of these small banks." Testimony of Chairman, Board of Governors, Federal Reserve System, *ibid.,* Vol. I, p. 610.

[15] Cf. Transamerica Hearings, Respondent's exhibit no. 188, for a detailed list of banking services.

pends on the effective rate of interest paid on time deposits and on the (absolute) volume of time deposits. Effective interest rates on time deposits decrease slightly as size of bank increases, although even this very slight tendency blurs considerably after 1944.[16] On the other hand, among the larger banks, the ratio of time deposits/ loans and investments decreases as size of bank increases. Except for the smallest category of unit banks, the lowest ratio of time deposits/loans and investments is found in the largest unit banks.[17] Therefore, any "economizing" of the interest cost (i.e., interest on time deposits/loans and investments) by the large banks was owing primarily to a somewhat smaller ratio of time deposits to loans and investments, and only secondarily to a possibly somewhat lower effective average interest rate paid on time deposits.

Miscellaneous economies.—The miscellaneous bill is a composite, including overhead, supplies, lawsuits and court costs, advertising, and the like. Since figures are not available for these individual components of the miscellaneous bill, nothing specific can be said about the individual items. For all these items taken together, however, proportionally less (i.e., per dollar of output— loans and investments) is spent by large than by small banks. So far as these are overhead items, that is not surprising. For example, the size and decorative features of a bank building do not necessarily increase *pari passu* with every dollar increase in the volume of business. Indeed, given appropriate changes in the product mix,[18] the loan mix, or the size mix, the volume of business could significantly increase quite consistently with a sharp fall in overhead costs connected with the bank building.

Branch Bank Costs

UNIT COSTS IN BRANCH BANKS

In this section, unit costs are compared among the branch banks themselves.[19] With one conspicuous exception (American Trust), unit costs of the individual branch banks vary with size of branch bank.[20] Except American Trust, the variation of unit cost with size

---

[16] Appendix table F.

[17] Appendix table G.

[18] The "product mix" refers to the relative proportion of loans as a percentage of total loans and investments.

[19] Under agreement by which the author received the figures pertaining to the individual branch banks, comparison can be made among the branch banks and between branch banks and unit banks, but the individual bank ratios cannot be published.

[20] When only four banks are compared, even one exception to the ranking of unit costs by size of bank cannot be ignored. The matter is examined in greater detail at a later point.

of branch bank reverses the pattern for unit banks. Specifically, the smallest branch bank (Anglo) almost invariably had the *lowest* unit costs; the largest branch bank (Bank of America) tended to have the *highest* unit costs, again with the exception of American Trust. The latter had the highest unit costs for more years than Bank of America, but the actual unit cost percentages were very similar for the two banks.

As a mechanical matter, the pattern of unit costs (viz., American Trust, Bank of America, Security, Anglo) among branch banks is the result of the pattern among the components of unit cost. Unit wage cost and unit interest cost on time deposits generally show the same ranking among branch banks as unit costs. For example, the smallest branch bank almost invariably had the lowest wage costs. The largest bank had the highest wage costs in the early part of the period, but American Trust held first place during the latter years of the period. In all years, however, the absolute figures for the two high wage cost banks (Bank of America and American Trust) were very similar. With the exception of American Trust unit wage costs vary directly with size of branch bank. Unit interest costs on time deposits exhibit a very similar pattern except that the absolute figures of the two banks with the lowest interest cost (Anglo and Security) were very close together rather than being differentiated by size of bank. Finally, the smallest branch bank (Anglo) showed some tendency to have the lowest miscellaneous costs. The largest bank had the highest miscellaneous costs in the first part of the period, and yielded first place to American Trust, the same bank with which Bank of America shared top place in other cost components. With these exceptions, the pattern of unit miscellaneous costs is a mixed one, but the absolute figures are often very similar where the pattern is mixed.

UNIT WAGE COSTS

It is necessary to understand the reasons for the observed ranking of the components of unit cost to interpret further the pattern of unit costs. The pattern of unit wage costs is basically explained in terms of: (1) the relative amount of loans in different branch banks, i.e., the product mix, and (2) the relative proportions of different size loans in different branch banks, i.e., the size mix.

Product mix.—In terms of product mix, the ranking of banks from 1938 through 1945 is the same as the ranking for unit costs and for unit wage costs. In other words, with the exception of American Trust, loans as a percentage of loans and investments

varied directly with size of branch bank. American Trust had the
highest percentage of loans over loans and investments through
1945. In the postwar period, the ratio of loans to loans and investments varied directly with size of bank, except that Security Bank
fell to the lowest place. In almost every year, the range from highest to lowest in the ratios of loans/loans and investments is at least
ten points. In many years it is considerably greater, especially in
the last two years of the study period when the range is as great as
30 percentage points. Except as stated above, the product mix
varies directly with size of branch bank. *Ceteris paribus,* a bank
with a higher percentage of loans as against investments has also
higher unit costs.

A priori, it would be difficult to predict how the branch banks
would have ranked in terms of their respective loan ratios.[21] On
the other hand, the observed ranking in which loan ratios do vary
directly with size of bank is not surprising. Under sufficiently restrictive assumptions, loan ratios would be expected to increase
as size of branch bank increases. The growth of a branch bank
increases not only its deposits but normally also extends its geographical coverage. Although greater geographical coverage need
not always mean greater diversification possibilities, California
offers precisely such opportunities. The larger the branch bank,
the more it can exploit the possibilities of diversification *within
its loan portfolio.* A smaller branch system would, other things
being equal, have to rely *relatively* more heavily on diversification
secured through open market investments.

The loan ratio pattern by size of bank that might be expected
from diversification considerations can be considerably affected by
other factors which are also important. For example, Anglo Bank
has the lowest loan ratio of any of the branch banks through 1945.
This ranking might be expected from Anglo's size as the smallest
of the California branch systems. However, the loan policy of
Anglo has also tended to reduce its loan ratio. The Annual Reports
of the Anglo Bank make repeated reference to its conservative loan
policy. In 1948, for example, when most banks were experiencing
a sharp increase in their loan portfolios, Anglo's annual report
stated: "Our loan volume has increased materially but its *growth
has been less than the opportunities afforded to expand it.* While
we have not and will not fail to care for the needs of customers
entitled to credit, we have not encouraged borrowings on the part

[21] In this section, "loan ratios" refers to loans as a percentage of loans and investments. In chapter v, "loan ratios" referred to loans as a percentage of total assets.

of those who have not established a satisfactory depositor relationship nor have we loaned where the need for borrowing was not
fully demonstrated."[22]

By contrast, the American Trust Company has clearly pursued
an aggressive loan policy. By 1948, American Trust was the eight-
eenth largest commercial bank in the country, with total resources
of slightly less than one billion dollars. Since American Trust is
only about one-sixth the size of Bank of America, but nevertheless
has as high or higher percentage of loans than the latter, there is a
strong presumption that this exceptionally high ratio is at least
in part a result of American Trust's loan policy. Still another factor accounts for the exceptionally high loan ratio of American
Trust Company. Normally, increasing size of branch bank con-
duces to a higher loan ratio because of the greater possibilities of
diversification within the loan division of the bank's total portfolio.
Although American Trust is concentrated geographically in about
fourteen counties of northern California, this area contains more
than 80 per cent of northern California's urban population and
industrial production.[23] The result is good diversification of their
commercial loans and lines of credit.[24] In other words, loan diversification can be secured through strategic placement of a limited
number of branches as well as through wide geographical disper-
sion of a larger number of branches. Both factors—an aggressive
loan policy and the particular geographical location of its offices—
have operated to produce an exceptionally high loan ratio in the
American Trust Company's portfolio.

Finally, Security–First National Bank had an exceptionally low
loan ratio in the postwar period. This is the result of a definite
policy of Security Bank to extend loans only to 30 per cent of its
deposits. At times, the management has permitted a ratio of loans
to deposits of 35 per cent. Security Bank's management deliberately holds down its loan ratio in the interest of greater liquidity.[25]

To repeat, the pattern of branch bank unit wage costs is very
similar to the ranking of their respective loan ratios. The loan
ratios are fundamentally a function of size of branch bank but
can also be materially affected by a bank's loan policy and the
particular placement of its branch offices. *Ceteris paribus,* the
higher the loan ratio, the higher are unit wage costs (and, *ceteris
paribus,* unit costs as well).

---

[22] Anglo-California National Bank, *Annual Report,* 1948, p. 4. (Italics mine.)
[23] American Trust Company, *Annual Report,* 1942.
[24] *Ibid.,* 1946.
[25] Statement made to the author by senior loan officers of Security Bank.

Size mix.—The other factor that significantly affects unit wage costs is the relative proportions of different size loans in different branch banks, i.e., the size mix. Other things being equal, the percentage of *small* loans tends to vary directly with size of branch bank. Among the California branch systems, the number of branch offices in each system varies directly with the size of the individual bank (as size is measured, say, by deposits). As the number of branches increases, an increasing percentage of offices usually will be situated in smaller towns and rural communities. Table 25 shows

TABLE 25

TOTAL CALIFORNIA BANK DEPOSITS OF INDIVIDUALS, PARTNERSHIPS, AND CORPORATIONS
AND BANKING OFFICES IN EIGHT CALIFORNIA METROPOLITAN AREAS AND OTHER AREAS
AS OF DECEMBER 31, 1947

(per cent)

Bank[a]	Eight metropolitan areas		Other areas	
	Deposits	Banking offices	Deposits	Banking offices
Bank of America	81.1	69.9	18.9	30.1
Security–First National	91.1	83.9	8.9	16.1
American Trust	93.7	92.0	6.3	8.0
Anglo-California	83.7	75.0	16.3	25.0

[a] SOURCES: Transamerica Hearings, Respondent's Exhibit No. 123. The eight metropolitan areas are Los Angeles, San Francisco, San Diego, Fresno, San Jose, Sacramento, Bakersfield, and Stockton.

the distribution of each branch bank's deposits and banking offices between eight metropolitan areas in California and all other areas. The deposits columns give a sense of the importance of the banking offices in different areas, since not all banking offices are of equal size. The branch banks are listed in the table from largest to smallest. As size of bank increases, the percentage of each bank's offices (as well as of deposits) located outside the metropolitan areas also increases. The only exception is the Anglo-California Bank. In 1947, Anglo Bank had a total of only twenty-five banking offices.[26] In other words, the number of Anglo's branches was so small that any particular distribution between metropolitan and other areas is partly fortuitous. Partly, too, the distribution is because of Anglo's particular policy in the location of its offices.[27] Presumably,

[26] *Rand McNally Bankers' Directory* (Chicago: Rand McNally and Company), 1948.
[27] "Of the frankly branch systems, *Anglo Bank has long followed a pattern somewhat different and distinct from that of its competitors.* It has not sought a large number of offices in the area of the city of its domicile, nor has it sought either to establish or to acquire many offices throughout the state. Rather, the pattern of having complete and substantial offices in key cities and towns, *generally not more*

as size of branch bank increases, the effects of a particular bank's policy on the distribution of its offices would tend to fade. The generalization seems reasonable, then, that as size of bank increases, the number of its offices in rural areas and small towns also would usually increase. Since borrowers in such areas are predominantly small borrowers,[28] the percentage of a branch bank's small loans tends to increase as size of bank increases. *Ceteris paribus,* a high percentage of small loans results in high unit wage costs.[29]

"Giant" banks.—Although branch bank unit wage costs vary directly with size of branch bank, American Trust is a conspicuous exception. In many years, unit wage costs of the American Trust Company were as high or even higher than those of the largest branch bank, Bank of America. This exception in the wage cost pattern is not fortuitous, and can be understood by an extension of the preceding analysis. Partly, as earlier explained, the high unit wage costs of American Trust are the result of its product mix, which is characterized by a high loan ratio. In part, however, the high wage costs of American Trust are related to its size mix.

It is easier to understand the reasons for the high wage costs in American Trust if, instead of thinking of American Trust as "pulling ahead" of the larger banks, one thinks rather of American Trust as holding its "normal" position on the wage cost scale, whereas Bank of America and Security–First National slip down below American Trust. It was observed earlier that as size of branch bank increases, so will the number of its small loans,[30] and, correspondingly, its unit wage costs. However, when a particular branch bank exceeds the size class of "large" and becomes a "giant" bank, it also becomes the only bank (or the most logical bank) to handle extremely large loans in which the output (i.e., dollar amount of loan) is very high per dollar of wage expense. Both Bank of America and Security–First National Bank are giant banks. Bank of America is the largest bank in the country, and Security–First National Bank is the eighth largest commercial bank.[31] Both are significantly larger than American Trust (18th largest) or

---

than one to a city except in San Francisco, has been closely followed with the thought in mind that the best job of banking, both for shareholders and for depositors, could thus be accomplished. Our policy has been one of conservative branch development." Anglo Bank, *Annual Report,* 1949, p. 1. (Italics mine.)

[28] Cf. n. 14, above.

[29] Cf. p. 86.

[30] It should be emphasized that this tendency holds primarily for giant *branch* banks. The size mix of the country's few giant *unit* banks in all probability contains only a small proportion of truly small loans.

[31] Security Bank, *Annual Report,* 1950, p. 2.

Anglo-California (36th largest).[32] In giant branch banks, the wage
cost (and, *ceteris paribus,* the unit cost) tendencies pull in opposite
directions because of the bimodal pattern of their size mix. At
times the effect of large loans predominates, and wage costs of giant
branch banks are no greater, and even lower, than the wage costs
of large but not giant branch systems.

Specialization and administration.—Large unit banks have lower
wage costs than small unit banks, partly because the labor-saving
(and cost-reducing) tendencies of increasing specialization of function only become possible with large size of bank. Although the
branch banks differ greatly in size, the pattern of unit wage costs
by size of branch bank is almost exactly reversed as compared with
the pattern for unit banks of different sizes. The basic pattern of
variation of wage costs in branch banks is determined by the respective product mix and size mix in the different branch banks.
In light of the earlier discussion of specialization, it seems likely
that whatever economies are possible by specialization of function
are almost as fully realized by the smallest branch bank as by the
largest. Beyond a certain point, size of bank can even produce cost-
raising tendencies because mounting administrative costs are incurred in coördinating very large organizations. Increasing absolute
size of bank thus generates conflicting cost tendencies. Whether
specialization results in significant cost disparities or is neutral in
different size branch banks is unknown. Whether potential marginal economies of specialization in very large branch banks are
outweighed by administrative diseconomies is also uncertain.
Whatever the cost tendencies from specialization and administration, they clearly are not important compared to the influence on
branch bank wage costs of the product mix and size mix.

UNIT INTEREST COSTS

The ranking of branch banks by unit interest cost on time deposits
tends to be the same as the ranking by unit wage costs, viz., American Trust, Bank of America, Security Bank, and Anglo Bank. The
particular pattern of unit interest costs on time deposits is explained by the fact that time deposits as a percentage of loans and
investments are in the same ranking for the various banks. In most
years, effective interest rates on time deposits show a slight tendency
for a similar ranking (except that the positions of Security and
Anglo are reversed from their positions in terms of wage costs).

[32] Cf. Anglo Bank, *Annual Report,* 1946, p. 7; and American Trust, *Annual Report,*
1948.

The significance of whatever pattern does emerge on interest rates is reduced to the extent that the actual figures are often identical for some of the banks. Moreover, in the postwar period, the earlier pattern is disturbed because Bank of America climbed to first place. Hence, the ranking of unit interest costs by size of bank is primarily conditioned by the pattern of time deposits/loans and investments and only secondarily by the rate of interest paid on time deposits.

Basically, the explanation for the ranking of unit interest costs is in terms of bank size and bank structure. In large measure, the pattern of unit interest costs is a function of the number of branches in the different branch banks. Banks located exclusively in metropolitan areas (e.g., the largest unit banks) have conspicuously low ratios of time deposits to loans and investments. Although all branch banks have offices in metropolitan areas, they also have branches outside the metropolitan areas. The larger the branch bank, the more branches it has; the more branches, the higher is the percentage of branches outside metropolitan centers. Hence, the larger the branch bank, *ceteris paribus,* the greater is its ratio of time deposits.[33]

The policy of an individual bank toward attracting and holding time deposit accounts (e.g., through advertising, leniency in abuse of time accounts, and so on) can also affect the particular ranking that size of branch bank would otherwise imply. For example, Anglo Bank deliberately adopted a policy of "refraining from the acceptance and retention of large deposits on which interest must be paid, without collateral advantages such as profitable commercial business, when there is no ready employment for the funds."[34] In general, however, the larger the branch bank, the greater is the percentage of its time deposits.

If size alone were involved, large banks would have a low percentage of time deposits and a correspondingly high ratio of demand deposits,[35] whereas branch structure alone would reverse this pattern. Beyond a certain large size, however, the tendencies from size dominate those from structure *within the same bank* and result in an increase of the relative proportion of demand deposits. As a branch bank grows very large, it attracts a disproportionate share

[33] "A fundamental difference between city and country banks is in the character of deposit liabilities ... country banks have a larger percentage of time deposits. . . ." Major B. Foster and Raymond Rodgers, *Money and Banking* (3d ed.; New York: Prentice-Hall, 1947), p. 168.

[34] Anglo Bank, *Annual Report,* January, 1940, p. 6.

[35] The Chase National Bank, for example, which is roughly comparable in size with Bank of America, had as of December 31, 1948, only 3.02 per cent of total deposits in the form of time deposits whereas Bank of America had 40.6 per cent.

of the large demand deposits of wealthy individuals and corporations in its market area, because of its ability to provide complete
banking services, its safety, its prestige, and so on. Beyond a certain
large size, therefore, the very large branch banks might have a
higher percentage of demand deposits to loans and investments
than other large branch banks. The very large size of Bank of
America and Security Bank explains why both slip in the ranking
of time deposits to loans and investments from positions which
they would otherwise hold as a result of their branch structure,
and actually rank lower than American Trust.

As compared with giant unit banks, e.g., Chase Bank of New
York City, the effects of Bank of America's branch structure dominate over the effects of its size in determining the relative proportions of time and demand deposits. As compared with another
branch bank, e.g., American Trust, Bank of America's size is the
determining factor rather than its branch structure. Like Bank of
America, Security Bank's ratio of time deposits to loans and investments is generally greater than that of large unit banks, because,
relative to unit banks, Security's branch structure is the dominating factor. However, compared to Bank of America, which has far
more branches than Security Bank, Security stands in the relation
of a large unit bank to a branch bank, with the result that Security's
time deposit ratio is lower than that for Bank of America. In short,
both size of bank and bank structure influence the ratio of time
deposits to loans and investments, and, hence, unit interest costs.
Both size and structure are relative terms, however. Necessarily,
therefore, the interpretation of empirical data must reflect the
relativity of the underlying determinants of pertinent statistical
patterns.

UNIT MISCELLANEOUS COSTS

In the early years of the study period, the smallest branch bank
tended to have the lowest miscellaneous costs and the largest bank
tended to have the highest. With these exceptions, unit miscellaneous costs are not clearly related to size of branch bank. In fact,
in some years, the miscellaneous costs of two or more branch banks
are very similar. Among unit banks, it will be recalled, miscellaneous costs decline as size of bank increases. Since miscellaneous
costs are to a considerable extent overhead items, the absence of a
clearly defined pattern of inverse variation between size of branch
bank and unit miscellaneous costs is not insignificant, and will be
further examined below.

COMPARATIVE COSTS OF BRANCH AND UNIT BANKS

The previous sections examined the cost ratios of unit banks and branch banks. This section extends that analysis and compares unit costs of both bank categories. This analysis of costs throws light not only upon the comparative nature of unit costs in different size unit banks and in branch banks, but also shows how structure (i.e., branch vs. unit) and size influence bank unit costs. Special attention is given to the comparison of branch banks with the largest category of unit banks in order to isolate the effects of structure on costs.[36]

COMPARATIVE UNIT COSTS

Unit costs of branch banks as a group were higher in every year but one (1944) than the unit costs of the largest unit banks. On the other hand, branch banks as a group had lower unit costs than the average of unit banks in every year studied. With only four exceptions, the branch bank average was also lower than that of any individual unit bank category, other than the largest unit banks. The penultimate size unit bank category is an important line of division. Unit banks of this size and smaller have higher unit costs than the average of branch banks, whereas unit banks larger than the penultimate category have lower unit costs than the average of branch banks.

Individual branch banks perform somewhat differently from the average of branch banks. For example, the costs of the lowest cost bank (Anglo) often were even a shade lower than the unit costs of the largest unit bank. The second lowest cost branch bank (Security) usually ran a bit higher than the largest unit banks, but lower than the penultimate size unit bank. The highest cost branch bank (American Trust) invariably had higher costs than the largest unit banks, and, after 1945, it even had higher costs than the penultimate size unit bank. The other high cost branch bank (Bank of America) always had higher costs than the largest unit bank, but in at least four years (1946–1949) had somewhat higher costs than the penultimate size unit bank.

Unit costs of the Big Four as a group and individually are usually about the same or higher than those of the largest category of unit banks. The relation of unit costs between large unit banks

---

[36] The largest unit banks are not entirely comparable with the branch banks as a group in terms of size, since at least two of the branch banks are among the ten largest banks in the country. However, the largest unit banks provide the best comparisons with branch banks for certain purposes.

and branch banks breaks the pattern mentioned earlier, in which unit costs decline as size of unit bank increases. Branch bank costs tend definitely to increase as size of bank increases.

The pattern of unit costs between large unit banks and branch banks depends upon the relative size of the component elements of unit cost, viz., unit wage costs, unit interest costs on time deposits, and unit miscellaneous costs. Branch bank wage costs were somewhat higher than for the largest unit banks in the early years of the study period and about the same or slightly lower in the latter years of the period.[37] The wage costs of the two highest wage cost branch banks were almost invariably higher than for the largest of the unit banks. The lowest wage cost branch bank had somewhat lower unit wage costs than the largest category of unit banks. For the period as a whole, unit wage costs were slightly higher in branch banks than in the largest unit banks in nine years and slightly lower in four. Unit interest costs on time deposits were invariably higher for the average of branch banks than for the largest unit banks. Figures for the lowest interest cost branch bank are very slightly higher than for the largest category of unit banks. Finally, the branch bank average of unit costs for miscellaneous expenses was about the same as for the largest unit banks. Although unit miscellaneous costs are about the same for branch banks and the largest unit banks, unit interest costs on time deposits and (to a lesser degree) unit wage costs are somewhat higher in the former than in the latter. Hence, branch banks have higher unit costs than the largest unit banks.

COMPARATIVE EFFICIENCY OF BRANCH AND LARGEST UNIT BANKS

Branch banks on the whole have higher unit costs than large unit banks although the branch banks are typically larger than the largest category of unit banks. As stated above, this is because both unit wage costs and unit interest costs on time deposits are somewhat higher for branch banks than for large unit banks, whereas unit miscellaneous costs are about the same for branch and unit banks. It is important to mention, therefore, that the higher unit costs of branch banks carry no necessary implication about the over-all relative efficiency of branch and large unit banks.

Unit wage costs.—Branch bank proponents have pointed out that branch banks economize labor, since each branch does not need a full complement of bank personnel as would a unit bank. The fact that branch bank unit wage costs tend to be somewhat higher than in large unit banks is not necessarily statistical refuta-

---

[37] See table 22, above.

tion of this contention. Indeed, the reverse tends to be true. The reason that wage costs in branch banks are as high or slightly higher than wage costs in the largest unit banks (despite the tendency for wage costs to decline as size of unit bank increases) is not inefficient use of labor, but is rather owing to the combined effects of different product mix, different size mix, and different loan mix in branch banks as compared to those in the largest unit banks.

In the first place, branch banks in California make a higher percentage of loans (as against investments) than the largest unit banks. Specifically, the branch banks as a group have considerably higher ratios of loans to loans and investments in every year than the largest category of unit banks (although the ratios are typically lower or, at best, about equal to those in the penultimate size category of unit banks). In fact, even the lowest ranking branch bank (viz., Anglo Bank) had higher ratios of loans to loans and investments than the largest category of unit banks.[38] This greater stress on loans among branch banks is partly responsible for the higher wage costs (and, thus, unit costs) in branch banks. This follows from the fact that loans are more expensive to transact than investments. Whereas the latter are generally rated by standard investment manuals (e.g., Poor's), each loan must be investigated separately. Even large loans where the credit check may be less important still must be formally negotiated through loan contracts, and so on.

In addition to a different product mix, branch banks have also a different size mix than the largest unit banks. Specifically, branch banks usually have a higher proportion of small loans than the largest unit banks. Security Bank, for example, has stated that, "The average size of 99 per cent of our loans, which number more than 94,000, is less than $1,600."[39] Similarly, more than 50 per cent of the commercial loans in Bank of America are less than $1,000; more than 90 per cent are less than $10,000; and only about 1 per cent of its commercial loans is more than $50,000.[40] It should be emphasized that these percentages refer to *numbers* of loans and not to dollar volumes. Although figures are not available for the size mix of the largest unit bank loan portfolios, it is reasonable to assume that the largest unit banks have far fewer small loans than do branch banks. Large unit banks are situated in metro-

[38] Appendix table H.
[39] Security Bank, *Annual Report,* January, 1947, p. 3.
[40] This breakdown of loans is for the period November 1, 1947 to October 31, 1948. Cf. Transamerica Hearings, Respondent's exhibit no. 149.

politan areas which have a large number of important (and large) borrowers. A large branch bank usually has its head office in a metropolitan area, but at least some of its branches are in smaller towns and in rural areas where small loans predominate. The importance of the alleged higher proportion of small loans in branch banks than in the largest unit banks is that small loans are notoriously more expensive to transact per dollar of loan than larger loans.

Finally, branch banks have higher unit wage costs than the largest unit banks because of the different loan mix in the portfolios of the two categories of banks. Branch banks make a variety of loans which large unit banks generally do not bother with, e.g., ICL loans, small mortgage loans, personal consumption loans, and so on. These are typically high cost loans. The fact that unit wage costs in branch banks are only slightly higher than in the largest unit banks is, under the circumstances, a tribute to the economy of labor in branch banks.

Unit interest costs.—Unit interest costs on time deposits are higher for branch banks than for the largest unit banks, and result, *ceteris paribus*, in higher unit costs of branch banks. The high unit interest costs in branch banks are the result of their high proportion of time deposits to loans and investments.[41] The ratio of time deposits to loans and investments in branch banks is related to branch bank structure. Checking accounts are not universally employed in this country even today. In part, checking accounts are expensive for the small depositor. In part, too, persons in lower income groups and those living in small towns and rural areas are simply less accustomed to the use of checking accounts than persons in higher income groups and residents of metropolitan areas. Since branch banks have branches outside major cities and in smaller towns and rural areas, they naturally attract a lower percentage of demand deposits (higher percentage of time deposits) than a large unit bank in a metropolitan area, dealing primarily with large depositors.

Unit miscellaneous costs.—Unit miscellaneous costs are about the same for the average of branch banks and for the largest unit banks.[42] This is rather surprising since miscellaneous costs are mostly overhead costs. Miscellaneous costs include items like depreciation on buildings and equipment, insurance, heat, light,

---

[41] Not only is the ratio of time deposits to loans and investments higher for the average of branch banks than for the largest unit banks, but, in almost every year, this is true as well for each of the individual branch banks.

[42] In different years, individual branch banks had slightly lower miscellaneous costs than the largest unit banks.

lawsuits and court costs,[43] advertising,[44] and even many items of supplies.[45] The branch banks (with the possible exception of Anglo Bank) are all very large banks, even by national standards, and they are typically much larger than the largest unit banks in California. Accordingly, they have a very large *absolute* level of output (loans and investments).

In the unit banks, absolute output increases as size of bank (measured, say, by deposits) grows. No doubt, too, absolute overhead costs also increase with size of bank. Since unit overhead costs decline as size of unit bank increases,[46] absolute overhead costs clearly increase less than proportionately with the increase in output. In branch banks, however, unit overhead costs are not lower—indeed, they are about the same—than the largest unit banks. Since the absolute output of most branch banks is considerably greater than that in the largest unit banks in California, it must be concluded that overhead costs increase *pari passu* with output as a bank moves from the category of the largest unit banks and into the category of large branch banks. In spite of their great size, branch banks as a group have no economies of overhead costs compared with the largest unit banks. Since overhead costs decrease among unit banks as size of unit bank increases, it would appear that, compared to unit banking, branch banking introduces diseconomies of overhead costs. Since cost data are not available for the individual components of miscellaneous costs, it would be more accurate to say that, *on balance*, branch banking involves diseconomies of overhead expenses. Even if there are economies in individual components of overhead costs, they are compensated by the still greater (relative to the largest unit banks) diseconomies of other overhead components.

COMPARATIVE LOAN COSTS

Generally, comparative unit costs among the firms of an industry are taken as a clue to their relative efficiency.[47] In banking, how-

[43] Certain exceptional lawsuits and court costs may not be considered fixed expenses, but most court costs are for legal disputes which inevitably arise when an institution enters daily into contracts with large numbers of people.

[44] Under modern banking attitudes, a certain minimum of advertising is probably taken for granted, but beyond this minimum level, advertising is a variable cost.

[45] To a certain extent, supplies are a variable cost and vary with the volume of business. In banking, however, numerous records must be kept even with no change or even a decline in business ("output").

[46] Cf. table 24 above.

[47] Many difficult problems in this area are being deliberately ignored; e.g., whether all firms in the industry must be operating at their respective optimum points before comparing relative efficiency.

ever, relative unit costs *per se* of different banks carry no automatic presumption of comparative efficiency.[48] The higher unit costs of branch banks as compared with the largest unit banks are clearly the result of branch bank structure, but, as already stated, this does not necessarily imply that branch banks are therefore less efficient than very large unit banks.

Branch vs. largest unit banks.—This analysis has shown that branch banks have higher unit costs than do the largest unit banks. These higher unit costs are primarily because of higher unit interest costs. However, interest costs are, in a sense, an artificial component of cost in spite of their importance in the total cost picture, because they are not directly related to efficiency of operations as narrowly conceived. As far as wage costs and miscellaneous costs are concerned, the analysis has revealed that branch bank miscellaneous costs are the same, and their wage costs are in many years only slightly higher than those of the largest unit banks. In other words, branch bank costs are almost equal to largest unit bank costs if the somewhat artificial[49] cost item of interest costs is ignored. This is an important conclusion and suggests one of two further conclusions.

On the one hand, it might appear that branch banks can negotiate a "large"[50] loan more cheaply than the largest unit banks.[51] As a result of their high specialization in different kinds of loans, branch banks may have a cost advantage over large unit banks. The branch banks in California are, after all, not merely "large" banks: they are among the largest banks in the country. Thus it is quite feasible for Bank of America to have a man specialize on, say, loans to sardine boats, or for American Trust to have a man who is expert on loans to turkey farmers.[52] Specialization to this extent is probably not feasible for large unit banks, unless such banks are also giant banks, and that is not likely to be true of unit banks except in the largest metropolitan centers or the money market centers. There is, after all, a considerable difference in the

---

[48] Unless, possibly, unit costs were broken down for different size loans, which our figures do not show directly.

[49] Again, from the narrow viewpoint of efficiency.

[50] The expressions "large," "small," and the like are obviously flexible. In this context, "large" loans specifically excludes prime loans. The direct costs of making prime loans are negligible. Thus, the notion of comparative efficiency of different banks does not arise when prime loans are concerned. The only important direct costs in prime loans are the "raw material costs," i.e., the cost to the bank of acquiring loanable funds. The matter is different, however, in large, but not prime loans.

[51] This discussion is limited to "large" loans since large loans predominate in the portfolio size mix of the largest unit banks.

[52] Parenthetically, neither example is hypothetical.

knowledge required to lend to truckers rather than to nurseries, to sardine boats rather than to turkey farmers. Loans to sardine-boat customers, for example, become involved with highly complex maritime laws. On the other hand, lending to turkey farmers requires, for example, detailed knowledge of the costs of raising turkeys at different stages of their growth. A nonspecialized credit man, even a very capable one, could hardly be expected to be expert in several such fields. Whereas the nonspecialist (or less highly specialized) banker would have to spend considerable time and costly effort investigating a proposed loan transaction, a banker specialized in that field might be able to make a sound decision in a fraction of the time.

These economies of specialization are not inconsistent with the statistics. Although the largest unit banks have a preponderance of large (but not prime) loans, the branch banks also service many small (high cost) loans. Moreover, the branch banks have a higher loan ratio (loans/loans and investments) than the largest unit banks, as well as a more costly loan mix. Despite the cost-raising tendencies of their product mix, loan mix, and size mix, average wage costs are only slightly higher (or equal), and miscellaneous costs of branch banks are equal to those for the category of largest unit banks. It would seem to follow, therefore, that the branch banks have a cost advantage in negotiating large loans as compared with the largest unit banks.

This possible conclusion must be qualified, however, because of an ambiguity in the preceding analysis. Branch banks, by virtue of their enormous size, can (even without syndication) negotiate loans which are incomparably larger than anything typically handled even by the largest unit banks in California. Unfortunately available statistics are lacking on the details of large loans by different banks. To the extent that branch banks in California do negotiate such giant loans, it is impossible to deduce with certainty from the total cost structure how they compare with the largest unit banks in the cost of handling *large* (but, again, not prime) loans of comparable size. However, in view of what has already been said about specialization in branch banks, it is eminently reasonable to think that branch bank costs on comparable large loans are, at worst, equal to those of the largest category of unit banks.

Branch vs. smaller unit banks.—Branch bank average unit costs are considerably lower than those of the smaller unit banks. This cost disparity is based on lower wage costs and on lower miscellaneous costs.[53] It is uncertain whether the lower wage and miscellaneous costs are *exclusively* owing to the size mix, i.e., to the fact that large loans are found in branch bank portfolios and not particularly in the portfolios of the smaller unit banks. Despite the absence of formal proof, there is a strong presumption that branch banks can negotiate small loans more cheaply than small unit banks. This presumption is predicated on numerous internal economies of the branch bank structure per se.

In the first place, branch banks economize on labor as compared to the ordinary unit banks. Although each unit bank must have its full complement of bank personnel, the branch bank does not need to duplicate in each branch office all the personnel who would be required if the branch office were an independent bank. For example, the personnel required in a unit bank to handle the investment portfolio are, in a branch system, entirely concentrated at the head office. In this manner investment personnel are economized. Moreover, the magnitude of the investment operations and the concentrated attention upon such problems by specially trained people results in greater expertise in making investments, which, in turn, means lower costs in managing the investment portfolio.

In similar fashion, a branch bank can afford a separate research department to conduct special industry studies, to analyze local and national economic trends and the like. The information developed by the head-office research department is made available to all the branches, thereby increasing their efficiency in their daily operations. By contrast, the typical small unit bank cannot afford a research department, and special information may require time of personnel who cannot be expert in all the projects they must undertake.

Quite aside from a formal research department which is available to all the branches, the branch loan officers can call upon expert assistance at the head office in transacting specialized loans (including small loans) in a variety of different fields, e.g., cotton, fabricated steel, wheat, corn, aluminum, and a host of others. As mentioned earlier, this kind of intensive specialization can give a branch bank a cost advantage even over a large unit bank, and a fortiori over smaller unit banks. In a small unit bank, one man may have to learn something about a wide variety of possible loans.

---

[53] Branch banks sometimes have higher unit interest costs than the smaller unit banks, but, for reasons stated earlier, unit interest costs are here ignored. Even when they are included, the conclusions are not affected, because branch banks have lower average costs (ATUC) than any but the largest unit banks.

Even the making of an ordinary real estate loan may require not only a knowledge of current real estate values in an area but also a familiarity with the considerable red tape connected with securing an FHA- or VA-guaranteed mortgage. The result is that the small unit banker is less efficient in making loans in many categories than the branch loan officer who has available the advice of specialists at the head office.

The branch type of organization offers still further economies of labor. The loan mix in a small unit bank probably contains a wider assortment of kinds of loans than in very large unit banks, though less than in a large branch bank. In many of these loans, the branch bank enjoys economies which are not available to the small unit bank. For example, in making installment credit loans, the branch bank enjoys economies in supervision and collection which a smaller unit bank cannot match. In a state with marked population mobility, the supervision and collection of such loans can involve the unit bank in considerable expense if the borrower moves to a different locality. The branch bank, however, need only transfer the credit to a branch in the vicinity where the borrower has moved.

Moreover, as a function of the large size of most intercity branch systems, the branch type of organization can employ labor-saving machines which are not feasible for smaller unit banks whose volume of business would not warrant them. By the same token, as indicated earlier, a branch system can negotiate bulk purchases of supplies and equipment, with corresponding reduction in their cost. Again, branch offices need not be so elaborate as their small unit bank competitors, since the prestige and strength of the head office support alike all the branches.

For all these reasons, it seems likely that the lower wage and miscellaneous costs of branch banks as compared with those of the smaller unit banks are not exclusively a function of the different size mix in the two categories of banks. The point should not be lightly passed, however, that this analysis can suggest only a presumption that lower costs in branch banks are functionally related to branch bank organization. The generally accepted statement that the branch bank organization per se provides net economies of operation has been based primarily on deduction, not on statistical evidence. Neither publicly available statistics nor those made available for this study provide proof that branch banks can negotiate a small loan more cheaply than a small (or medium) unit bank *because of cost economies integrally related to branch banking*. There is, after all, a considerable difference in a bank's having lower average costs because of its size mix instead of its particular organization. To repeat, however, there is certainly a strong presumption that branch banking per se as compared with smaller unit banks, provides net economies in making small loans.

It has often been observed that branch banks can enter small towns and rural areas and operate profitably where unit banks could not survive. This possibility would be obvious if branch banks have demonstrably lower costs than their small unit rivals on comparable (small loan) output. Numerous reasons have already been suggested in support of this contention. In spite of the circumstantial evidence, the statistics per se could not prove this point. It is worth commenting, therefore, that the ability of a branch bank to enter a small town where unit banks could not survive does not necessarily prove a branch bank's cost advantage by inference. Although branch bank entry *may* be related to lower costs of the branches than of the smaller unit banks, it *need* not be so. Branch banks could enter such towns if their unit costs of production were the same as, or, indeed, even higher than those of unit banks. The main problem in such towns is the absence of a sufficient potential volume of business to support even a minimum-size unit bank.[54] Whereas a unit bank would have to find most of its loan output in its local community, a branch could shift such excess reserves for lending through other parts of the system.

BANK STRUCTURE AND COMPARATIVE COSTS

A comparative cost analysis of branch and unit banking can follow either or both of two major lines of investigation. First, the investigation can consider the over-all performance of each bank category as this performance is reflected in its unit costs. An extension of this first approach also involves an analytical breakdown of the components of unit costs and also of the real factors which lie behind the individual cost components. Second, a cost investigation might attempt to determine statistically the cost relations among different banks for comparable output. Specifically, this second approach would attempt to discover exactly how branch

---

[54] With reference to small, bankless, rural communities, the Comptroller of the Currency has stated that, "In many of these situations a new bank is not the answer for the amount of available business is inadequate to permit profitable operation, and an unprofitable bank cannot long retain competent employees, and hence it gradually deteriorates and becomes a hazard to the economic life of the community. On the other hand, these communities could, in a great number of instances, readily support a branch office of a sizable institution." Patman Report, Vol. II, p. 927.

bank costs compare with those of any particular size unit bank in making some particular size (or kind) of loan as against some other size (or kind). Public policy deliberations about branch bank concentration require background information provided by both approaches.

The comparative cost analysis of this chapter has concentrated primarily on the over-all performance of branch and unit banks and on their comparative performance as measured by the individual cost components. Bank operations are not sufficiently detailed in available statistics to make precise evaluations between branch and unit banks on specific size (or kind) of loans. The general observations made on these latter costs were based on a combination of circumstantial evidence and inference from the statistical record of over-all cost performance.

In terms of over-all performance, the largest unit banks have a cost advantage over branch banks. However, if the somewhat artificial cost item of unit interest costs is ignored,[55] branch banks are (practically) equal to the largest unit banks both on wage costs and on miscellaneous costs. This statement has at least two important implications. On the one hand, it qualifies the commonly vaunted claims of branch bank proponents that branch banking is "superior" to unit banking because of alleged cost advantages.[56] If interest costs are included in the full cost comparison, branch bank costs are actually higher than those of the largest unit banks. Even when interest costs are ignored in the comparison, the remaining costs of branch banks are at best only equal to those of the largest unit banks. Again, the similarity of wage costs between branch banks and the largest unit banks implies economies of actual labor in branch banks relative to the largest unit banks. By contrast, the similarity of miscellaneous costs implies diseconomies in the use of actual overhead items as compared to unit banking.[57] The alleged cost superiority of branch over unit banking holds, strictly speaking, only when branch banks are compared to any but the largest unit banks. Branch banks then have lower full costs and lower cost components, with the possible exception of interest costs.

The investigation of comparative costs in terms of specific output was suggestive but statistically inconclusive. There is reason

---

[55] Unit interest costs might be ignored in a public policy appraisal of branch and unit banks because the high interest costs of branch banks are primarily a function of their high ratio of time deposits.

[56] As far as I know, these claims have been based primarily on broad considerations, but not on direct statistical evidence.

[57] Cf. p. 100.

to infer that branch banks can outperform the largest unit banks on their most nearly comparable output, viz., large business loans. At the very least, it would appear that their costs on such output are similar. By the same token, there is a strong inference that branch banks can outperform the smaller unit banks on smaller loans.

In a discussion of the cost "superiority" or "inferiority" of various banks, the relevant consideration is the basis on which the cost comparisons are made, i.e., over-all operations, specific cost components, actual factor use, or specific output. Clearly, too, a summary evaluation must take into account the particular bank categories under comparison. In most, but not all these comparisons, branch banks appear to have a cost advantage over unit banks. The cost advantages of branch banks are in turn specifically related to their large size as well as to their branch structure.

From one point of view, it is often difficult to isolate the effects of size from the effects of structure, because these two characteristics are interrelated. For large banks in particular, size is related to structure. The branch structure of a giant bank is typically the medium by which such growth has been achieved. With very few exceptions, it is hard to conceive of a giant bank that is not also a branch bank. At least some of the apparent exceptions are not really exceptions at all. Some of the giant banks in money market centers have branch offices in their head-office city, but are generally regarded as unit banks. In a city like New York, with a metropolitan population larger than that of many states, such "unit" banks are really multiple-office (or "branch") banks operating in a "city-state."[58] Alternatively, or additionally, some giant unit banks are bankers' banks (i.e., correspondents) for numerous other banks in other parts of the country. From a growth standpoint, even large correspondent banks might be regarded as pseudo-branch banks.

---

[58] Branch banks restricted to the head-office city do not necessarily have all the other characteristics of bona fide branch banks; e.g., the mobility of funds among different lending areas.

VII

Pricing Practices and Price Policy

THE REVENUES of a manufacturing firm are primarily a function of the price of the product and the total volume of sales during a given period. In analogous fashion, the revenues of a bank are primarily a product of the interest rate paid by the borrowers and the total volume of credit made available by the bank. Moreover, like many manufacturing enterprises, banks are multi-product firms. A bank's output can be divided into two main categories: (1) loans and discounts, and (2) investments. Each of these, in turn, can be further subdivided to explain given revenue patterns. Bank revenues are also available from service charges on checking accounts, from fees and commissions in providing financial services for customers, and so on. For most banks, such sources of revenue are comparatively minor.[1] Since bank revenues stem primarily from earnings on loans and investments, bank revenues directly involve a bank's price policy and pricing practices.

The interest rate policy of branch banks[2] is of concern in this study for at least three reasons. First, the rate structure on loans is directly related to earnings, and, other things being equal, to the profitability of a bank. Second, the rates charged by different banks affect their business borrowers. Most important of all, perhaps, the rate structures and rate policies of branch banks are clues to the kinds of markets in which these banks operate. Since banking directly affects the public interest, all three considerations are relevant for public policy.

---

[1] Certain small banks, however, depend heavily on such fees, e.g., those state banks which avoid membership in the Federal Reserve because membership would require par collection of checks.

[2] The factual information in this chapter is mostly based on personal interviews with senior loan officers of the Big Four branch banks in California. The analysis and interpretations are mine. At the request of the loan officers interviewed, the anonymity of individual statements is preserved. There was a very high degree of uniformity in the information supplied by different loan officers.

AVERAGE RATES OF INTEREST

Table 26 shows earnings on loans and discounts as a percentage of total loans and discounts. The percentage figures describe effective average rates of interest on loans and discounts. These interest rate figures are automatically properly weighted, since they reflect the relative volumes of different size and kind of loans and the corresponding rates of interest charged. In order to approximate the effective average rates of interest charged[3] by banks, the figures in table 26 have not been adjusted for losses and recoveries. Among unit banks, the table reveals a clear-cut progression in which the average interest rates charged on loans and discounts vary inversely with size of bank. It is worth stating, too, that interest rates in the smallest-size banks are significantly higher than for the largest category of banks throughout the period of study. This pattern of rates on loans and discounts by size of bank is similar to that for different size banks in other parts of the country.[4] This pattern is basically related to the size mix of different size banks. For example, small banks, largely because of their size and location, usually make a preponderance of small loans, whereas the large loans are preponderantly transacted by big banks. Furthermore, small loans are made by small borrowers who do not have a significant number of alternative sources of supply. The weakness of their bargaining position is reflected in the higher rates they must pay.

The tendency among unit banks for average interest rates to vary inversely with size of bank is exactly reversed for branch banks. Highest average rates were almost invariably earned by the largest branch bank, and the lowest rates, by the smallest branch bank. The intermediate-size branch banks earned average rates intermediate between the highest and the lowest among the branch banks. The range among all the branch banks was considerably less than among the extremes of the unit banks. The intermediate-size branch banks, in particular, were extremely close together in rates. In every year during the period under investigation, the branch bank average rate of interest was higher than the average rate of interest for the largest of the unit banks. Curiously, too, whereas the branch bank average is higher than that of the largest unit banks, it is invariably lower than that for the penultimate size unit banks. Finally, the smallest of the branch banks, with the lowest rate among branch banks, is only slightly higher than

[3] As contrasted with ultimate net earnings.
[4] Cf. chapter iii.

TABLE 26

EARNINGS ON LOANS AND DISCOUNTS AS A PERCENTAGE OF TOTAL LOANS AND DISCOUNTS, BY SIZE AND KIND OF BANK, CALIFORNIA, 1938–1950

Unit banks[a] (by size)	1938	1939	1940	1941	1942	1943	1944	1945	1946	1947	1948	1949	1950
Smallest	8.4	7.2	7.2	7.3	7.4	6.8	6.9	6.0	6.0	6.5	6.8	7.2	7.5
2	7.2	7.0	6.6	6.4	6.2	6.4	6.1	5.9	5.9	5.9	6.0	5.9	6.1
3	6.3	6.4	6.3	6.4	5.8	6.3	5.7	5.5	5.5	5.4	5.5	5.5	5.8
4	6.2	6.4	5.7	5.9	5.4	5.4	5.0	4.6	4.6	5.0	5.0	5.2	5.2
5	5.9	5.9	5.4	5.3	4.0	5.4	5.0	4.7	5.0	4.9	4.9	5.3	5.7
6	5.5	5.3	5.4	5.4	....	3.7	3.7	3.3	3.5	3.5	3.4	3.1	4.0
7	5.5	5.3	4.2	3.9	....	....	....	....	....	....	....	....	....
8	4.3	4.4	....	....	....	....	....	....	....	....	....	....	....
Unit bank average	6.2	6.0	6.1	6.1	6.1	6.0	5.8	5.4	5.4	5.5	5.7	5.6	5.9
Branch bank average	5.0	5.0	5.0	4.9	4.6	4.5	4.2	4.0	4.2	4.3	4.4	4.6	4.8

For sources and notes to table, see Appendix.
[a] See notes to table 16.

the rate of the largest unit banks, although it is invariably lower in rate than the penultimate-size unit banks.

The results, on the surface at least, are curious. If size of bank (without distinction between branch or unit) were plotted along the abscissa and average rate of interest along the ordinate, a curve joining the two would (generally speaking) fall throughout most of the range and then begin to rise at the very end of the curve. Such a chart would actually blur the facts of the situation somewhat, since at least some unit banks are larger (whether measured by assets, deposits, or capital) than the smallest of the branch banks. In such a chart, the influence of the smallest branch banks would cancel out. If, however, the chart was plotted with two curves, one for unit banks and the other for branch banks, the unit bank curve would fall as size of bank increases. The branch bank curve would begin to the left of the end of the unit bank curve and rise above the lowest point of the unit bank curve. The suggestion is inescapable that the higher average rates earned by branch banks are in some sense related to their structure, in spite of their size, whereas for unit banks, size alone is a sufficient clue to the rates they earn. This conclusion is particularly curious since it has sometimes been alleged that branch bank structure results in low loan rates, whereas it has just been observed that branch bank structure is statistically associated with high average rates!

In fact, the actual loan rates charged by different banks are only imperfectly revealed in table 26. The average character of interest rates in the table masks the considerable heterogeneity of loan rates even in the same bank, as well as between different bank categories. The price policy of unit banks has been sketched in chapter iii. This chapter concentrates primarily on branch bank price policy and pricing practices. Unfortunately, detailed statistical information beyond what is shown in table 26 is unavailable. Bankers do not readily divulge specific data on the sacrosanct field of interest rates. It is necessary, therefore, to precipitate the desired information on prices from the data in table 26. The indispensable catalyst in the process is the factual information collected in interviews with branch loan officers.

INTEREST RATE POLICY OF BRANCH BANKS

It is convenient to break down the analysis of interest rate policy of branch banks in at least two ways. Business loans, which are of direct concern in this study, can be divided into two main categories—commercial and industrial loans, and agricultural loans.

This division is desirable because government agencies operate in the agricultural loan field and have no counterparts to the same extent in ordinary commercial loans. The analysis in earlier chapters suggests another division of the interest rate policy discussion, viz., among the different kinds of markets in which banks operate in making business loans.

The interest rate structure in any bank or in any region is a complex entity affected by myriad forces which constantly play on that structure. This chapter deals with the immediate determinants of interest rate structures. Later chapters examine the broader, underlying factors which affect interest rates by their influence on the over-all demand and supply of short-term credit. Although these latter factors affect customer loan rates indirectly, their impact is often as powerful and as important as the immediate determinants. Indeed, at least some customer loan rates respond quite promptly to changes in the basic demand and supply conditions for credit.

The immediate determinants of loan rates include the size of the borrower or the size of the loan, the quality of the credit, the type of credit, the duration of the loan, the degree and nature of the risk, the cost of administering the credit, the average balances maintained at the bank by the borrower, the nature and extent of competition among banks, the kind and amount of collateral if any, the character and length of the banker-customer relation, and the general worth of the account to the bank. Based on these considerations, the loan rate structure for business loans ranges from the low level of open market commercial rates (and sometimes even lower) to the legal limit of 8 per cent.

The problems of retailing credit differ in one critical aspect from the retailing of physical commodities. In the latter, an established price at any moment of time confronts the prospective buyer, and the consummation of a sale depends upon the buyer's reaction to the price and other terms of sale. In banking, however, there is no set rate of interest nor even a set series of rates at which different categories of borrowers can exercise the option of borrowing or not borrowing. Each loan transaction is individually negotiated between banker and borrower. Moreover, each loan is likely to differ in at least some details from any other loans made by the bank. If no common denominator could be found among the multifarious loans made by banks, the situation would be hopelessly chaotic for economic analysis. Fortunately, however, the immediate determinants of loan rates, though numerous, are often interrelated. To illustrate, a given size of loan will usually imply given conditions of risk, costs of administering the loan, size of balances, and general worth to the bank. It is no doubt for this reason that size of loan emerged in the earlier analysis as an important determinant of the structure of loan rates. This, however, is only part of the explanation. At least part of the explanation for the high correlation between size of loan and the levels of different rates of interest is that size of loan has distinct implications for alternative sources available, and, hence, for the kind of market in which the borrower must operate. Flexibility (as distinct from level) of different rates in the rate structure is almost exclusively a function of the market structure in which the loan is negotiated, and, hence, is a clue to the nature of that structure.

COMMERCIAL AND INDUSTRIAL LOANS

PRIME LOANS

Rate policy of branch banks on commercial and industrial loans can be subdivided, at least initially, into prime loan rates and rates on all other loans. A prime loan is one made by a very large corporation (or an important individual) whose operations are generally national in scope. Prime loans are short term, usually for ninety days. The corporation negotiating the loan must have a financial status which places its loans in the most highly preferred risk category. There is usually no real question about the safety of the loan. Prime borrowers negotiate loans in all parts of the country and even (though not necessarily) on the open market for commercial paper. Prime loan paper is also eligible for rediscount at the Federal Reserve Banks.

Prime rates.—Rates to prime borrowers are competitive because these borrowers have numerous alternative sources of supply and correspondingly strong bargaining positions. Moreover, prime rates respond reasonably promptly to changes in demand and supply conditions for credit as reflected in money market conditions. Indeed, for prime borrowers who can borrow on the open money market directly, rates charged by banks on prime loans must be competitive with open market commercial paper rates. During the past decade and a half, the prime rate has fluctuated between 1½ per cent and 3¼ per cent, a range of more than 100 per cent. The details of this fluctuation are shown in table 27.

As will be seen shortly, the prime rate is the key rate in the whole interest rate structure. Accordingly, the method of its determination is pertinent. As discussed above, the prime rate reflects changes in basic demand and supply conditions of credit. These short-run changes are most sensitively recorded in the open money market for short-term funds. The prime rate thus fluctuates with changes in open market short-term rates, and, to a lesser degree, with changes in the Federal Reserve rediscount rate. For banks all over the country, the prime rate is determined under a system of price leadership[5] in which the leadership rotates among the large New York City banks whose operations involve them constantly

TABLE 27

FLUCTUATIONS OF PRIME LOAN RATE, NEW YORK CITY, 1935–1953[a]

Periods	Per cent
1935–December, 1947	1½
December, 1947	1¾
August 10, 1948	2
September 21, 1950	2¼
January 5, 1951	2½
October 17, 1951	2¾
December (middle), 1951	3
April 27, 1953	3¼

[a] SOURCE: Compiled for the author by the Research Department, Federal Reserve Bank of San Francisco.

in the open money market. The price leadership usually rotates among the National City Bank, the Chase Bank, the Chemical Bank, the Guaranty Bank, and Bankers Trust Company. Occasionally the initiative is taken by a large bank in Chicago. When a change in the prime rate is publicly announced by one of the price leaders, the rest of the banks in the country which make prime loans fall in line within a matter of days, and, often, as fast as the change can be read on the ticker tape.[6] The prime rate is thus always a low interest rate and one with sufficient flexibility to reflect important changes in demand or supply conditions with reasonable promptness.

Impact of prime rates on other loan markets.—The situation is somewhat different for other than prime borrowers. Since the cate-

[5] Banking statistics simply do not provide the kind of detailed information on rates and timing necessary to establish the exact extent and consistency of a price leadership system. As used in this study, "price leadership" connotes a *general* pattern of leader-follower relationships.

[6] On April 27, the large New York City banks raised the prime rate to 3¼ per cent. Bank of America increased its prime rate to exactly the same figure on the same day, and other banks in San Francisco indicated they would increase rates shortly. Cf. *San Francisco Chronicle,* April 28, 1953, financial page.

gory of other than prime loans covers a wide assortment of transactions, the responsiveness of such rates to changes in underlying
money conditions varies. It is a legitimate simplification, however,
to divide such loans into two categories by size of loan, viz., medium-size loans and small loans.[7] Generally speaking, in an interest
rate structure which varies between 3 per cent and 8 per cent on
business loans, the medium-size loans are those which pay a rate
somewhat higher than the prime rate and up to about 4½ per
cent. The small borrowers pay from 5 per cent up to the legal
limit.[8] These distinctions are arbitrary but not unrealistic.

As soon as a branch bank has taken official recognition of the
change in prime rate announced in the money market centers, the
rate is promptly communicated to all its branches. Since the com-
munication is often by telephone, the transmission of the intelligence is practically instantaneous. The impact of this intelligence
in the branches depends upon the particular market in which the
branches are operating. The loan officer in each branch has in
mind a schedule or pattern of rates which is determined in its broad
outlines at the head office. Obviously there can be no hard and
fast formula for setting rates on intermediate- and small-size loans,
since the particular circumstances of each case will vary. Notwithstanding, there is sufficient homogeneity of the rate-determining
variables among different loans to group them into categories, and,
as discussed earlier, particularly into size categories. Thus, for each
category of loan, and allowing a certain amount of flexibility for
particular circumstances of the loan, the loan officer in each branch
knows what rate of interest to charge.

The uniformity of rate structure among different branches of a
branch bank is not difficult to maintain even where no formal
schedule is supplied to the branch loan officers by the head office.[9]
A loan officer of a branch will usually have had many years (possibly fifteen) of experience with the bank before assuming the
discretionary role of rate decision. During this apprenticeship, the
future loan officer has ample opportunity to review loans made by
branches all over the system and to gain a very clear conception
of the rate structure of the bank for different categories of loans,
even allowing for the heterogeneity of loans. Again, in most branch
banks, loan officers are subject to loan limitations above which

---

[7] Cf. p. 41 for definition of different size loans.

[8] For necessary qualifications to the above, see again pp. 112 and 113.

[9] At least some branch systems do provide such schedules which specify suggested
rates by size of loan, kind of collateral, and so on. Even where a formal schedule is
supplied, there must obviously be an element of judgment and discretion by the
branch loan officer.

they must secure head-office approval. These loan limits vary with the character of the business done by the branch and the experience and competence of its loan officer. The limits may be as low as $1,000 or as high as $100,000. Since many loans, even small loans in many instances, must be referred by the branches to the head office for approval, the head office has ample opportunity to ensure that uniformity is maintained in the rate structure. Even where no formal loan limit is imposed, all loans above a certain size (say, $25,000) must be submitted for ex post facto head-office review. If the loan officer is out of line with head-office loan policy, he is notified. Finally, even where the loans are not subject to loan limits, the branch loan officers are in constant touch with the head-office loan supervision department whose function it is to maintain a continuous review of loans made in the branches and to inform loan officers of deviations from head-office policy. Moreover, the loan officers are in frequent contact with the loan supervision department and with other branch loan officers. In big cities, such conferences may be held as often as twice a week.

Although at any moment the rate structure is uniform for different categories of loans among all the branches of a bank, there is considerable disparity in the *flexibility* of rates for different loan categories over time. The prime rate, as earlier observed, responds with reasonable promptness to changes in open money market rates. This cannot be said, however, for either medium-size or small loans. When the prime rate is changed, the rates on medium-size credit may also change but not to the same extent. Indeed, on medium-size loans above 4 per cent, the rate change not only fails to match the prime rate change on a percentage basis; it often is not matched even on an absolute basis. The sluggishness in these loan rates is such that rate changes are almost never made in less than one-half of one per cent moves. Thus, if the prime rate changes by only one-fourth of one per cent (which is not uncommon), the medium-size loan rate may not move at all. As prime rate changes accumulate over time, however, the medium-size loan rate will eventually move, too. What has here been said of the 4 per cent rate would also hold, *mutatis mutandis,* for rates above the prime rate and extending up to, or possibly even short of, the 5 per cent loans.

SMALL BUSINESS LOANS

The small business loans that pay a rate of (say) 6 per cent or 7 per cent may respond not at all to changes in the prime rate. In areas distant from metropolitan centers, the small loan rates of 6 per cent or 7 per cent have held with perfect stability for two decades, despite the wide fluctuations (percentagewise) of the prime rate.[10] Whereas a moderate sluggishness characterizes the medium-size loan rates, many small loan rates are practically frozen for years on end, despite significant changes in the over-all demand and supply for short-term credit.

Risks.—Branch bankers in California explain the considerable differences in the levels of prime and small loans in terms of risks and of costs. Prime rates are riskless and, per dollar of credit, cheap to negotiate; small loans are presumably neither. For economic analysis, however, the matter is perhaps not quite so simple as it appears on the surface. Consider the question of risk. It is certainly true that prime loans are riskless. Of course, in an uncertain world, even an outstanding national concern could conceivably default on its short-term credit and, on very rare occasions, that happens. In the overwhelming number of instances, however, the risk of default is negligible.

On the face of the matter, it is obvious that the risks of default in small loans are almost inevitably larger than in prime loans. The management in small concerns is not likely to have the same experience nor to be so competent as the prime borrowers; moreover, the financial position of small borrowers is neither so strong nor in all probability so liquid as that of the prime borrowers. Nevertheless, it is true that the branch banks in California take considerable pride in the very small number of losses on small loans. For several years now, losses on small loans have not averaged more than .0015 per cent of the total volume of such loans, according to the estimate of one branch loan officer. On a 6 per cent rate, this statistical loss would account only for a negligible amount of the total rate. Whether the estimate of .0015 per cent of losses on small loans is strictly accurate is not crucial except to illustrate the kind of magnitudes involved in the risk factor, at least statistically. All loan officers were agreed that losses on small loans have been negligible during the prosperity of the last decade.

It might be argued, however, that a much larger risk premium, say 1½ per cent, might have to be charged on small loans even during prosperity in order to cover the losses anticipated with a change in business conditions. These funds could then be placed

---

[10] In view of the analysis presented thus far, these facts are not surprising. The reader is reminded, however, that the factual information in the text has been confirmed in interviews with the loan officers of the Big Four branch banks.

in reserves to cushion the losses of depressed periods. Although there is certainly merit in this general approach, it needs careful examination to see whether it conforms to the facts of the real world. First, the tax-allowed amounts placed in reserves for possible loan losses are restricted by law so that a heavy risk premium in the small loan rate might go into tax payments rather than into reserves. Second, the branch loan officers do not even pretend to calculate a risk premium on the small-loan rate to accord with any statistically realized losses nor even with any specific anticipations of losses on such loans. Although all bankers are agreed that the small-loan rate contains a risk factor, none could specify what part of the small-loan rate represented the risk premium. Finally, although the Big Four branch banks differed in their respective loan policy, they did not (as will be shown later) differ on rates charged for the same category of loans. Specifically, at least one of the branch systems in California follows a policy of selective credit risks, which means that the bank in question calculates its expected earnings on the assumption that ascertainably risky loans will have been rejected at the outset. By contrast, others operate on a volume policy in which it is hoped that earnings will cover losses resulting from attempting to secure large volume. Notwithstanding this basic difference in loan policy, both banks charge the same rates for comparable loans. In short, it seems difficult to explain the disparity in level between the prime rate and small loan rates during the past decade to any significant extent in terms of a risk premium.

Costs.—The cost difference in administering small loans as contrasted with prime loans is a far more substantial explanation for the disparity in rate levels. Whether it is a full explanation remains to be determined. In dollar terms, a large loan may cost as much to negotiate as a small loan. A small loan is expensive to administer because of the extensive credit check and follow-up involved. On the other hand, large loans may also be expensive because such loans may be embodied in a formal loan contract that must be carefully examined by lawyers. Furthermore, the terms of large loans must often be negotiated on a point-by-point basis, and such negotiations are naturally handled by top loan personnel. In other words, whereas the time-consuming and costly credit check of the small borrower need not be conducted for the large borrower, full reports may yet be necessary for the latter. Moreover, the large borrower employs the time of the bank's most expensive personnel. In some instances, the bank must even place its own employees with the large firm if something untoward develops.[11] Although there may be no important difference in the absolute cost of negotiating a small loan compared with a large loan, the unit cost (cost per dollar of credit) is probably negligible for the large loan but may loom very sizably for a small loan. To this extent, a difference in level between the two categories of loans is definitely warranted by bona fide cost differences.

It remains to inquire if cost differences are a sufficient explanation for the rate differences between large and small loans. It is significant in this connection that the costs of handling many large loans are separately covered by a loan fee charged by the bank and paid by the borrower. By contrast, the costs of administering a small loan, although they may be important in terms of the size of the loan, are included in the rate. There could be no material objection to these different ways of handling the costs involved if there existed clear evidence about the amount of the rate which represented cost factors. In fact, however, as in the case of risks, the small-loan rate must cover the high costs of such loans, but it appears that the magnitude of the costs per se of the small loans has never been determined in any of the branch banks, nor have such cost data been explicitly introduced with precision into the rate. Also, bank costs are not constant. Labor costs, for example, which are the most important cost factor in administering small loans, vary with the cycle, but small-loan rates often do not. It is, of course, true that risks increase during depressed periods, and to this extent the risk premium on small loans might be expected to rise. However, it would be remarkable indeed if during two decades, covering a period of extreme depression and intense inflation, the risk premium always changed exactly to balance cost changes.[12] Moreover, this would assume that risk premiums fluctuate with the cycle, and yet bankers claim that risk premiums must be charged even during prosperity to cover the anticipated losses of depressed periods.

The resort to the greater costs of small loans as the major explanation for the difference in level between small and large loan rates encounters still another curious aspect. The analysis of branch bank and unit bank costs in chapter vi strongly suggests that branch banks can negotiate and follow through on a small loan at a lower unit cost than can most unit banks, especially the small unit banks.

---

[11] One bank reported a case where two of its employees worked with one of the bank's borrowers for eight months.

[12] What has been said of risks can be applied also to the other factors affecting rates.

Notwithstanding this cost advantage of branch banks, the same rates are charged on comparable small loans by both branch banks and unit banks.[13] If unit banks with high unit costs on small loans can cover those costs and earn a normal return on their capital, the suggestion is inescapable that something more than costs is responsible for the difference in rate levels between small loans and prime loans.

Finally, the resort to the cost factors as the only really important element in the level of small-loan rates is doubtful in view of the extreme stability of the small-loan rate, despite changes in over-all demand and supply conditions of credit sufficient to change the prime rate more than 100 per cent in ten years. Even if costs were stable over time, or if there were compensating variations in the other variables which determine interest rates, the small-loan rate might still be expected to fluctuate at least by the same *absolute* amount as the prime rate. And even if this fluctuation would not occur with every movement of the prime rate, it might certainly appear after two decades! Yet the small-loan rate, especially away from metropolitan centers, has exhibited a most remarkable stability over time.

It seems fair to conclude that although costs are undoubtedly an important element in the small-loan rate, something else is also important. That something else, as the reader has undoubtedly realized, is the nature of the market in which the small borrower must operate as contrasted with the market in which prime and other large borrowers deal.

Price policy.—Prime-loan rates are the lowest and most flexible rates in the entire rate structure for business loans, because prime borrowers are in every sense the strongest and most desirable borrowers of business credit. As a function of their desirability and strength, they have numerous alternative sources of supply and thus operate in a reasonably competitive market for business credit. At the opposite extreme, the small borrowers are the weakest and least desirable (creditwise) of all business borrowers. Accordingly, their alternative sources are extremely limited, and the markets in which they must deal are semimonopolistic, duopolistic, or, at best, oligopolistic. In these markets, all the branch banks are agreed that *rivalry must never take place on a rate basis*. In the banking markets for small borrowers, competition has shifted completely from the price variable to the product variable. Rate competition is explicitly disavowed even by the California branch bank reputed to be the most aggressive bank in the state.

---

[13] This point is discussed later.

In economic theory, an oligopolistic rationale can lead to tacit collusion among the oligopolists in which price rivalry is excluded. This results in an approximation to a monopoly price or to a "live and let live" price which, barring strong changes in the underlying conditions of demand and supply, exhibits great stability. Bankers admit that strong psychological barriers prevent price flexibility in the small-loan market. Once a rate has been established for particular categories of small loans, that rate acquires the aura of a "customary, fair, and just price," and cannot be easily changed by the action of any single bank. Bankers recognize, too, that if any one of them were to raise the rate, he would probably find himself in a unilateral move. On the other hand, to lower the rate would invite retaliation by the other banks. As one banker put it: "Price-cutting is a two-way street; we can shave prices, but so can the other fellow." The result is the kind of price rigidity implied by the kinked-demand curve analysis.

Price cutting in banking is avoided for two further reasons. In the first place, bankers prefer loans to investments because loans are usually more profitable despite their higher costs. However, a banker could not be forced to cut loan rates below a certain point, because he always has the alternative of shifting part of his resources into investments. But there is a still more compelling reason that precludes price cutting. The usual motivation for price cutting is to expand sales, but it is a peculiarity of the banking business that, in general, banks are safest when they keep in step with other banks. In an ordinary business, if one firm's sales expand more rapidly than those of its rivals, the result may simply be more profits. In banking, however, if one bank expands its loans more rapidly than the rest of the banks in the area, the expanding bank is likely to experience severe pressure on its reserves. This would quickly call a halt to the excessive expansion, with the result that rates would rise to their former level. One important exception would be the bank whose resources are growing more rapidly than those of other banks in the area. Under such circumstances, the bank might safely expand its loans at a greater rate than its rivals, through the inducement of rate cutting. In fact, however, although there has been a striking difference in the rates of growth of different branch systems in California, the disparate rates of loan expansion in various banks has taken place within a fixed rate structure for small loans.

Small-loan prices are not only rigid, they are also highly uniform for comparable categories of small-loan credit. As stated above, this uniformity results from tacit collusion induced by an oligopolistic rationale, which recognizes the mutual dependence of the rivals and instinctively eschews rate competition. In a field where each transaction is individually negotiated and is likely to differ in at least some details from other similar transactions, the achievement of a uniform price may require more than just tacit collusion among the oligopolists. Although each loan transaction is secret, the rates charged are not necessarily secret to other bankers. This becomes clear when a small borrower attempts action beyond the limits of his innate bargaining strength. Shopping for rates by small borrowers is distinctly discouraged by banks, but occasionally, some small borrower will try it. If, therefore, a bank's rates have fallen out of line with those of other banks, the customer will notify the bank. Often, however, the customer will be referred back to his home bank. Moreover, should the small borrower attempt a bluff which is not consistent with his essentially weak bargaining position, the bank in question need only call the other bank and in most cases would be readily told what rate had been offered to the customer. Again, the uniformity of rates is no doubt assisted by the numerous opportunities for informal exchanges among bankers. This sort of exchange occurs quite naturally at banking conventions, meetings, and so on. In these informal exchanges, there need be no overt collusion, since as one bank loan officer expressed it: "Rates are jelled by the uniformity of thinking of everybody in the banking profession." And the numerous opportunities for informal discussion of common banking problems helps to bring about this uniformity of thinking.

The oligopolistic structure of the small loan market is further implied in the following excerpt from a policy letter to his branch managers by the president of a large branch bank in California:

The necessity of having to reduce interest rates on some loans has, I fear, developed a tendency in many cases for officers to be a little too ready to drop rates when it is not essential to do so. It is my wish that you resist, as far as practicable, all attempts made to reduce interest rates both on present and future loans. I realize that concessions are necessary under some conditions in order to hold valuable business but I would like to see such concessions made only in isolated cases and where full justification exists.[14]

It is worth mentioning the date of this letter, August 3, 1937. The date is important because the letter was written during a period

[14] Transamerica Hearings, Respondent's Exhibit no. 357, President to Managers, Policy Letters, no. 1, August 3, 1937.

of business uncertainty and recession. Even the kinked-demand curve explanation of price rigidity under oligopoly cannot pretend to hold during periods of sharp instability, whether inflationary or deflationary. During deflationary periods, in particular, it is well known that the price structure in an oligopoly market often begins to crumble through secret price concessions. These subsequently become generally known and emulated until official prices come trailing after actual prices. The banking industry is superbly organized for secret price arrangements because of the traditional secrecy that envelops the entire loan transaction. In the light of the foregoing, the president's policy letter merits further examination.

The letter acknowledges the necessity to reduce rates on "some" loans, not on all loans. In a competitive market the option of engaging in price discrimination by reducing rates on some loans but not on all loans would not exist, even though bank loans are heterogeneous. That would be possible only in the event of a significant change in the demand for different category of loans. However, even if that were so, a bank in a competitive market could not "resist" rate reductions. In a competitive market, the pressures for a reduction in rates would lead to a fall in the competitive market price (which, remember, tends to uniformity for the various categories of loans). A single competitor has no option about resisting a fall in market price because market price is for him a parameter. Under oligopoly, however, rival firms may well resist a deterioration in market price at such points along the price front as the price can be held. In the case in point, rates were to be reduced only where necessary "to hold valuable business." Valuable business is at least in part presumably the business of large and important borrowers. They are the borrowers with alternative sources, the "isolated cases where full justification" exists. Small borrowers, however, have no alternative sources; hence, it would not seem "essential" to drop rates for such borrowers. Along their price front, the line might be held. Since the branch bank in question is extremely large and aggressive, the expressed attitude of this bank's management on the rate question presumably holds a fortiori for other branch banks as well.

MEDIUM-SIZE LOANS

The position of intermediate-size borrowers lies between that of prime borrowers and small borrowers. So far as the medium-size borrower resembles the prime borrower, in terms of the general worth of his business to the bank, his financial capacity, and other rate-determining characteristics, the medium-size borrower tends to operate in a more nearly competitive market than if he resembled more nearly the small borrower. So far as the medium-size borrower resembles the prime borrower, his alternative sources of supply are increased; so far as he resembles the small borrower, his alternative sources are narrowed. The kind of banking market in which he must operate is conditioned accordingly.

There is at least some evidence to suggest that the medium-size borrowers in California operate in somewhat less competitive markets than in other parts of the country. If this be true—and the evidence is only suggestive, not conclusive—it presumably reflects the high concentration of banking resources in California. In this study, medium-size borrowers have been defined as those whose size and other characteristics enable them to borrow outside the city of their residence, but who cannot go far beyond the state boundaries. Since the banking resources of any state are more or less reflected in the banking facilities available in the metropolitan centers of that state, this means in practice that the medium-size borrowers have complete mobility among all the banks in the metropolitan centers. It was suggested earlier, however, that the dominant position of the Big Four branch banks in the state as a whole is naturally reflected, too, in the highly oligopolistic structure of banking markets in the principal cities of Los Angeles and San Francisco. The concentration is particularly striking in comparison with the very large number of banks operating in New York City—an area which offers its medium-size borrowers maximum possible scope in their borrowing operations.

The result of the high degree of oligopolistic concentration of banking resources in California is that the markets in which medium-size borrowers must operate are characterized by somewhat greater rate rigidity than is true for medium-size borrowers in New York City. This rigidity can be gauged by comparing rate changes for medium-size borrowers with those for very large (including prime) borrowers. For prime borrowers, the rate charged is a pure interest rate that covers money costs only but has no risk premium nor cost factor added. Any costs involved in prime loans are typically covered by a separate loan fee. For any but prime borrowers, the rate technically covers not only money costs but also such other costs and risks as the loan may involve. If all loan markets were equally competitive, or, more accurately, as competitive as the market for prime loans, a given absolute change in the prime rate would be communicated intact to the other markets as well. In fact, however, the oligopolistic elements in other than prime-loan markets tends to rigidify rates on those markets. The result is that a given absolute change in the prime-loan market is not necessarily communicated in full to the other markets.

This failure of absolute changes in prime-loan rates to be transmitted in full to the other loan markets is aggravated by the concentration of California banking. Specifically, a greater part of the absolute change in the prime rate tends to be transmitted to the medium-size loan market in New York City than is transmitted in the more oligopolistic medium-size markets in California. This fact is illustrated in table 28. For purposes of this table, the average loan rate for loans of more than $200,000 is representative of the large-loan rate and is employed in lieu of the prime rate. Between September, 1950, and September, 1952, the large-loan rate in New York City rose 1 per cent. During the same period, the large-loan rate in California rose 0.99 per cent.[15] If the absolute change in the large-loan category in New York City and California, respectively, is taken as a base for the measurement of changes in the other loan markets in the two areas, the two intermediate categories[16] in New York City were more affected by the change in the large-loan rate than was true in California.[17] In other words, the figures in the table are consistent with the interpretation that the medium-size loan rate is more rigid in California than in New York City. To repeat, the greater rate rigidity in the medium-size loan market in California than in New York City is presumably a function of the high concentration of banking resources in California. Since the data are crude, however, the validity of this conclusion is uncertain.

---

[15] Thus the absolute change in the two areas was practically identical, differing by only .01 per cent.

[16] Incidentally, the rate to the smallest category of borrower was least affected by the change in the large-loan rate. However, it was affected much more in New York City than in California, reflecting again the larger absolute number of objective sources of supply in New York City than in California's major cities. The reader will notice that even the smallest borrowers may feel some effect of changes in money market conditions if they are in metropolitan centers, whereas rates for comparable loans in outlying areas (away from metropolitan centers) may remain absolutely fixed for years and irrespective of changes in over-all credit conditions in the country. To this extent, as discussed in chapter iii, the absolute number of alternative sources can affect the nature of the market structure in a community even for the smallest category of borrowers.

[17] It is true that prime rate changes are not necessarily transmitted to medium-size loan rates as soon as the change occurs. Often the changes must accumulate over a period of time before they finally make themselves felt in the rate to medium-size borrowers. However, two full years would appear to be sufficient allowance for this time lag.

AGRICULTURAL LOANS

The analysis of branch bank rate policy on commercial and industrial loans applies with minor modifications to agricultural loans as well. The only important modification of the earlier discussion concerns the influence of governmental farm-lending agencies, and especially the Production Credit Association. Loans made by the Production Credit Association are effective substitutes for many

TABLE 28

COMPARATIVE MOVEMENT OF AVERAGE LOAN RATES, NEW YORK CITY AND CALIFORNIA, SEPTEMBER 1950–SEPTEMBER, 1952

Size of loan	Sept., 1950, rate	Sept., 1952, rate	Net change in rate (absolute)	Change in each category (per cent of largest category)
New York City				
Less than $10,000	4.06	4.66	0.60	60
$10,000–$99,999	3.33	4.06	0.73	73
$100,000–$199,999	2.72	3.60	0.88	88
$200,000 and more	2.15	3.15	1.00	100
California				
Less than $10,000	4.75	5.21	0.46	46
$10,000–$99,999	3.89	4.42	0.53	54
$100,000–$199,999	3.24	3.97	0.73	74
$200,000 and more	2.58	3.57	0.99	100

bank agricultural loans, and, therefore, bank rates on such loans must compete with PCA rates. Rates charged by PCA for moderate-size loans currently range between 5 per cent and 5½ per cent, depending upon the particular association, its financial position, and its desire to build reserves.[18] Since PCA credit constitutes an alternative source of supply for agricultural borrowers, rates charged by the PCA place an absolute ceiling upon rates that can be charged by banks on comparable loans.[19] Indeed, ". . . generally speaking, . . . Production credit rates tend to establish the pattern

[18] Testimony of Jesse W. Tapp, Transamerica Hearings, p. 9862.

[19] There may be a small discrepancy between PCA rates and bank rates because a farmer who borrows from the PCA must purchase stock in the association to the extent of 5 per cent of his loan. Also, borrowing from the government agency involves a certain amount of red tape which some farmers prefer to avoid even at a somewhat higher rate charged by banks.

for normal day-to-day lending in moderate amounts."[20] In other words, for loans of "moderate" size, Production Credit Association rates establish not only a ceiling but the actual rates at which commercial banks, including branch banks, actually lend in normal operations. As might be expected from the earlier analysis, there is one important exception to this general rule: ". . . (for) farmers who have financial statements which enable them to borrow without the crop and chattel mortgage type of loans, and for loans of that character, the rates may be below the rates charged by the Production Credit Association . . ."[21] In short, for borrowers whose financial standing gives them alternative sources of supply, rates may fall below the ceiling rates of the federal lending agency.[22]

Branch Bank Structure and Average Interest Rates

It was stated earlier that average rates of interest charged on loans decline as size of bank increases, with the conspicuous exception of branch banks, where the pattern is reversed. The preceding survey of branch bank loan rate policy helps to explain this pattern. Although many factors no doubt influence the loan rate, the one factor that cuts across all loans and appears to be the decisive determinant in a given context is the alternative sources of supply available to the borrower. This latter factor, in turn, reflects the size of the borrower or, alternatively, the size of the loan. Alternative sources of supply are apparently as important in branch bank loan rate policy as in unit banks. Furthermore, the evidence of this chapter suggests that, for different size borrowers, branch bank loan rates are similar to those charged by unit banks.[23] The higher average loan rate in branch banks than in the largest category of unit banks thus reflects primarily the higher percentage of small (higher yielding) loans in the former. Similarly the fact that average earnings on loans and discounts increase as the size of the

---

[20] Tapp, Transamerica Hearings, p. 9862.

[21] *Loc. cit.*

[22] Although the factual information concerning the relation between agricultural loan rates and PCA rates was based on testimony by Mr. Tapp in the Transamerica Hearings, substantially the same information was provided in interviews with the lending officers in the other branch banks.

[23] This is not to deny the possibility often asserted by Bank of America, for example, that at the time of entry, they have lowered loan rates. Thus, in 1916, Bank of America took over the Hollister Bank and reduced interest rates on mortgage loans from the then usual rate of 7 to 8 per cent down to 6 per cent. Cf. Transamerica Hearings, *op. cit.*, p. 9963. Once a branch is established in a community, however, loan rates are stabilized and all banks charge comparable rates, whether they are branch or unit banks. Otherwise, *new* borrowers would, *ceteris paribus,* always prefer the low-rate banks.

branch bank increases reflects primarily a higher percentage of small loans as size of branch bank increases.[24] On the other hand, the fact that the average interest rate for the average of branch banks is below that for any of the unit banks except the largest is owing to the weight of the large (low-yielding) loans in branch bank portfolios.

As explained earlier in this study, the portfolio composition of branch banks described above is not fortuitous, but rather is related to the branch-banking structure. It must follow, therefore, that the loan earnings of a bank are partly conditioned by the bank's structure.

---

[24] In both cases, of course, the percentage refers to dollar-volume of small loans.

VIII

Pricing and the Open Market

THE PREVIOUS chapter on the pricing practices and price policy of branch banks demonstrated that the prime rate is a key loan rate in business loan markets. In the market for the very largest borrowers, the prime rate is a controlling rate in all parts of the country. Prime rate changes have a lesser impact on the medium-size loan market, and their impact is least on the small-borrowers' loan market. So far as rates are flexible in the different customer loan markets, the initiating impulse for a change comes to a great extent from the prime rate. There is a price leadership situation in the prime rate with leadership rotating (usually) among four of the large New York City money market banks. In changing the prime rate, the price leader banks in New York City take their cue from rate changes on the open money market for short-term funds. Indirectly, therefore, the level of interest rates in all loan markets is, in greater or lesser degree, related to open money market rates.

It is the purpose of this chapter to investigate the nature of this critical relationship between customer loan rates and open market rates. We wish to know *why* the price leader banks take their cue in changing the prime rate from open market rate changes. In a sense, of course, the price leader banks are forced to change prime customer rates with changes in open market rates because at least some prime borrowers have access to the commercial paper market of the open money market for short-term funds. It will be shown, however, that to drop the matter at this point would miss the essential nature of the relationship between open market rate changes and rate changes on the prime customer loan market. Moreover, this inquiry should disclose whether the role of the open market is strictly *passive* (in the barometer sense of merely indicating the time for a change in the prime rate) and whether its *direct* influence is limited to the prime rate.

The basic character of the interrelation between the open market rates and customer loan rates can be demonstrated by selecting any one of the short-term open market rates to represent them all, since the various open market rates for short-term funds tend to move together. The commercial paper rate for short-term prime paper is from one viewpoint the most logical candidate to represent all open market rates, because open market commercial paper is a substitute for certain prime customer loans. On the other hand, the very closeness of the relation between the commercial paper rate and the prime customer rate may mask the underlying relation between the open market and the customer loan market. As will be seen, this relationship is much broader and more fundamental than the mere substitutability of open market commercial paper and prime customer loans. Since the most important submarket of the open money market is the Treasury bill market, the bill rate will be used to represent all open market rates in explaining the relation between the open market and the customer loan market for short-term funds. Accordingly, this chapter investigates the possibilities and circumstances under which changes in the bill rate could be expected to influence a change in the customer loan rate.[1]

In figure 1, the fluctuations of the Treasury bill rate and of the average customer loan rate, New York City, can be compared for the twenty-year period from 1931 to 1951.[2] The chart reveals that in most years during this study period, the two rates moved in the same direction. Significantly, too, there is evidence of a lead-lag relationship in which movements on the customer loan market follow changes in the bill rate. There are, however, two important exceptions. In 1937, the Treasury bill rate fluctuated whereas the customer loan rate was impressively stable. By contrast, from 1942 to 1945, the Treasury bill rate was perfectly stable whereas the customer loan rate fluctuated.

Since the pattern of relationship is not homogeneous throughout the period, it will be convenient to conduct the analysis by a process of successive approximations. The first approximation will

[1] To avoid possible confusion, it should be stated explicitly that this chapter does not appraise the efficacy of customer loan rate changes in influencing the volume of business borrowing. That is an important problem, but it is properly the subject of a separate investigation.

[2] Until a later point in this analysis, average customer loan rates throughout the country will be represented by average customer loan rates in New York City. Although the Treasury began to issue bills in 1929, the starting date of 1931 was selected because no series is available until that year. The customer loan series was plotted on a monthly basis through March, 1939, but was available thereafter only on a quarterly basis; the bill rate was plotted monthly for the entire period.

try to explain why the two series move together as much as they
do. In a second approximation, the basic analysis can be modified to account for the extent of divergent movement between the
two series.

COMPARISON OF OPEN MARKET AND CUSTOMER LOAN RATES

An understanding of the mechanics of the relationship between
the Treasury bill market and the customer loan market is aided
by first considering the relation between the customer loan market
and the open money market for short-term funds. The Treasury
bill market is only one of the submarkets of the open money market, and, in large part, its relationship with the customer loan
market derives from its characteristics as an open money market.
Furthermore, the fact that there are other submarkets in the open
market modifies the nature and extent of the interaction between
the bill market and the customer loan market. A few comments are
thus in order to highlight the important distinguishing characteristics of the open market and the customer loan market.

The open market for short-term funds is actually a conglomera-
tion of submarkets, including the markets for prime bankers' acceptances, commercial paper, call and time loans on stock exchange
collateral, and Treasury bills. Each of these submarkets is, in a
sense, a self-contained unit, with one common characteristic unit-
ing them for purposes of analysis—complete impersonality. In such
markets, buyers and sellers are completely indifferent to each other.
A lending bank feels no sense of responsibility nor any continuing
obligation toward those to whom it makes funds available. Borrowers likewise understand that they can expect no special consideration in the event of a credit stringency.

The expression "customers' loan market" is also merely a label
which encompasses a vast number of submarkets in all parts of
the country. These submarkets are all bound together in varying
degree. In the largest financial centers or in big cities, the ties are
very close and such banks participate in what is broadly a common
market. By contrast, the country banks incline to be somewhat
more autonomous in their policies and activities. Although the
open market is characterized by almost complete impersonality,
the personal element is often of dominating importance in the
customer loan market. Each customer loan is negotiated as an individual case, both with regard to price and to the terms of the loan,
and, in the normal course, the customer will become a regular
client.

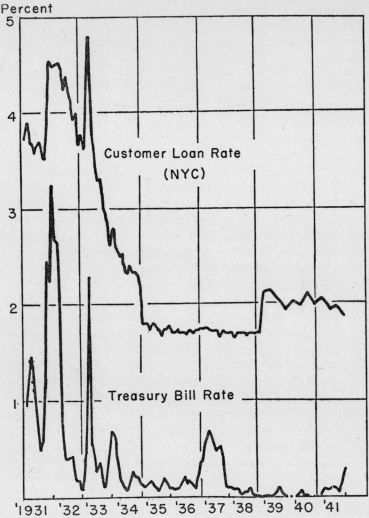

Fig. 1. Customer loan rate (NYC) and Treasury bill rate, 1931–1951.
Sources: Board of Governors, Federal Reserve System, *Banking and Monetary Statistics* (Washington, 1943), pp. 460, 463–464, for the period 1931–1941.
Discontinuities in the Treasury bill rate series indicate periods during which the bill rate was negative.

A corollary of the banker-customer relationship is the almost universally held opinion that, as one prominent banker stated it: "(Banks) *always* would prefer to lend to commercial borrowers than to hold Government securities. That is our permanent business. We want to do business for our customers."[3] By contrast, the

---

[3] Testimony of Randolph W. Burgess, formerly chairman of the executive committee, National City Bank of New York, Douglas Hearings, p. 193. (Italics mine.)

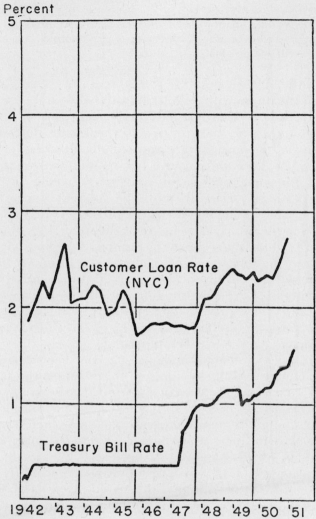

Fig. 1. Customer loan rate (NYC) and Treasury bill rate, 1931–1951.
Sources: Board of Governors, Federal Reserve System, *Federal Reserve Bulletins,* for the years 1942–1951.
Discontinuities in the Treasury bill rate series indicate periods during which the bill rate was negative.

open money market is the repository of the country's surplus funds, i.e., "funds not needed or demanded by local business activity, or by the customer bank-loan market."[4] Randolph W. Burgess, a vigorous proponent of this view, has stated this position clearly:

[4] The definition of "surplus funds" is that used by Benjamin H. Beckhart, *The New York Money Market* (New York: Columbia University Press, 1932), Vol. III, p. 5.

The New York money market is the national market for *surplus* funds. As the leading money market of the country, it is the center towards which the *idle money* of all sections gravitates to find employment, pending the time when it is needed.[5]

THE OPEN MARKET—A PASSIVE MARGIN

The fundamental nature of the relationship between the customer loan market and the open market (and, thus, with the Treasury bill market) can now be set forth. In a very real sense, the customer loan market and the open market are a common market for short-term funds. The basic unity of the two markets is suggested not only by the foregoing analysis but also by the parallel routes of fluctuation of the two series. It should be observed, however, that although the routes of fluctuation of the two series are similar, the *level* of rates in the two markets is clearly different. This difference in level can be understood partly in terms of the objective differences between the kind of loans made on the open market and those made on the customer loan market—differences in risk, liquidity, and the like. Partly the difference is due to noncompetitive influences in the various markets. Finally, these differences in level are partly the result of different methods of allocating costs under alternative marketing techniques.

Although the open market and the customer loan market constitute a common credit pool for short-term funds, the latter is substantially more important than the former in terms of volume of funds. The significance of the open market inheres not in its size, however, but in its marginal nature and in the high sensitivity which that marginal nature implies. Basically, the open market is marginal in Marshall's sense of the term.[6] The open market simply *measures* the broad forces of supply and demand for short-term funds in the entire country. The margin does not determine prices in the national short-term market; prices are determined by demand and supply. The margin, in this view, is analogous to the pressure gauge on a boiler.

This conclusion about the relation between the customer loan market and the open market holds tentatively also for the Treasury bill market. The foregoing analysis thus explains the observed pattern between Treasury bill rates and customer loan rates. According to this analysis, sequence does not evidence causation, because rates in both markets are commonly determined. The only sig-

---

[5] Randolph W. Burgess, *Reserve Banks and the Money Market* (New York and London: Harper and Brothers, 1927), p. 110. (Italics mine.)

[6] Cf. Alfred Marshall, *Principles of Economics* (8th ed., London: Macmillan, 1947), p. 410.

nificance to the sequence of rate changes is that, in general, restrictive (or expansionary) tendencies make themselves felt first in the marginal (Treasury bill) market and only with a lag in the broader (customer loan) market for short-term funds.

This analysis, which is consistent with traditional views on this subject, explains the *basic* (and historical) relationship between the two markets. The analysis needs qualification and elaboration on at least two grounds: (1) the preceding explanation is silent on the possibility of a causal nexus between the two markets; (2) although common movements are explained, there is no explanation for important divergent movements, e.g., 1937, 1942–1947, nor, indeed, for the lack of a better correlation than actually exists even during periods of common movement. Since generalized explanations are sought, ephemeral and transitory influences which could account for short-run erraticisms can be ignored. This inquiry is concerned with generalized causes which can explain divergent movements above and beyond those explicable in terms of specific and transitory influences. Such generalized explanations for divergent movements should, preferably, also provide the key to the possibility of the aforementioned causal nexus.

The theory as thus far developed rests on two cardinal propositions: (a) that the open market (and, hence, the Treasury bill market) is the repository for exclusively surplus funds and is thus a *marginal* market; and (b) that the open market is marginal in a *passive* sense. If both of these characteristics perfectly inhered in the open market, the lead-lag correlation between the Treasury bill rate and the customer loan rate (New York City), allowing for a frictional blur in the lead-lag period and barring transitory influences, would also be perfect. Although the actual correlation appears to be high, it is far from perfect. The lack of perfect correlation must, therefore, be owing (previous exceptions noted) to generalized factors which compromise the marginal aspect of the open market and its passive nature. The following investigation is divided accordingly.

MODIFICATIONS OF THE SURPLUS FUNDS DOCTRINE

Secondary reserves and the open market.—In his discussion of the open market, Burgess pointed out that "The money in the money market may thus be thought of *not simply as surplus funds, but as the secondary reserves of banks* and business all over the country."[7] Banks invest secondary reserves in the open market because

---
[7] Burgess, *loc. cit.* (Italics mine.)

open market paper is highly liquid, practically riskless,[8] and is sold in suitable (meaning short) maturities and convenient denominations. Further, open market investments are normally preferable to non-interest-bearing excess reserves.

Although it is true that surplus funds invested in the open market can serve as secondary reserves for banks, not all funds invested in the open market are surplus, nor are all secondary reserves surplus funds. A banker's ability in his profession is most clearly revealed in the composition of the bank's portfolio, since it is in the bank portfolio that the conflicting demands of profitability and safety of a bank must be reconciled. In the allocation of a bank's funds, secondary reserves take priority over customer loans.[9] After insuring its liquidity and fully satisfying the local demand for customer loans, the bank can again enter the open market to invest its surplus funds for whatever income is possible. This emphasis on protective investment suggests an important qualification to the earlier analysis. Since Treasury bills are an important form of protective investment, banks would not, as has been alleged, "*always* prefer to lend to commercial borrowers than to hold Government securities." Accordingly, open market securities held for protective investment do not represent surplus funds from the customer loan market, and are not, therefore, a marginal supply of funds.

Burgess has emphasized that, "In the New York market we are dealing with what economists call the marginal supply and the marginal demand, which are the first to show any changes in conditions."[10] At least one qualification to this statement is now apparent. The short-term open market investments are all available as secondary reserves, but only part of these investments represent surplus funds. Under "normal" circumstances, when the open market

---

[8] The risk here refers to risk of default and not to fluctuations of market prices. Commercial paper, for example, has a record of negligible losses to the holders. This is no doubt owing to the fact that prospective borrowers on commercial paper are most rigidly scrutinized, and only companies which are very large and eminently sound are accepted as clients by the commercial paper houses. Call and time loans are also very secure because they are backed by stock exchange collateral in a manner which varies the collateral with any variation in the market value of the securities. Bankers' acceptances are "two-name paper," and one of the names is that of a large, strong bank. Treasury bills are safe for the obvious reason that they represent the credit of the United States government, and, in any case, are eligible for rediscounting. Finally, open market paper is bought with no consideration other than the soundness and yield of the paper; customer loans are frequently influenced by personal considerations which can outweigh possible technical inadequacies of the loans.

[9] Cf. Roland I. Robinson, *The Management of Bank Funds* (New York: McGraw-Hill, 1951), pp. 12–18.

[10] Burgess, *op. cit.*, p. 112.

contains bona fide marginal (surplus) funds, pressure on bank reserves can be relieved by liquidating some of the open market
investments with a resultant stiffening of open market rates, a
stiffening that is subsequently felt also in the customer loan market.
During a period of sustained credit stringency, however, it is entirely possible that the investment-for-income securities of the open
market will have been liquidated, leaving only funds for protective investment. Under these circumstances, any further pressure
would, *ceteris paribus,* hit the customer loan market (specifically,
marginal customer loans), but the further stiffening of customer
loan rates would not (again *ceteris paribus*) also be felt in the open
market. In other words, the marginal funds would be those invested in the marginal customer loans and not those funds which
remained invested in the open market.

In practice, positive identification of such a situation is difficult.
In the first place, bank statements do not distinguish between open
market investment for income and open market purchases for protective investment. Furthermore, in a real life situation, many
other factors (especially central bank intervention) would likely
be in the picture at the same time, making it difficult to isolate the
effects of particular forces. Present difficulties of empirical identification should not, of course, preclude attempts at theoretical
exposition of underlying tendencies.

Federal funds.—The existence of Federal funds also compro-
mises the marginal character of the open market. Federal funds
arise from the excess reserves of banks. A bank that is experiencing
a temporary deficiency of reserves can make up this deficiency by
purchasing the excess reserves of other banks. Such negotiations
are typically transacted by negotiation between the banks concerned, although there is a going rate for Federal funds. The use
of Federal funds became prominent during the 'thirties when the
banking system had large excess reserves. Although the banking
system as a whole had excess reserves, the large money market
banks of New York City would often find themselves under pressure. Such banks could have secured the required reserves by borrowing from the central bank or liquidating open market investments. With abundant excess reserves in the interior banks, however, it was definitely cheaper to meet a temporary reserve shortage
by purchasing Federal funds.[11] During the decade of the 'forties,

---

[11] For a description of a typical instance, see Federal Reserve Bank of New York,
Monthly Review, September 1, 1937, p. 65. Federal funds at that time were mostly
purchased at the rate of 1/4 per cent.

and, indeed, even at the present time, many banks continue to
resort to Federal funds to meet a reserve deficiency of two or three
days, or even overnight. As mentioned earlier, member bank borrowing from the System has been negligible for many years; significant reserve deficiencies are typically met today by sale of
Treasury securities in which most banks are heavily invested. However, to meet a temporary deficiency of reserves, large banks in
Central Reserve and Reserve cities often find it cheaper to buy
Federal funds, because "The sale and repurchase of securities contains an element of cost in the commissions that they have to pay
in the buying and the selling."[12] In such cases, Federal funds are
the marginal short-term funds and short-term pressures would be
absorbed in the Federal funds market without necessarily being
reflected in the open market, or, what is of particular interest in
this chapter, in the Treasury bill market.

Excess reserves.—Under present circumstances, "It is impossible
to maintain more than about three-quarters of a billion of excess
reserves, which are maintained largely by . . . country banks."[13] Although excess reserves do not today reach the levels of the 'thirties,
a consideration of the effect of excess reserves is pertinent to this
analysis for at least three reasons. First, excess reserves must be
considered in understanding the relationship of Treasury bill rates
and customer loan rates in previous periods. Second, although
excess reserves are not large today, there is no guarantee against
some future "credit deadlock." Most important of all, however,
excess reserves can affect the relation of Treasury bill rates and
customer loan rates even when the excess reserves are not of the
huge magnitudes of the Great Depression. The experience of the
'thirties demonstrated that when the banking system is holding
large excess reserves, the excess reserves, and not the open market
investments, are the marginal funds which are the first to feel
changes in credit conditions. Thus, in June, 1937, when the banks
held heavy excess reserves, "Movements of reserve funds of as much
as \$500,000,000 to \$1,000,000,000 occasioned little or no disturb-
ance in the money market."[14] With large excess reserves in the system, a pressure on an individual bank's reserves is reflected first
in Federal funds and not at all in open market short-term rates.
That was actually the situation in August, 1937, when New York
City banks experienced a reduction in their excess reserves with

[12] Testimony of Marriner S. Eccles, then member, Board of Governors, Federal
Reserve System, Douglas Hearings, p. 225.
[13] *Ibid.,* p. 226.
[14] Federal Reserve Bank of New York, *Monthly Review,* July, 1937, p. 49.

the result that the rate on Federal funds rose as high as 1/2 per cent
on some transactions, whereas there was virtually no change in
open market rates.[15] If the pressure on reserves is sustained or is
large enough, the effects will, of course, eventually be felt, too,
on the open market. For example, on January 30, 1937, the Board
of Governors announced an increase in reserve requirements to be
effective on March 1 and on May 1. Most banks were able to meet
the increase from their excess reserves, but at least some banks
had to borrow from other banks and a certain number were obliged
to liquidate some open market investments.[16]

During the depression years of large excess reserves, customer
loan rates were remarkably stable. With the conspicuous exception
of 1937, Treasury bill rates were also relatively stable during that
period. Although the demand for customer loans did fluctuate,
even during the depressed 'thirties, this variation was absorbed,
first, in a shift of excess reserves, with an accompanying rise of
Federal funds rate, and, second, in fluctuation of open market rates.
The fluctuation in demand did not affect the customer loan rate.
The economic revival during the early months of 1937, for example, stimulated an increased demand for business loans. This increase normally would have firmed rates in the open market and
then, with a lag, in the customer loan market. Nevertheless, customer loan rates did not rise. Many banks met the increased demand for customer loan funds partly by reducing excess reserves,
and, since the excess reserves of many banks were relatively low,
partly by liquidating their government securities. The result was
a mild firming of Treasury bill rates but continued stability in the
customer loan market.

The Federal Reserve and its "nonmarginal funds."—In still another sense, it is inaccurate to describe Treasury bill rates as the
rates determined by the marginal demand and marginal supply
of short-term funds. During the war period, the demands of war
finance dominated central bank policy with the result that the
government securities market was not a free market. The central
bank not only established repurchase provisions for Treasury securities; it also engaged in open market operations with the aim
of exactly setting their price. Since the central bank's portfolio is
managed not for profit but for purposes of credit control, the funds
employed in open market operations are hardly "surplus" in the
usual sense.

[15] Cf. *ibid.*, September, 1937, p. 66.
[16] Cf. *Federal Reserve Bulletin*, April, 1937, p. 283.

Organized voluntary credit restraints.—In March, 1951, a National Voluntary Credit Restraint Committee was organized under the aegis of the Federal Reserve. Its purpose was to organize commercial bankers to restrain inflationary expansions of credit.[17] Such voluntary credit restraints amount to credit rationing. Now, credit rationing is hardly new to the banking community; it goes on all the time. The relevant point here is that ordinary credit rationing to commercial borrowers may be the result of the credit unworthiness of a particular borrower, or of considerations of portfolio diversification in a particular bank. This special credit rationing held down the demand for commercial loans in the interests of a government program of anti-inflation credit control.[18] Such credit rationing would, of course, "release" funds from the customer loan market which would then be available for investment in government securities. Again, such released funds are hardly marginal or surplus in the sense of the passive margin theory of the open market.

Summary.—Because of the kind of factors listed above, it is inaccurate to claim that the open market is the repository for the marginal funds of the economy, especially if this statement is interpreted to mean that *only* surplus funds find their way to the open market. To the extent that other than surplus funds are invested in open market securities, the traditional explanation of the observed pattern of relationship between customer loan rates and open market rates must be modified. In other words, the lack of perfect correlation between the Treasury bill series (or any open market series) and the customer loan rate series is in part owing to the fact that open market funds are not always and exclusively marginal (in the surplus sense). Specifically, if the open market contains only protective investment, the marginal short-term funds in the economy are the least desirable customer loans. A pressure on reserves could thus force liquidation of marginal customer loans (with a corresponding tendency toward firmer rates on the customer loan market) whereas open market investments for protective purposes are left untouched and open market rates, stable.

If the system has excess reserves, the excess reserves and not the open market funds are marginal. An increase in the demand for funds need occasion no increase in customer loan rates. However, if individual banks expand more rapidly than all the others, they may suffer adverse clearings with a consequent reduction or even

---

[17] For example, "refrain from financing inventory increases above normal levels relative to sales, or reasonable requirements by other conservative yardsticks." *Ibid.*, April, 1951, p. 379.

[18] Cf. "Programs for Voluntary Credit Restraint," *ibid.*, March, 1951, p. 264.

elimination of their excess reserves. Such banks might then borrow the excess reserves of other banks, and the rate on Federal funds would increase. A sustained pressure of this sort might even force liquidation of open market investments, so that rates rise in the open market. If, however, the pressure does not continue, it need not hit the customer loan market, and customer loan rates would be left unchanged. Such a development would be another generalized explanation for a lack of perfect correlation between open market and customer loan rates.

Another factor, which can account in part for the lack of a perfect correlation between open market and customer loan rates, is the influence of the central bank on the open market. It would be possible, for example, for the central bank to engage in open market operations to lower Treasury bill rates while at the same time taking restrictive action on the customer loan market by raising reserve requirements.[19]

Finally, the existence of *organized* voluntary credit restraints by commercial banks in the interests of restraining inflation may remove funds from the customer loan market to the open market. Accordingly, low (or even falling) rates on the Treasury bill market would be perfectly compatible with tight credit (with or without rising customer loan rates) on the customer loan market.

The above list of factors is not, of course, comprehensive of all the elements that could at different times compromise the marginal character of open market funds; the above list is rather suggestive of some important qualifications to the alleged marginality of open market funds. To the extent that open market funds are not surplus (and, hence, not marginal), the traditional explanation of the relation between the open market and the customer loan market must be modified.

QUALIFICATIONS AS TO THE PASSIVE NATURE OF THE OPEN MARKET

It has been thus far assumed that the open market is marginal in a *passive* sense, i.e., it simply measures the broad forces of supply and demand operating all over the economy.[20] In fact, the sub-

[19] A conflicting use of central bank credit controls is, of course, not unknown. In 1937, for example, the Federal Reserve Board feared an inflation owing to the large excess reserves in the banking system, so it raised reserve requirements. At the same time, however, it willingly purchased securities from individual banks put under pressure by this action, since the goal was to reduce excess reserves and not to penalize individual banks.

[20] The previous section raised objections to the "marginal" nature of open market funds; this section questions whether the idea of a *passive* margin is entirely accurate.

markets of the open market do more than measure at the margin the demand and supply from the whole country, since each sub-market is endowed with a semi-independent (autonomous) existence. Thus, for example, there are special demand and supply forces in the call loan market which are essentially peculiar to itself, viz., its relation to the stock market, and which may be shared, if at all, only to a much less degree with the rest of the economy. Or, again, the bankers' acceptance market may be particularly active because of foreign trade transactions which are being negotiated in dollars through the New York market, but such transactions need not be tied to a general movement within the rest of the economy. The special demand and supply forces in the Treasury bill market would include any central bank or Treasury activity on that market which is motivated by the government's economic policy, e.g., government policy toward inflation, deflation, war finance, debt management, and so on.

It is still correct that, basically, the open markets are marginal in a passive sense, because these markets are to a considerable extent an integral part of the broader money market for the short-term funds of the country. Within the framework of responding to broader demand and supply forces, however, the individual sub-money markets also respond to the forces of demand and supply which are, more or less, peculiarly their own. Since the submarkets are endowed with a semi-autonomous existence, open market rates may become out of line with rates on the customer loan market. When it is further recognized that not all open market investments are made with surplus funds, the stage is set for an interaction between the submarkets of the open market and the customer loan market.

In short, there is a duality in the marginal nature of the open markets. In a basic sense, these marginal markets are passive and reflect common forces of demand and supply. Beyond this basic limit, these marginal markets become *active* and do compete with the customer loan market.

IMPACT OF THE OPEN MARKET ON CUSTOMER LOAN MARKET

In their active character, the open markets can affect customer loan rates directly or indirectly. A specific example of direct influence can be found in the movement of the call loan rate. As with all the submarkets of the open market, the call loan rate and the customer loan rate move roughly together with the call market in a passive role. But in 1928–1929, when call money was in great demand because of extensive speculation on the stock market, rates on call money were very high and attracted more than just the surplus funds from the customer loan market.[21] By draining non-surplus short-term funds from the customer loan market, the call market was partly responsible for raising customer loan rates also.[22]

Sometimes a change in open market rates can indirectly affect customer loan rates through anticipations which are aroused by open market rate changes. A full analysis of the role of anticipations and uncertainty upon interest rates is beyond the scope of this study. In general, it may be observed that a change in open market rates can arouse expectations of a general interest rate movement. The expected movement might then be anticipated in the customer loan market although a change is not justified by any alteration in the reserve position of the banks or in the demand for loans. The degree of reaction on the customer loan market to open market changes is partly determined by the force of the indirect impact.

Rate changes in the Treasury bill market illustrate the possibility of both direct and indirect influence on the customer loan market. With today's huge national debt, Federal Reserve activity in the Treasury bill market reverberates throughout the entire banking structure. Toward the end of 1947, for example, the Federal Reserve System dropped the supports on government bonds by one or two points. This was the so-called Christmas present by the Federal Reserve to the banks. The resulting increase in Treasury bill rates was followed a few months later by an increase in customer loan rates.[23] The increase in customer loan rates was owing

[21] This action was deliberately planned by the Executive Committee of the Stock Exchange Clearing Corporation (in coöperation with the large New York City banks and the Federal Reserve Bank of New York) in attempts to stabilize the market for call money. For a merely transitory discrepancy between demand and supply, the Executive Committee would request the New York City banks to make more funds available and thereby prevent the rate from rising. When the disequilibrium was considered to be more than temporary, the Committee would arrange for only part of the supply to be made available to borrowers at a fairly high rate of interest. It was hoped that when news of this high rate was flashed to the entire world, it would attract the necessary funds to New York. This procedure could be repeated until the requisite funds were forthcoming. If the response continued inadequate, the Committee would call upon the New York City banks to supply enough funds to keep the call rate from abnormal rises. Cf. Beckhart, *op. cit.*, p. 55.

[22] Cf. *ibid.*, pp. 10 ff.

[23] In his testimony before the Douglas Subcommittee, Burgess reported that the increase in Treasury bill rates "slowed up the process of new financing, made people who were planning investment programs—I mean business people who were going ahead with accumulating inventory or building new plants or buying machinery—go a little slower." Douglas Hearings, p. 182.

at least in part to the competition between customer loans and Treasury bills. In order to compete successfully with the higher bill rate, customer loan rates had to rise also.[24] In part, too, the increase in customer loan rates reflected the bankers' belief that a general increase in interest rates was forthcoming. In other words, the raising of the Treasury bill rate with official sanction served as an announcement of Federal Reserve credit policy and also as an indicator of the future course which interest rates would take.[25]

Wartime relation of Treasury bill and customer loan rates.— The purchase of short-term open market securities for income purposes takes lowest priority in the allocation of commercial bank funds. Since such investment normally presupposes that protective investment and the demands of commercial borrowers have already been met, the funds so invested would be surplus funds. During the war period, however, the funds invested in Treasury bills were clearly not exclusively marginal funds. From the middle of 1940 to the end of 1945, commercial banks purchased $95,000,000,000 of United States government securities. Many of these bonds were purchased under a combination of pressure and cajolery by official sources.[26] In order to encourage bank purchase of Treasury bills, the Treasury "tailored" the debt to the needs of different investors; hence, the offer of bank-restricted bonds and of short-term securities designed for commercial banks. The Federal Reserve Banks agreed to repurchase provisions at a fixed rate of $3/8$ per cent. To eliminate uncertainty further, the System also undertook to peg the bill rate, and, indeed, to freeze the entire interest rate structure on government issues. Although government securities carried

---

[24] A similar development occurred recently in the market for long-term funds. When the Federal Reserve unpegged long-term rates, mortgage money became tight and continued to be tight. The higher rates on government long-terms would normally force an upward revision in (competing) mortgage rates. Since mortgage rates are "frozen" under FHA- and VA-insured mortgages, mortgages are unable to attract funds away from government securities.

[25] This situation was described in the Monthly Letter of a large New York bank: "... the possibility that the authorities will continue to draw back their support levels and allow short-term interest rates to rise further has entered into bankers' calculations and provided an inducement to continued holdings of short-term Governments in anticipation of a further improvement in short-term yields. Some hardening has been apparent in loan rates and banks are less eager to enter into term loan arrangements." National City Bank of New York, *Monthly Letter*, November 1947, p. 131.

[26] Apropos of the wartime responsibility of banks, the president of the Federal Reserve Bank of Philadelphia has remarked: "The position of the banks—I think they all understood it—was they were to be residual buyers of anything and they were to provide the funds we could not obtain by taxation and borrowing from the rest of the economy." Testimony of Alfred H. Williams, Douglas Hearings, p. 40.

very low rates, the virtual guarantee during the war of their market prices, together with their huge volume, made them a profitable source of investment for other than surplus bank funds. In November, 1949, the president of the Philadelphia Reserve Bank even speculated that in the event of a departure from a policy of a fixed price structure, with an accompanying adjustment of market values, ". . . it may well be that banks would prefer to remain in governments rather than to enter into the field of commercial credit extension."[27] In this context, the accuracy of this conjecture is less important than the testimony by a competent observer of *competition between commercial credit and Treasury securities*. Such competition clearly modifies the surplus funds doctrine of open market investments, and, more important, qualifies the *passive* margin notion of open market investments.

Reference has already been made to the wartime fluctuation of customer loan rates despite the complete stability of Treasury bill rates. Specifically, from May, 1942, through June, 1947, the Treasury bill rate was perfectly stable, but the customer loan rate fluctuated within a range of 1 percentage point. Although there was active competition between Treasury bills and customer loans, the Treasury bill rate was immobilized by the central bank's "freeze" of the rate structure. Accordingly, any variation in the demand or supply situation was reflected in the customer loan market. In late 1941, however, the Treasury bill rate rose and the New York City average customer loan rate also rose somewhat, with a lag, in early 1942. In 1947, the Treasury bill rate again began to climb, and again the customer loan rate followed with a lag later in the year.

The pegging of Treasury bill rates had another effect on customer loan rates. So far as there is a fluidity of funds between the Treasury bill market and the customer loan market (i.e., so far as the bill market is active in either the direct or indirect sense), our analysis would suggest that the customer loan rate was probably more rigid than it would have been had the Treasury bill rate been free to fluctuate at the impetus of uncontrolled demand and supply.

Finally, it is worth noting that the customer loan rate fluctuated at a generally lower level during the war period than at any previous time. The customer rate had already begun to decline after 1929, reflecting the reduced demand for funds during the depression and also the huge excess reserves resulting from the gold inflows during the 'thirties. During the war period, the low level of rates no doubt is partly explained by the enormous increase in reserves (i.e., increase in the supply of funds) which were created

[27] *Ibid.*, p. 50.

simultaneously with the growth of the national debt. This analysis
would suggest, however, that at least in part the low level of customer rates during the war and postwar period has been influenced
by central bank and Treasury policy which held Treasury bill rates
at historically low levels over a period of years.

Nonhomogeneity of the open market.—It has long been recognized that "interest rates are the thermometer of credit." Furthermore, this analysis has shown that typically (but not always) open
market rates are more sensitive to changes in credit conditions
than customer loan rates. Actually, of course, the open market
includes various submarkets, and these submarkets are not homogeneous in their degree of sensitivity to general credit changes.
In large measure, the sensitivity of the various submarkets is a
function of their size. During the decade of the 'twenties, for example, the call loan market was the most sensitive [28] and also overwhelmingly the most important submarket of the open market,
approaching the $7,000,000,000 mark in 1929. After the stock mar-
ket crash, however, its importance declined considerably, and the
largest market during most of the 'thirties was the Treasury bill
market, which in 1937 reached $2,300,000,000.[29] Corresponding to
the change in the position of call loans and Treasury bills in commercial bank portfolios, the Treasury bill rate soon became the
most sensitive indicator of changes in money market conditions.[30]

In short, whereas all the submarkets of the open market are
broadly speaking marginal markets, some are more sensitive at different periods than others. The Treasury bill market has been the
dominant submarket of the open market during most of the period
studied in this chapter. Thus, although it is legitimate to explain
general movements in all the submarkets by subsuming them under
the open market, it must be recognized that even this general explanation would need modification to allow for the varying sensitivity of the submarkets at different periods.

*Choice of New York City customer loan rates to represent entire
country.*—It is now convenient to explain the choice of the New
York City customer loan market to represent the generalized relationship of all customer loan markets with the open market. Actually there are numerous local customer loan markets all over the

---

[28] During the 'twenties, "a transfer of as little as $25,000,000 from New York may
cause an increase of 1/2 per cent in the call-loan rate." Burgess, *op. cit.*, p. 112.

[29] At the wartime peak, Treasury bills outstanding amounted to more than $17,000,-
000,000.

[30] Cf. Federal Reserve Bank of New York, *op. cit.*, October, 1937, p. 74; Federal
Reserve Bank of New York, *Annual Report for 1937,* p. 10.

country. The Federal Reserve bulletins provide data on average customer loan rates for New York City, northern and eastern cities, and southern and western cities. Broadly speaking, these three series have common fluctuations, though at distinctly different levels. Since, however, the large New York City banks directly serve the open market, they are the *most sensitive reactors* to changes in credit conditions, as reflected in open market rate changes. To a considerable degree, the greater rigidity (lesser sensitivity) of average customer loan rates outside New York City is the result of noncompetitive features in the market structures of the various local markets throughout the country. New York City markets generally are characterized by a greater degree of competition, and, therefore, of greater price (or, in this case, interest rate) flexibility.[31] Moreover, New York City rates are key rates because price leadership in the customer loan market rotates among the large money market banks in New York City.

The selection of the New York City average customer loan rate as a representative customer loan rate was, partly, too, an expository convenience which revealed most sharply the nature of the relationships discussed in this chapter. However, in customer loan markets characterized by relative rate rigidity, the direct and indirect impact of changes in the Treasury bill rate may take the form of credit rationing rather than a change in customer loan rates.

CONCLUDING OBSERVATIONS

The analysis of the relation between the open market and the customer loan market has revealed that, under normal circumstances, parallel movement of rates in both markets is owing to the fact that both markets respond to a common set of forces, the broad forces of demand and supply of short-term funds in the economy as a whole. Fundamentally, the open market is marginal in a passive sense. However, were it true (as has been so often alleged) that bankers *always* prefer customer loans to open market investments, and, thus, only bona fide surplus funds are invested in the open market,[32] changes in the open market could have no *direct* impact on rates charged in the customer loan market. If banks always give priority to customer loans over open market investment-for-profit, and if banks hold no excess reserves, then the funds tossed on the open market are truly surplus funds. Under such

[31] Cf. chapter iii for a survey of the market structure in various types of customer loan markets.
[32] Above and beyond the amount necessary for protective investment, of course.

circumstances, a (say) rise in open market rates would not directly affect customer loan rates, since there is no competitive interaction between them; bankers would not withdraw funds from the customer market to invest them in the open market. Therefore, the impact of open market changes on the customer loan market would, if anything, be indirect, e.g., changes imposed on the customer loan market resulting from anticipations aroused by open market changes, i.e., the open market changes might (especially if accomplished with official sanction and coöperation) act as a storm signal or fair-weather flag.

Although the lead-lag relationship between open markets and customer loan markets during earlier periods is fundamentally explained in terms of the passively marginal nature of the open markets, this explanation is inappropriate for what is roughly the same statistical relationship during the decade of the 'forties and up to the present. During this latter period, the Treasury bill market in particular has grown to immense proportions and is very important in commercial bank portfolios. It is inaccurate to assume that only bona fide surplus funds are invested in Treasury bills; clearly, commercial banks hold Treasury bills because they are (risk considered) relatively profitable. Should the Treasury and/or the central bank permit (or bring about) an increase in bill rates, active competition for bank funds would ensue between the Treasury bill market and at least a part of the customer loan market. The existence of an indirect impact is by its nature less certain. Under this new set of conditions, a causal impetus from the government market to the customer loan market would exist, and both interest rates and availability of credit on the customer loan market would be influenced by conditions on the open money market.

Price leadership and the open market.—Price leader banks in New York City take their cue in prime loan rate changes from rate changes on the open money market. This analysis has shown, however, that this action by the price leader banks is by no means exclusively related to the substitutability between open market commercial paper and prime customer loans. Indeed, the analysis has shown that the character of interaction between the open market and the customer loan market would exist even if there were no such thing as a commercial paper market on the open money market. In fact, ever since the 'thirties, the customer loan market has followed primarily the Treasury bill market rather than the commercial paper market.

Furthermore, although banks all over the country may follow

the price leadership of the large New York City banks, the first category of banks has been already prepared for the rate changes. Open market rate changes are barometers of changed credit conditions which in varying degree will have already affected all banks. Moreover, the direct and indirect impact of open market rate changes will also have conditioned banks in all parts of the country for a change in rate and credit policy. The change in the prime loan rate by the price leader banks in New York City is thus an official signal for a general change in price and credit policy by all banks. In other words, the price change by the leader banks typically recognizes a generally prevailing consensus of the need or desirability for a change.

In the prime loan market all over the country, prime rates promptly follow the leadership of the New York City banks. The price leadership in the prime loan market is not fully effective in other markets, because the various customer loan markets are only loosely connected. Rates are sluggish in the medium-size loan market and may not change so promptly nor so much as prime rates. Rate rigidity is still greater on the small loan market, and prime rate changes may have no impact on small loan rates. Presumably, however, the broad demand and supply forces which induced the prime rate change will affect availability of credit in medium and small loan markets even when rates are not affected. In the prime loan market, the price leadership tends toward a competitive level in the prime rate.

The alleged coexistence of competition and price leadership in the prime loan market deserves further explanation, since price leadership is normally expected to characterize only oligopoly markets. In fact, the prime loan market is oligopolistic in *structure* since the majority of prime loans is granted by a comparatively few giant banks. Notwithstanding, the prime loan markets exhibit reasonably competitive rate *behavior*. The explanation for an oligopolistic structure with competitive behavior reverts to the distinction made early in this study between the Chamberlin and Triffin approaches to market structure. In the Chamberlin sense, the prime loan market is oligopolistic, because it is dominated by a comparatively few large banks. In the Triffin sense, however, the cross-elasticity of demand of the oligopolists for prime loans approaches infinity. The reason, of course, is the existence of a close substitute for prime loans in the form of open market commercial paper—and, at least indirectly, thousands of banks in the country are involved on the open market.

IX

Pricing and the Federal Reserve

CUSTOMER LOAN rates are affected by many influences. The preceding chapter revealed the passive relation between customer loan rates and open market rates. It revealed further the general, active impact of open market rates on customer loan rates. An analysis of bank price policy would be seriously incomplete, however, without an examination of the possible influence of the Federal Reserve on bank price policy and customer loan rates. The examination is twofold. Initially, the possible influence of the Federal Reserve upon the open market is examined, since open market rate changes tend to be transmitted with varying force throughout the structure of banking business loan markets. A final section of this chapter examines the possibility of a *direct* impact of the central bank on customer loan rates and availability of credit in a given market area. Where possible, it will also be desirable to ascertain whether central bank influence is permissive or compulsive. The results, it will be seen, are uniform neither among different markets nor within the same banking markets at different times. The analysis of this chapter thus attempts to complete the tracing of the channels of influence on the customer loan markets back to their institutional sources. Since the media of possible central bank influence are well known, the need is for a critical examination of existing preconceptions and a synthesis between the results of this survey and the problem in question.

If the central bank has any influence over open market rates and customer loan rates, that influence is exercised through its broad instruments of credit control. As is well known, the central bank's ability to exert such influence inheres primarily in its power to change reserve requirements, to manipulate the discount rate, and to engage in open market operations. Reserve requirement changes are unquestionably a powerful credit control device, but, historically, this power has been sparingly employed by the Board of Governors of the Reserve System. Between June 21, 1917 and August 15, 1936, there were no changes in the reserve requirements because the Board had no power to change them. After the Banking Act of 1935, reserve requirements were successively raised three times between August 16, 1936, and April 15, 1938, in an attempt by the Board to cope with the unprecedented volume of excess reserves that resulted from the gold inflows during the decade of the 'thirties. Legal reserve requirements were somewhat reduced April 16, 1938, but were again raised in 1941. Central Reserve City requirements were reduced on October 3, 1942, for reasons of war financing,[1] and increased again in 1948.[2] Reserve requirements were lowered somewhat in 1949, but have since been restored almost to the 1941 levels.

The history of the Board's use of its power to change reserve requirements would seem to conform to the view that "This power . . . should be used, not as an instrument of short-period credit control, for which it would be much too rigid and hazardous, but only at rare intervals when it is necessary to make a fundamental readjustment of required reserves."[3] Accordingly, for purposes of this analysis, the central bank's ability to affect open market and customer loan rates by altering reserve requirements can be ignored.

FEDERAL RESERVE INFLUENCE ON OPEN MARKET RATES

THE DISCOUNT RATE AND OPEN MARKET RATES

The problem in this section is to ascertain whether, and to what extent, open market rates are "controlled" by the Federal Reserve. For a market structure analysis, it is important to know to what extent (if at all) the prices established on the open market are subject to the influence of a dominant firm (in this case, the Federal Reserve). If open market rates are significantly controllable by the Federal Reserve, banking markets would exhibit another layer of price leadership[4] operating to affect prices on the customer loan markets. Thus stated, the problem suggests a double line of attack: (1) to ascertain the possible existence of central bank control of

---

[1] Cf. Rollin G. Thomas, *Our Modern Banking and Monetary System* (1st ed., New York: Prentice-Hall, 1946), p. 134.

[2] Cf. Charles R. Whittlesey, *Principles and Practices of Money and Banking* (New York: Macmillan, 1948), p. 251.

[3] John H. Williams, *Postwar Monetary Plans* (2d ed., rev.; New York: Alfred A. Knopf, 1945), p. 121. For a similar statement by the Chairman, Board of Governors, Federal Reserve System, cf. Patman Report, Part I, p. 297.

[4] The reader should again note the limitations of this term as used in this study. See chap. vii, n. 5.

open market rates, and (2) in the event of such control, to examine the possible methods by which this control is exercised.

A suggestive approach to the question of possible central bank influence on open market rates involves a comparison of the dis-

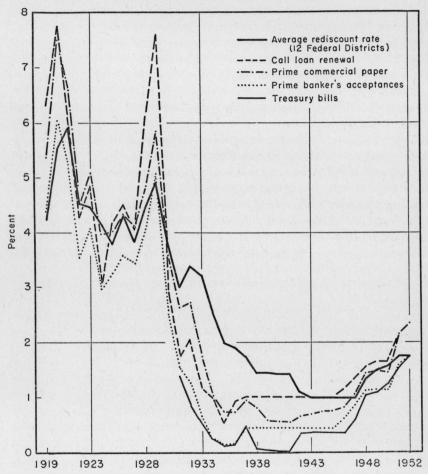

Fig. 2. Short-term open market rates compared with Federal Reserve rediscount rate.

count rate and the open market rates. Figure 2 shows open market rates with the average discount rate of all Federal Reserve Banks. The most obvious feature of the more than thirty-year series is the similarity in the lines of fluctuation of the open market and discount rates. The similarity is by no means so striking as between the Federal Reserve buying rate on acceptances and the acceptance rate.[5] Moreover, although the discount rate and open market rates move closely together, their level is by no means identical. Furthermore, the discount rate is sometimes below and sometimes above the open market rates. Notwithstanding, the correlation would appear to be sufficiently high to warrant further investigation on the chance of discovering a causal nexus. At the outset, therefore, the hypothesis is tested that causation runs from the discount rate to the open market rate, i.e., that the discount rate "controls" the open market rate. Evidence can then be marshaled to support a hypothesis of reverse causation, or, possibly, of no causal connection.

Since a commercial bank is a profit-making institution, the presumption is that it will avail itself of every legitimate opportunity to increase its earnings. If the discount rate per se is to be an effective and precise instrument to control open market rates,[6] it must operate via the profit motivation of the private banks. When the open market rate (i.e., the weighted average of short-term rates) is above the discount rate, a profit-making opportunity presumptively exists to be exploited by the banking system. Banks can borrow from the Federal Reserve Banks at the (lower) discount rate and then re-lend on the open market at the higher rate. The increased supply of Reserve funds thus made available would tend to lower the market rate toward the discount rate. Similarly, when the market rate is below the discount rate, it is no longer profitable to borrow from the Reserve banks. Instead, private banks would curtail their lending in order to repay indebtedness incurred at the central bank. Funds are thus withdrawn from the market, and the resulting credit tightness would tend to drive market rates up toward the discount rate.

Another examination of figure 2 makes it quite clear, however,

---

[5] For long periods, these two rates moved very closely together and constituted in effect a single series.

[6] The discount rate has been historically considered one of the most important instruments available to the central bank to influence the market rate of interest. In 1921, a former Governor of the Federal Reserve Board remarked that: "Control over discount rates, as exercised by the Federal Reserve Banks and the Federal Reserve Board, is one of the most important and far-reaching powers ever delegated by Congress to another instrumentality. *The grant ranks with the power given the Interstate Commerce Commission to regulate railroad rates.*" Remarks by Governor W. P. G. Harding at the opening session of the joint conference of the Federal Reserve Board with the Federal Reserve Agents and Governors of Federal Reserve Banks held at Washington, D.C., October 25–28, 1921, in Annals of the American Academy of Political and Social Science, *The Federal Reserve System—Its Purpose and Work* (Concord, 1922), Vol. XCIX, no. 188, p. 183. (Italics mine.)

Whether this position can be accepted at face value can be determined after examining the mechanics by which the discount rate is assumed to influence market rates.

that the type of activity considered above does not adequately describe the attitude of the commercial banking system to borrowing from the Reserve banks. If private banks were motivated exclusively by profit considerations and had no reluctance to become indebted at the Reserve banks, the rather considerable deviations between the discount rate and the open market rates could not have existed. Such deviations in fact exist, and conclusions as to the efficacy of the discount rate as a regulating instrument must be accordingly modified. From an inconclusive test, it is obviously impossible to derive definite conclusions. Negatively, the discount rate cannot *completely* dominate the market rate. But the test does not preclude the possibility that the discount rate has *some* influence on the market rate. This possibility is further considered in the discussion of the "tradition against borrowing" which follows shortly.

The discount rate can exert its influence on open market rates in still another manner, which is regarded by some writers as the discount rate's most decisive effect. Although the Federal Reserve System is young compared to the central banks of other countries, it enjoys considerable prestige among private bankers. Changes in the discount rate are respected by the banking community as an indicator of the judgment of the monetary authorities about the economic situation. Accordingly, "The psychological effect of a rate change is very great."[7] When the banking system has ample reserves and can thus act without recourse to the central bank, the psychological impact of discount rate changes is the most important means available to the Reserve banks for influencing market credit conditions.[8] To reinforce this effect, the Federal Reserve System publishes many reports, analyzing business and credit conditions and explaining the reasons for its credit policies. These publications also serve as a liaison between the central bank, the numerous private bankers, and businessmen, and help to establish among these groups a coöperative approach to the monetary problems of the economy. This coöperative spirit helps to mold a banking tradition, and "A firmly established and rational banking tradition is in the long run the greatest safeguard against continuous or widespread practices leading to unhealthy credit expansion."[9]

[7] Ray B. Westerfield, *Money, Credit, and Banking* (New York: Ronald Press, 1938), p. 639.
[8] E. A. Goldenweiser, *Federal Reserve System in Operation* (New York: McGraw-Hill, 1925), p. 168.
[9] *Loc. cit.*

Tradition against borrowing.—It is impossible to measure the quantitative impact of a tradition, but there is evidence that various banking traditions have a powerful influence upon the activities of private bankers. W. W. Riefler has adduced one such tradition to support his contention that the discount rate *cannot* affect market rates through the mechanism of profit borrowing by member banks from the Reserve banks. This tradition is the "tradition against borrowing."[10] The antiborrowing tradition allegedly precludes member banks from becoming large and continuous debtors at the Reserve banks. Such indebtedness would be contrary to the intent of the Federal Reserve Act which held that "The funds of the Federal Reserve banks are primarily intended to be used in meeting the seasonal and temporary requirements of members . . ."[11]

This official injunction merely formalized a long-standing conviction of private bankers even before the Federal Reserve System was established. Under the correspondent relationships which historically characterized American banking, it was considered a sign of weakness for a bank to be too long or too much in debt. Every effort was made by private bankers to avoid such adverse reflections on their credit. And it was more than a matter of pride, though pride was also involved. When a bank's credit became thus impaired, it was difficult for the bank to borrow from its correspondent although a loan might be desperately needed. When the Federal Reserve System was established, it was intended to perform the usual functions of a central bank and especially to be available as a "lender of last resort." The inherited tradition against borrowing was very strong, however, and in the early years of the System, private banks were loath to become indebted to the Reserve banks even when such indebtedness was necessary to meet the legitimate needs of business. The Federal Reserve Board had to undertake a campaign to educate bankers to borrow from the System for authorized purposes. On the other hand, the Reserve Board made it explicitly clear that ". . . Reserve bank credit should not be used for profit, and that continuous indebtedness at the Reserve banks except under unusual circumstances, is an abuse of Reserve bank facilities."[12] To reinforce this injunction against profit borrowing, the Reserve banks employ a variety of methods, including moral suasion, the issuing of warnings to offending

---

[10] W. W. Riefler, *Money Rates and Money Markets in the United States* (New York: Harper & Brothers, 1930), pp. 29–30.

[11] Board of Governors, Federal Reserve System, *Annual Report*, 1926, p. 5.

[12] Charles O. Hardy, *Credit Policies of the Federal Reserve System* (Washington, D.C.: Brookings Institution, 1932), p. 231.

banks, requiring excess collateral to discount, and a flat refusal to discount "eligible" paper if it is not "acceptable."[13]

So far as the tradition against borrowing, supported by various auxiliary central bank controls, prevents borrowing for profit, the discount rate per se can have no direct effect (other than psychological) on open market rates, because the efficacy of the discount rate is predicated on profit borrowing. It is nevertheless true that the banking system as a whole is almost always, to a greater or less extent, indebted at the Federal Reserve Banks. Under the present hypothesis, this indebtedness could not have been incurred primarily under a profit motivation. It follows, therefore, that the indebtedness was incurred because banks were in "need" of Reserve bank credit. By way of projecting the analysis, if the need theory turns out to be valid, the original problem of whether and how the central bank can influence open market rates is a step closer to solution. Hence, if banks borrow only for need, it is only necessary to discover whether the central bank has some way of affecting the magnitude of member bank "needs."

"NEED" THEORY OF BORROWING

The need theory has been most vigorously espoused by Winfield Riefler. His argument, very much in brief, is as follows: If banks borrow for need, then open market rates will reflect the ease or pressure of their position. Open market rates rise through liquidation of open market investments when member bank borrowings (motivated by their needs) are large, and vice versa.[14] Figure 3 shows the fluctuation of member bank discounts at the Reserve banks against the fluctuation of open market rates. The chart shows that the rate and volume series have moved very closely together, each duplicating the rise and fall of the other. Riefler accordingly concludes that "The motivation for member bank borrowing is the need for funds rather than the opportunity for profit."[15] It follows, therefore, that "money rates would be affected as they have been affected more by the mere fact that member banks found it necessary to borrow at the reserve banks than by the rate which they paid on that borrowing."[16] Finally, the Reserve banks (usually) have it within their power to influence the needs of member banks through exercise of open market operations and, if necessary, through changing reserve requirements.

---

[13] Cf. Lawrence E. Clark, *Central Banking Under the Federal Reserve System* (New York: Macmillan, 1935), pp. 278–279.

[14] Riefler, *op. cit.*, chapter ii.

[15] *Ibid.*, p. 32.

[16] *Ibid.*, p. 33.

Criticism of the need theory.—The acceptance of Riefler's position would, in its strictest form,[17] imply a complete rejection of the profit theory of borrowing. The rejection of the profit theory, in turn, suggests that the discount rate per se cannot directly (again, except for psychological influences) affect open market rates by

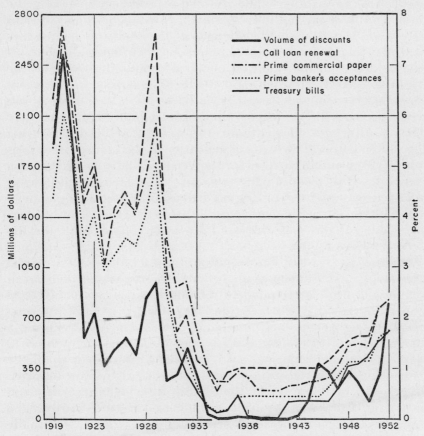

Fig. 3. Short-term open market rates and volume of member bank discounts.

any profit-motivated reaction to discount rate changes, as the original theory of discount rate changes would have assumed. Any vestigial influence of the discount rate on open market rates is discounted by Riefler in putting heavy emphasis on the *mere fact of indebtedness.*

[17] A careful reading of Riefler's analysis would show that his acceptance of the need theory is not unqualified. Cf. *ibid.,* p. 25. It seems fair to conclude nonetheless that his emphasis on the need theory amounts to an almost total rejection of the profit theory.

Although the mere fact of indebtedness seems clearly established as an important factor influencing open market rates, Riefler's almost complete rejection of the possible direct influence of the discount rate (other than psychological) seems unduly pessimistic. The validity of the need theory involves not only a virtual demolition of the profit theory but also considerable confidence in the inviolability of the tradition against borrowing. Serious questions have been raised about the strength of the tradition against borrowing. Robert Turner, for example, has mentioned the weakening influence on the tradition of the schizophrenic policy of the Reserve banks. On the one hand, the Reserve banks try to maintain the tradition against borrowing; yet their *raison d'etre* was to provide elasticity to the system—an elasticity that implies member bank borrowing.[18] Furthermore, the concept of need borrowing can be ambiguous; it is not always easy to distinguish need borrowing from profit borrowing. Practically all borrowing by member banks at the central bank is ex post facto. Hence, it is difficult to determine whether the original extension of credit by the member bank was to accommodate the legitimate demands of business or whether it was done because borrowing conditions at the Reserve banks were easy.

As discussed earlier, the tradition against indebtedness existed before the establishment of the Federal Reserve System and was an outgrowth of the correspondent relationships which characterized American banking. The relations between a bank and its correspondent are not unlike those between a borrowing client and a bank. The correspondent bank is under no legal compulsion to lend to another bank, and such lending is contingent upon the borrowing bank's remaining sound and using its borrowing privileges with discretion. Under the Federal Reserve System, although it is true that a member bank has no legal right to borrow, the idea prevails that the System, as a lender of last resort, is virtually obliged to make credit available as long as the technical requirements of "eligibility" are fulfilled. This spirit is not the one that historically fostered the borrowing inhibitions.

Another influence weakening the tradition is the change in the technique of borrowing under the Federal Reserve System from what it was before the establishment of the central bank. Under a correspondent system the personal relationships between bankers were important. By contrast, borrowing from the Reserve banks

[18] Robert C. Turner, *Member Bank Borrowing* (Columbus: Ohio State University, 1938), chapter iv.

is highly impersonal and the mechanics of borrowing make the process almost automatic. Essentially this point involves the distinction between the atmosphere in which a personal loan is made and that in which there is a mere "adjustment of reserves."[19]

Seymour Harris also has questioned the validity of the tradition against borrowing:

Undoubtedly, too much has been made of the point . . . In the years 1928 and 1929, the authorities frequently pointed out that market rates rose because member-bank indebtedness had increased. But the relation between the two variables has at times perplexed the authorities, and *member banks have not always evinced any strong desire to liquidate open market investments merely because they had increased their borrowings*. Open market investments increased to a marked extent in a period (1927–29) in which indebtedness increased to an unprecedented level. Banks are more willing to remain in debt when the returns on open market investments increase rapidly. Moreover, the enforcement of restraint by reserve banks is not easy when the evidence of increased indebtedness is merely an increase in the period during which member banks stay in debt, and a somewhat higher level of debts for banks in debt; and when permanent indebtedness is still not the rule.[20]

Because of the above criticisms, the need theory of borrowing cannot be unqualifiedly accepted. However, any qualifications of the need theory are necessarily an implicit admission of (at least) some borrowing from a profit motivation. It will be recalled that the discussion of the profit hypothesis demonstrated that borrowing was *not exclusively* on a profit basis; the analysis could not prove that no borrowing was done for profit. It now seems probable that at least some borrowing is done for profit.

CONCLUSION: NEED VERSUS PROFIT THEORY

The foregoing analysis suggests that banks borrow both for profit and for need. This further implies that open market rates are influenced directly both by the discount rate and by open market operations. Many writers have observed that discount rates *follow* open market rates. How, then, it might be asked, can the discount rate influence open market rates? The apparently reversed sequence of events does not impair the analysis, because as Lauchlin Currie put it: ". . . rediscount rate changes 'back up' open-market opera-

[19] *Ibid.*, pp. 77–78.
[20] Seymour Harris, *Twenty Years of Federal Reserve Policy* (Cambridge: Harvard University Press, 1933), Vol. I, pp. 262–263. (Italics mine.)

tion."[21] Through a joint manipulation of open market operations and the discount rate, the central bank can influence the range within which open market rates can vary. Although the discount rate is not completely effective in controlling open market rates, the market rates can deviate from the discount rate only to the extent that the Reserve banks are unwilling (or unable) to engage in open market operations.[22]

"PRICE LEADERSHIP" BY THE FEDERAL RESERVE

This analysis of the ability of the central bank to influence open market rates suggests that another price leadership system ultimately affects rates on the customer loan market. Under most circumstances, the Federal Reserve holds the place of a "dominant firm" in the open money market. Moreover, the dominance of the central bank is a function not only of its size, but also (again, under ordinary circumstances) of its ability to influence profoundly the reserve position of the member banking system, and indirectly, of all banks in the country. Customer loan rates in many areas tend to follow the lead of the prime rate of the large money market banks. The prime rate, in turn, tends to follow the open market rate. The central bank is clearly able (under most circumstances) to influence the *zone* within which open market rates can vary. To this extent, therefore, the central bank exercises a qualified price-zone leadership over the money market.[23] It is worth emphasizing that although the central bank can affect customer loan rates via its influence on open market rates, it does not have corresponding influence over customer availability of credit. The ability of the central bank to restrain availability of credit is manifest, but its ability to induce an expansion of credit is far weaker.

FEDERAL RESERVE INFLUENCE ON CUSTOMER LOAN RATES

Interest rate structures in customer loan markets are the net product of a variety of complex forces which play on those markets. The nature of the price leadership systems that affect rates on

[21] Lauchlin Currie, *Supply and Control of Money in the United States* (Cambridge: Harvard University Press, 1934), p. 102. An excellent sketch of the complementary functioning of open market and discount policy can be found in Patman Hearings, p. 295 ff.

[22] Sometimes, too, open market operations are ineffectual, e.g., large excess reserves in the banking system.

[23] The equivocation in the phraseology of this sentence is both deliberate and necessary. This analysis cannot support the unequivocal contention that the central bank can control with precision what rates shall rule on the open market. On the other hand, the analysis does suggest that the central bank can influence those rates within a zone.

customer loan markets has been described. Similarly, this analysis has examined the manner in which the open market can *actively* influence customer markets. The particular market structure in various markets is, of course, a critical element in rate determination in those markets. One final, important influence remains to be explored—the ability of the Federal Reserve to affect customer loan markets, not circuitously by affecting open market rates, but by exerting a direct influence on the customer loan markets. The banks dealing directly on the New York money market are essentially the large New York City banks. Other banks throughout the country participate indirectly through the correspondent relationships which they maintain with the New York banks. Therefore, developments in the open market probably reflect the attitudes and financial position of the New York banks primarily, and only secondarily of the indirectly participating banks throughout the country. On the other hand, all banks take part directly in granting customers' loans. Therefore, the attitudes and conditions surrounding *all* banks are directly involved in the determination of customer loan rates. Accordingly, it is necessary to examine the attitudes toward Reserve bank operations not only of the large New York City banks but also of other banks all over the country.

The various aspects of the central problem of market structures and performance are all interrelated. For systematic analysis, however, it is necessary to deal with artificially autonomous units of study. Since this discussion is closely connected with that of the preceding section, the analysis already developed will be repeated in this section only as far as seems necessary to ensure clarity of exposition.

THE DISCOUNT RATE AND THE CUSTOMER LOAN MARKETS

It is convenient to open the investigation of the possible direct influence of the Federal Reserve on customer loan markets by considering whether there is any evidence that the Federal Reserve discount rate in any way influences the rates on customer loan markets. This possible influence can be examined by assuming a change in the discount rate and tracing the possible impact on the customer loan market. As a first approximation, the possibility that a change in the discount rate can affect customer loan rates depends on the following: (1) whether the cost of funds to the bank is affected by the change in discount rate, (2) whether the possible change in the cost of funds to the bank are passed onto the bank's customer, and (3) whether there is a psychological impact of discount rate changes which affects the customer loan market independently of any cost effects. The analysis of the effect of discount rate changes on customer loan rates and availability stresses primarily these possible channels of influence.

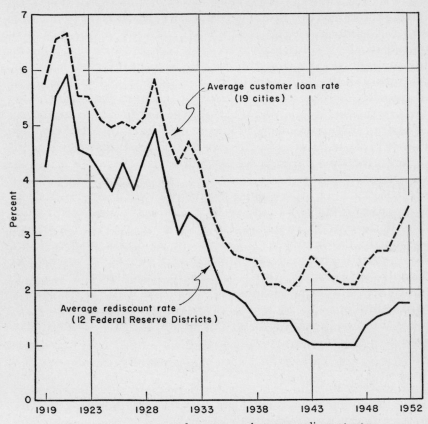

Fig. 4. Average customer loan rates and average rediscount rates.

In the early stages of this investigation, it seems useful to consider the customer loan market as a single unified market. At a later stage, the differences among the various customer markets can be admitted into the analysis. Figure 4 shows the fluctuations of the customer loan rate (based on an average of rates in 19 cities) and the discount rate (computed as an average of the discount rates in the twelve Federal Reserve districts). Although the level of rates in the two series clearly differs, the *routes* of fluctuation are impressively similar *during part of this period*. Between 1919 and 1935, the two series moved quite closely together. Thereafter, however, the average customer loan rate moved with considerably greater independence from the discount rate. A priori, the fact that both series are averages could account for either more or less similarity between them. Although the correlation between the two series is clearly not perfect, the similarity of fluctuation, especially during the early years of the period, is sufficiently great to warrant an investigation into the possibility of a causal nexus. There is, of course, no automatic presumption that even perfect correlation implies causality between the variables. In this case, however, the theory of discount rate use lends support to the presumption of causality, and the matter is investigated from that angle.

As in the earlier analysis, the ability of the discount rate in and of itself to affect customer loan rates is predicated upon the assumption of profit borrowing by the member banks. In its original conception, the discount rate was supposed to be set at a level "to accommodate commerce and business." If a bank's reserve position precluded further loans to business, new reserves could be obtained by borrowing from the central bank at the nonpenalty discount rate. If the central bank authorities wished to restrict further expansion in the money supply, an increase in the discount rate would force higher rates on bank loans because of the increase in bank costs. Customer loans would thereby be discouraged.[24] The possibility of profit borrowing by the member banks at the central banks thus provides (at least, tentatively) a partial explanation for the similar fluctuations of discount rates and customer loan rates.

REHABILITATION OF THE DISCOUNT RATE

The analysis thus far has considered whether the discount rate per se could affect customer loan rates. Clearly, however, the discount rate can have none but a psychological impact on customer loan rates unless the discount rate actually enters into the cost calculations of commercial banks either directly or indirectly. In turn, member bank borrowing at the Reserve banks is a necessary condition for the discount rate to be effective. As everyone knows, however, the discount rate has not by itself been an important credit control device (except for psychological influence) for at least two decades. Throughout most of the 'thirties, member bank borrowing at the Reserve banks was very small and even negligible because of the huge volume of excess reserves which piled up dur-

---

[24] Cf. Raymond P. Kent, *Money and Banking* (rev. ed., New York and Toronto: Rinehart, 1951), pp. 459–460.

ing that depressed decade. During the war decade of the 'forties, too, the banks of the country had only slight occasion for borrowing at the central bank.[25] The enormous swelling of the money supply to finance the war resulted in a huge increase of government securities in commercial bank portfolios. Under the Federal Reserve's wartime policy of freezing the rate structure on government securities, the banks of the country had independent control over the expansion of the money supply by the simple process of liquidating securities whose prices were virtually guaranteed.[26] The conviction among Federal Reserve authorities that this policy of rigid support of the government bond market was seriously hindering any attempt to control the postwar inflation led finally to the celebrated "accord" between the Federal Reserve and the United States Treasury.[27] Under the agreement, the Federal Reserve was committed to no more than the "maintenance of orderly conditions" in the government market. That commitment was sufficiently flexible to permit the Federal Reserve to resume a flexible monetary policy freed from the overriding necessity of maintaining a rigid rate structure on government securities.[28]

The resuscitation of monetary policy has resulted in a striking resurgence of central bank loans and discounts.[29] In 1929, Reserve bank discounts and advances amounted to slightly more than $1,000,000,000. Although such discounts and advances had been

---

[25] These facts are pertinent in trying to understand why the parallelism of movement between the series for customer loan rates and discount rates (fig. 4) became much less pronounced after about 1935. Until the early 'thirties, the member banking system was continuously in debt at the Reserve banks. Cf. also Patman Report, Vol. I, p. 283.

[26] The National City Bank stated that: "As long as the authorities supported government security prices at fixed points, there was little need for banks to use the discount window." National City Bank, *Monthly Letter*, February, 1953, p. 15.

[27] On March 4, 1951, the Federal Reserve System and the Treasury announced the following agreement: "The Treasury and the Federal Reserve System have reached full accord with respect to debt management and monetary policies to be pursued in furthering their common purpose to assure the successful financing of the Government's requirements and at the same time, to minimize monetization of the public debt." Cf. Patman Report, Vol. I, p. 293.

[28] It was also the stated purpose of this "accord" to "restore the discount mechanism as a restraint on inflation." National City Bank, *loc. cit.*, p. 15.

[29] In his testimony before the Patman Committee, Chairman Martin took the position that "Member bank borrowing at the Federal Reserve should be the principal means of obtaining additional bank reserves. Discount rate changes and open market operations should be the main instruments through which credit and monetary policies are adapted to changing conditions in the economy. This means increased use of the discount mechanism, increased importance of discount rates in comparison with credit policy experience of the past decade, and reliance on open market operations to reinforce discount policy." Cf. *ibid.*, p. 17.

trivial during most of the 'thirties and the 'forties, by July, 1952, Reserve bank discounts and advances stood at $1,200,000,000 and in August, they rose to $1,300,000,000.[30] Indeed, "at the seasonal peak of pressure on the money market in December, bank borrowing from the Federal Reserve . . . ran up as high as $2 billion."[31] This development, in retrospect, has seemed inevitable. It was unthinkable that the central bank should be permanently stripped of its ability to influence general credit conditions. During the long siege when the commercial banks were independent of the central bank or could exploit the central bank's self-imposed passivity in controlling credit, the traditional methods of influencing the money supply were effectively paralyzed. With the revival of a flexible monetary policy, the central bank has resumed its function as a lender of last resort.[32] That means, in turn, as the experience above suggests, that the banking system as a whole has again become indebted at the Reserve banks.[33] It is not surprising, therefore, that the reaction of member banks to discount rate changes and central bank open market operations has increasingly resembled the operating experience of the 'twenties rather than that of the 'thirties or the 'forties.[34]

This resumption of indebtedness at the Reserve banks by the commercial banking system points up the importance and the

[30] "Greater reliance by member banks on borrowing to obtain reserve funds has pervasive restrictive effects on credit expansion throughout the banking system even though at any one time the number of borrowing banks and the dollar volume of borrowings is comparatively small." Patman Report, Vol. I, p. 396.

[31] National City Bank, *loc. cit.*, p. 15.

[32] The chairman of the Board of Governors noted that as a result of the "accord," "Temporary reserve needs of banks were met to an increasing extent through borrowing at the Federal Reserve." Patman Report, Vol. I, p. 293.

Cf. also Madeline McWhinney, "Member Bank Borrowings from the Federal Reserve Banks," in Federal Reserve Bank of New York, *Money Market Essays*, March, 1952, p. 9.

Reliance on the central bank was enhanced by the tremendous loan expansion of banks following the outbreak of hostilities in Korea. The loan expansion increased dependence on the Federal Reserve Banks by reducing the liquidity of the commercial banks. Cf. Patman Report. Vol. I, p. 384.

Even the Council of Economic Advisers conceded that: "Some increase in discounting might result from continuation of the policy of allowing greater flexibility in the movements of prices and yields in the market for Government securities than prevailed during the period of close support of the market." *Ibid.*, Vol. II, p. 863.

[33] Cf. Winfield W. Riefler, "Debt Management, Fiscal Policy, and Monetary Controls," in *Proceedings*, Twenty-Seventh Annual Conference, Western Economics Association, Redlands, California, September, 1952. p. 7.

[34] After the accord, "it was possible to conduct open market operations more flexibly . . . and to exercise more effective restraint on loan expansion to private borrowers." Patman Report, Vol. I, p. 293.

relevance of the earlier analysis.[35] If the banking system is again
indebted at the Reserve banks, such indebtedness must have been
incurred either for profit or for need. The earlier discussion has
shown that an unqualified acceptance of the profit theory of borrowing is impossible in view of the strength of the tradition against
borrowing. To the extent that borrowing is not profit motivated,
however, it must, by the logic of the analysis, be need borrowing.
The ability of the discount rate per se to affect customer loan rates
depends on whether borrowing is for profit or for need. The profit
theory has been examined above; the need theory is analyzed further in the following section.

FURTHER ANALYSIS OF THE NEED THEORY

Riefler's analysis would suggest that profit-motivated borrowing
would no more characterize banking operations in the customer
loan market than vis-à-vis the open market. He would point out,
for example, that if banks borrowed primarily for profit, then the
discount rate and the customer loan rate would move very closely
together, and certainly more closely than the actually observed
movement. It is no doubt true, too, that the discount rate moves
more closely with the average of open market rates than with the
average of customer loan rates.[36] Moreover, customer loan rates
fluctuate more closely with open market rates than with the discount rates. All this suggests to Riefler that banks borrow for need
rather than for profit. In other words, Riefler would hold that
any effect (other than psychological) of discount rates on customer
loan rates is an indirect effect, because customer loan rates respond
to changes in general credit conditions (and the latter are reflected
first in open market rates).[37] Discount rates thus affect customer
loan rates only incidentally. The primary influence is by open

---

[35] For a discussion of the renewed importance of monetary controls, including quite
specifically the discount rate, cf. Robert Roosa, "The Revival of Monetary Policy,"
Review of Economics and Statistics, XXXIII, no. 1 (February, 1951): 32.

[36] Goldenweiser has apparently also accepted the need theory. "That discount rates
are more closely related to open market rates than to customers rates reflects the fact
that banks borrow from the Reserve Banks principally for the purpose of replenishing
reserves when they fall below the legal minimum and not for the purpose of relending
at a higher rate." E. A. Goldenweiser, "Instruments of Federal Reserve Policy," in
Board of Governors, Federal Reserve System, *Banking Studies* (Baltimore: Waverly
Press, 1941), p. 395.

[37] Incidentally, Riefler notes that "Banks and others make loans in these markets
when they have *surplus* funds to put out ..." Riefler, *op. cit.*, p. 10. (Italics mine.) In
fact, as shown in chapter viii, there are also nonsurplus funds in the open money
markets, and, to this extent, pressures on reserves could *directly* hit the customer
loan market first instead of the open market and maybe not even touch the open
market at all. Cf. p. 140.

market operations which place pressure on the reserves of member banks and force them to borrow at the Reserve banks. This pressure is felt first in the open market and subsequently in the customer loan market.

As before, the importance of need borrowing can be conceded. The issue is whether profit-motivated borrowing is as negligible as Riefler's analysis would suggest. Since Riefler puts great stress on the tradition against borrowing to preclude profit-motivated borrowing, the real question is how much faith can be put in the strength of this tradition. Some compromising aspects about this tradition have been mentioned earlier, but its importance in this context warrants further examination.

In addition to the objections already given concerning the tradition against borrowing, it is not a constant factor but rather varies according to the bank concerned and the time in question. Lauchlin Currie has drawn a distinction between "sensitive" and "nonsensitive" banks, i.e., sensitive or otherwise to indebtedness at the central bank. He found an "extreme reluctance of the large New York banks to remain in debt."[38] The country banks are least sensitive to indebtedness. All other banks range somewhere between these two extremes.

Various explanations have been proposed for this varying degree of sensitivity to indebtedness.[39] The large New York City banks put a very high premium on liquidity. They act as correspondents for country banks and are subject to sudden drains into the interior whenever the country banks wish to withdraw their funds. Second, the New York City banks can more readily discharge indebtedness because many of their assets are held in the form of highly liquid open market securities. Country banks, on the other hand, are overwhelmingly involved with customer loans, and the sudden calling of such loans threatens a rupture of long-standing banker-customer relationships. A final explanation is political. The Reserve banks are sensitive to criticism from agrarian areas—the charge that they favor the highly developed at the expense of less developed areas—so they perhaps put less pressure on country banks to liquidate their central bank indebtedness. The preceding points, properly modified, would also apply to those banks ranging between the two extremes of sensitivity and insensitivity.

Sensitivity to borrowing is also a function of the period involved. Currie has shown that even for the same class of banks, sensitivity

---

[38] Currie, *op. cit.,* p. 93.
[39] Cf. *Ibid.,* p. 94.

to indebtedness is least during prosperity and greatest during depression.[40] As Currie suggests, this is probably the result of the fact that, in good times, liquidity is not likely to be a bothersome problem and the opportunities for profit are good; the reverse would be true during the downswing of the cycle.

Some reluctance to borrow, which is ascribed to the tradition against borrowing, is more accurately explained on other grounds. A customer loan rate above the discount rate is not always prima facie evidence of an opportunity for profitable borrowing. The cost of funds to the bank is by no means the only, and not even necessarily the most important, cost of borrowing. High-rate loans in particular must also consider the elements of risk, labor costs, liquidity, and the like, and such factors can more than negate the profit gap between the market rate and the discount rate. For these reasons, a fall in the discount rate of (say) $\frac{1}{2}$ per cent may be quite negligible and would not stimulate further borrowing.

The profit gap between the market rate and the discount rate can be especially deceptive in country districts. Country bank rates are usually higher than those in large cities, but there is not an unlimited market for such loans. Since the banks in country districts are generally not under a regime of pure competition, any extension of their loans might require a drop in their price (rate of interest). But if the demand for loans in that district has an elasticity of less than unity, an increase in their loan portfolio would reduce their total revenue. Under these circumstances, the profit gap is more apparent than real.[41]

BANK COSTS AND LOAN RATES

These and earlier mentioned qualifications of the tradition against borrowing preclude an exclusive acceptance of the need theory of member bank borrowing. By the logic of the problem, any qualifications of the need theory are an implicit admission of (at least) some borrowing from profit motivation.[42] The evidence indeed suggests that borrowing is done both for profit and for need. In need borrowing by debt-sensitive banks, customer loan rates

[40] Cf. *Ibid.,* pp. 96–97.

[41] Cf. Goldenweiser, *op. cit.,* p. 50.

[42] In their discussion of member bank borrowing, the Reserve Bank presidents noted the inhibiting influence of the tradition against borrowing. On the other hand, they also stated that: "The restraining influence of borrowing will be enhanced if discount rates are high enough to reduce *the profitability of using borrowed funds for the extension of credit.* The lower the discount rate the less the effectiveness of such a policy." Patman Report, Vol. II, p. 702. (Italics mine.)

are liable to be influenced by the mere fact of indebtedness. In addition, customer loan rates are liable to be affected if the costs of debt-sensitive banks are affected by the necessity of borrowing at higher discount rates. In profit borrowing, however, loan rates are affected only if the change in bank costs can be transmitted to borrowers. If costs can be passed on, then customer loan rates are, for example, raised in response to a rise of the rediscount rate. If increased costs cannot be passed on—suppose that customer rates are, for whatever reason, rigid—then customer rates are not affected; bank revenue is affected; and probably the marginal customer loans are dropped. In practice, both situations are encountered.

It seems clear that the traditional theory relating loan rate changes to discount rate changes via transmitted cost effects cannot be completely accepted. The largest banks, and particularly those connected with the financial centers, tend to pass on changes in money costs to their customers. This is practically automatic for many large borrowers who negotiate long-standing term loans. A common clause in term loan contracts provides for interest rate changes on a sliding scale with discount rate changes. Interest rates of large banks are flexible and respond to changes in money costs because large banks deal mostly with large borrowers. Since large borrowers have many alternative sources of supply, including the open money market, their bargaining position is strong. Hence, they operate in a competitive loan market and secure the most competitive rates which the country affords.

On the other hand, country banks tend to have rigid rates, because they operate in monopolistic or oligopolistic loan markets. Since rates are rigid, changes in bank costs are not readily reflected in the prices charged for short-term credit. A bank occupying a sole position in a town is in a semimonopolist position, a monopolist position compromised primarily by the extent to which prospective borrowers have alternative sources of supply in near-by towns. Despite its semimonopolistic position, such a bank is not always free to vary its customer loan rates in response to central bank pressure. If the central bank is trying to accomplish a reduction in customer loan rates, the lone banker can successfully resist this pressure to a great extent by exploiting his (semi) monopolist advantage.[43] When the central bank is trying to induce a rise in customer loan rates, the small-town monopolist is confronted with

[43] Not irrelevantly, a sustained decline in his customer loan rates may drive the small-town banker into bankruptcy.

a serious obstacle. Bank loan rates in small towns have acquired over the years the historic sanction of a customary or fair price, not unlike the medieval notion of the "fair and just price." Not even the small-town monopolist can affront this entrenched notion without risking ultimate reduction of profits.

When country banks occupy an oligopoly position in the loan market, the price of customer loans is stabilized (again, at the customary or fair price) by a recognition by the oligopolists of their mutual dependence, or, in certain instances, by outright collusion in the form of informal agreements and understandings. At the stabilized price thus achieved, each of the oligopolists faces a kink in his demand schedule.[44] The kink in the demand schedule implies a corresponding discontinuity in the marginal revenue schedule. Hence, any but the very largest changes in the marginal cost curve are "lost" in the discontinuity of the marginal revenue schedule. Only the most severe changes in the cost of member bank borrowing at the central bank can escape the discontinuity of the marginal revenue curve and actually influence customer loan rates.[45] Both in monopolistic and oligopolistic small loan markets, rates on customer loans are relatively fixed and bank profit margins are alternatively expanded and squeezed as bank costs vary.

SUMMARY

Rediscount rates and open market operations.—Central bank influence on customer loan rates is exercised through the use of the discount rate and open market operations. The effect of central bank influence on customer loan rates through the exercise of these two instruments can be summarized as follows:

1. To the extent that member banks respond psychologically to a change in discount rates, the central bank can affect customer loan rates by exploiting this psychological impact.

2. Closely allied to the psychological impact of discount rate changes is their prestige impact as indicators of changed credit conditions. Prime commercial loan rates tend to vary with discount rate changes. Term loan contracts commonly carry provision for

---

[44] "When an oligopolistic firm raises the price above the conventional level, the other firms in the group do not react, but when it lowers its price below the conventional level, the others follow suit to 'keep their own' or to penalize the transgressor against the social consensus. In consequence, the demand schedule confronting each firm has a kink at the level of the conventionally established price and the marginal-revenue schedule is discontinuous at the corresponding output." Oskar Lange, *Price Flexibility and Employment* (Bloomington: Principia Press, 1944), pp. 40 ff.

[45] In this connection, cf. p. 168, where it was pointed out that moderate changes in the discount rate may have a negligible effect on the cost of making a bank loan.

changing customer loan rates in accordance with changing discount rates. Since term loans are growing in importance, this direct impact of discount rates on customer rates is important.

3. To the extent that member bank borrowing is profit motivated, customer loan rates are *potentially* influenced when discount rate changes affect member bank costs. Such changes in cost are passed on to customers, generally speaking, only by the larger banks in the large cities. Rates of country banks tend to be fairly rigid because of monopolistic elements in the internal structure of the markets in which these banks operate. Since their rates tend not to vary, the effect of changes in their costs is deflected to their profit margins and affects also, no doubt, the availability of credit by affecting decisions regarding negotiation of marginal loans.[46]

4. So far as concerns member banks that borrow only for need, the central bank can potentially affect customer loan rates indirectly by forcing need borrowing through open market operations. Customer loan rates of debt-sensitive banks can be expected to reflect the fact of their indebtedness. There is, however, a considerable range in the sensitivity to indebtedness exhibited by different elements of the banking community. The large New York City banks are extremely sensitive to indebtedness; the country banks are least so; and all others are ranged somewhere between. Furthermore, sensitivity to indebtedness is not invariant with the business cycle. During good times, even "sensitive" banks are less concerned about indebtedness than during bad times. This cyclical variation in sensitivity to indebtedness tends to reduce (or at least to delay) the impact of Reserve bank action on customer loan rates. The Federal Reserve System is most likely to exert a restrictive pressure on the banking system when it feels that a prosperity threatens to degenerate into an inflation. But this is precisely the phase of the business cycle when even sensitive banks are least agitated about their central bank indebtedness. Thus the reinforcing effect in raising customer loan rates, which large bank sensitivity to indebtedness would otherwise induce, tends to be diminished or delayed. Conversely, the central bank is likely to

---

[46] The credit instruments of the Federal Reserve System are normally made effective by their impact on marginal loans. Cf. Patman Report, Vol. I, p. 383.

It is well to keep in mind that, as stated by the Reserve Bank presidents, "It is never possible to measure quantitatively the effects on the volume of bank credit of general credit control actions. To so measure the effects would require definite knowledge of what would have happened had no action been taken, and that must necessarily remain a matter of informed opinion rather than knowledge." Patman Report, Vol. II, p. 690–691. Accordingly, this analysis has stressed lines of causation rather than specific quantitative impacts.

use its powers to ease the credit situation during the deflationary phase of the cycle. During this period, normal sensitivity is accentuated and the reduction of customer loan rates is delayed. Eventually, reduced indebtedness would tend to lower customer loan rates, though probably with a lag.[47]

5. Discount rate changes and open market operations are manipulated jointly by the central banks. Accordingly, the customer loan rates of debt-sensitive banks which have been forced to borrow by central bank open market operations may reflect the change in member bank costs as well as the mere fact of indebtedness. Debt-sensitive banks are thus under a double pressure.

---

[47] The lagged effect on customer loan rates is owing to the fact that in the first instance, an improved reserve position enables "sensitive" banks to reduce their indebtedness at the Reserve Banks, *after which* they can "breathe more freely."

X

Profitability of Branch and Unit Banking

An examination of the profitability of different banks serves to integrate some of the earnings and cost analysis of branch and unit banks in earlier chapters. In a certain sense, profit data summarize the major activities of a business enterprise, because they reveal the net position of the firm in the interplay of prices, costs, and output. Hence, profit data are an important index of the degree of success that a firm achieves in its operations. Profit data are interesting for other reasons, too. Some consider profit figures as a clue to over-all firm efficiency; others, as a clue to market behavior. This chapter compares the profitability of branch and unit banks and tries to discover the reasons for the patterns that emerge.

Bank profitability can be measured in various ways: (1) net earnings on loans and investments, (2) net earnings on assets, and (3) net earnings on capital. The different profit ratios illuminate diverse aspects of bank operations and behavior. Earnings on loans and investments describe the net markup on bank output. Earnings on assets measure the basic earning power of a corporation. Earnings on capital measure profitability from the viewpoint of entry and exit. Accordingly, all three measures are examined in this chapter.

In each profit measure, the net earnings figures are *not* net of taxes. To exclude taxes might easily distort the underlying pattern of real earnings in various size banks, since absolute earnings are taxed at progressive rates. Similarly, the net earnings figures do not show charge-offs for losses and depreciation, nor do they take account of recoveries, because bank policies vary widely in such matters. In short, the net earnings figures are not strictly net profit

TABLE 29

Net Earnings from Current Operations Before Taxes as a Percentage of Loans and Investments, by Size and Kind of Bank, California, 1938–1950

Unit banks[a] (by size)	1938	1939	1940	1941	1942	1943	1944	1945	1946	1947	1948	1949	1950
Smallest	2.97	1.48	1.65	1.34	1.41	1.12	0.90	0.73	0.85	0.43	1.26	0.79	1.56
2	1.93	1.55	1.77	1.72	1.31	0.97	0.99	0.83	1.07	1.19	1.36	1.28	1.30
3	1.76	1.78	1.41	2.04	1.89	1.08	0.95	0.92	1.02	1.13	1.20	1.27	1.35
4	1.95	2.00	1.87	1.95	1.44	0.89	0.95	0.67	0.92	1.06	1.05	0.95	0.99
5	1.73	1.70	1.49	1.53	1.15	1.11	1.07	0.90	1.26	1.39	1.45	1.38	1.47
6	1.69	1.48	1.99	2.00	....	0.90	0.74	0.72	0.71	0.65	0.83	0.83	0.83
7	2.09	1.44	1.36	1.33	....	....	....	....	....	....	....	....	....
8	1.47	1.32	....	....	....	....	....	....	....	....	....	....	....
Unit bank average	1.84	1.70	1.67	1.79	1.54	1.00	0.95	0.83	1.01	1.11	1.24	1.16	1.29
Branch bank average	1.29	1.08	1.34	1.46	1.17	1.03	0.89	0.84	0.84	0.98	1.16	1.30	1.30

For sources and notes to table, see Appendix.
[a] See notes to table 16.

figures, because profit figures would introduce non- or extra-economic factors which reduce comparability for purposes of this study. In this study, the expression "profitability" must be interpreted with the foregoing qualifications.

NET EARNINGS ON LOANS AND INVESTMENTS

ALL BANKS

Net earnings from current operations as a percentage of loans and investments (table 29) are not strongly related to size of unit bank. In almost every year, the largest category of unit banks earned less on loans and investments than the smaller unit banks. Generally, however, earnings on loans and investments are not closely related to size of unit bank. Private examination of the profit data for the four branch banks also reveals no strong relationship between size of branch bank and net return on loans and investments. Furthermore, like the different size unit banks, the branch banks among themselves exhibit a wide range of variation in returns on loans and investments. With the exceptions of 1938–1940, branch banks as a group earned a higher return than the largest unit banks. In every year, however, the average figure for the branch banks was less than for the penultimate size group of unit banks. Specific attention is given to the comparison between branch banks and the largest category of unit banks in order to distinguish where possible between the effects of branch banking as a structural form and those from mere size of bank.

The pattern of earnings on loans and investments in the various bank categories depends upon: (1) the rates of return on loans and on investments, (2) the product mix, i.e., the relative importance of loans and investments (loans/loans and investments, and investments/loans and investments), (3) the size and relative importance of other current earnings, i.e., other current earnings/loans and investments, and (4) comparative unit costs in different categories of banks.

UNIT BANKS

Net earnings on loans and investments are not related to size of unit bank. This fact can be accounted for approximately as follows: In the first place, and contrary to some observations, different size unit banks earned similar rates of return on securities as a whole, with some exceptions in the earlier years.[1] Moreover, the

[1] Cf. Appendix table I.

relative volumes of securities (i.e., investments/loans and investments) in different size banks is also not related to size of bank (except that the large unit banks had the highest investment ratios).[2] Approximately, therefore, the contribution of the earnings on securities to the net returns on loans and investments for different size unit banks tends to cancel out.

By contrast with securities, average returns on loans and discounts tend to vary inversely with size of bank, although the relative volume of loans and discounts is not related to size of bank, except that the largest unit banks consistently had the lowest ratios. On the basis of loan earnings alone, net earnings on loans and investments would tend to vary inversely with size of bank, and would be particularly emphasized in the case of the largest unit banks.

The analysis of price policy (chapter vii) has shown that the pattern of loan earnings is a function of the different loan mix, different size mix, and different market structures of banking markets in which different size unit banks operate. The particular loan mix and size mix which predominate in small unit banks tend to produce high returns on loans. Although high loan rates are partly related to the high costs and (possibly) high risk factors in small-bank loan portfolios, the high return is partly the result of the semimonopolistic or oligopolistic markets in which the loans of small unit banks are predominantly made. At the other extreme, the loan mix of the largest unit banks tends to be more heavily concentrated in business loans. Moreover, the size mix of large banks is heavily weighted (in dollar volume) with large loans. Both cost and risk elements in the loan rate are minimal for very large business loans. In fact, the risk on prime loans is all but absent, and direct loan costs are separately covered by a loan fee. The low loan return in large unit banks implied by the foregoing is further accentuated by the presence of more competitive market structures than those which characterize small borrower markets. The market structure tendencies thus reinforce similar tendencies stemming from the loan and size mix which typically characterize large unit bank loan portfolios. Hence, the largest unit banks have lower earnings on loans and investments than the small unit banks.

The influence of other current earnings (miscellaneous earnings) tends to confirm the pattern just described. Generally, miscellaneous earnings are not clearly related to size of bank except that the small*est* banks have the highest ratios and the larg*est* banks have

[2] Cf. Appendix table J.

the lowest ratios.[3] This pattern is no doubt owing to the fact that "other current earnings" include items like service charges on checking accounts and collection charges. Among the depositors of the largest unit banks, service charges are not explicitly paid by many large depositors whose accounts are very large and valuable to the bank, whereas the reverse is true in the smallest unit banks. Moreover, the smallest unit banks are often not members of the Federal Reserve System and can enhance their earnings by collection and other charges which are prohibited to member banks. In the middle-size bank categories, miscellaneous earnings are often very similar. Generally, then, miscellaneous earnings leave the pattern of net earnings on loans and investments unchanged. Similarly, the exceptionally high miscellaneous earnings of the smallest banks and the very low miscellaneous earnings of the largest banks confirm tendencies given by the earnings on loans and discounts.

The earnings pattern indicated by the various components of earnings is compensated, however, by the unit cost pattern of different size unit banks. Because of the different loan mix and size mix in different banks, unit costs tend to vary inversely with size of bank. The inverse variation of unit costs cancels any tendency of the individual earnings components to produce a distinctive yield among different size banks. Hence, the pattern discussed earlier in which no particular relation is evident between net return on loans and investments and size of bank. The only exception is the case of the *largest* unit banks which almost always have the lowest net earnings on loans and investments. Their very low earnings are owing to the multiple impact of low average interest rates on loans and discounts, low volume of loans and discounts, and low earnings from miscellaneous sources. Even the comparatively low unit cost ratios of the largest unit banks cannot sufficiently counteract the combined tendency of these factors for low earnings. The largest unit banks are thus left with a distinctively low ranking in their net earnings on loans and investments as compared with other unit banks.

BRANCH BANKS

Net earnings on loans and investments are not particularly related to size of branch bank. Except for some of the early years, the effective interest rates on securities do not show much variation, and, in any case, there is no pattern between rate of return on securities

[3] Cf. Appendix table K.

and size of branch bank. The relative volume of securities is inversely related to branch bank size with the exception of American Trust in the early years and Security in the later years. With these exceptions, if security earnings dominated net earnings, they would tend to produce a pattern of inverse variation between net earnings per dollar of loan and investment and size of branch bank. However, the large branch banks generally earned higher average interest rates on loans and discounts than the small branch banks. The large branch banks have numerous branch offices in small towns and rural areas, and, to this extent, their loan and size mix tend to resemble those of small unit banks. The large branch banks thus earn higher rates on their loans than small branch banks because of their particular loan and size mix. Furthermore, with the exceptions given earlier,[4] loans/loans and investments also tend to vary directly with size of branch bank. Like the loan and size mix, the product mix, too, is directly related to the branch organization for reasons analogous to those set forth in connection with loan earnings. If loan earnings and relative loan volumes dominated net earnings, net earnings on loans and investments would be directly related to size of branch bank.

With the exception of Security–First National, this also would hold for miscellaneous earnings, which vary directly with size of branch bank. The absolute range of miscellaneous earnings in different years varied between .228 and .661 percentage points, with a mean absolute difference of .363 percentage points. This pattern of miscellaneous earnings among branch banks is directly related to their branch type of organization. Miscellaneous earnings of the large branch banks resemble those of small unit banks. However, in the case of branch banks another consideration is involved. Miscellaneous earnings include earnings from trust accounts, and the large branch systems have an important trust business. Moreover, the very large branch banks have a higher proportion of bona fide prime loans than the smaller branch banks. This is a function, not directly of bank structure, but rather of size, since prime borrowers are very large borrowers and naturally turn to the largest banks to transact their business. This affects miscellaneous earnings, because the cost of handling such loans is typically covered by a separate loan fee rather than being included in the rate of interest—and the loan fee appears under the heading of miscellaneous earnings.

[4] Cf. p. 88.

As in previous comparisons, the high earnings from loans and discounts and from miscellaneous earnings are compensated by the high unit costs of large branch banks, by the random relation of percentage earnings on securities to size of banks, and by the exceptions to the direct relation of loan rates and size of bank discussed above. As a result, there is no distinctive ranking pattern of net earnings on loans and investments among different size branch banks.

BRANCH AND UNIT BANKS

Although net earnings on loans and investments are not related to size of unit bank, it is useful for this analysis to compare earnings ratios of branch banks with those of the largest category of unit banks. As a group, branch banks usually enjoyed higher net earnings on loans and investments than the largest category of unit banks. This earnings pattern can be explained by a procedure similar to that employed for unit and branch banks separately. On both government securities and other securities, branch banks usually earned less than the largest unit banks (though the differences were often small). Although branch banks had a higher percentage of higher yielding "other securities," they had a lower percentage of lower yielding United States government securities, and a generally lower percentage of total securities than the largest unit banks. It appears probable that the contribution of the total earnings on securities to net return on loans and investments would account for no significant distinctions between the two groups in profitability on loans and investments, because differences in securities earnings were often small. If anything, there is a presumption of lower profitability on loans and investment for branch banks based solely on their securities earnings.

The situation is different for loans and discounts. Branch banks earned more on loans and discounts than the largest unit banks, because the former earn higher average rates on their loans and sustain loans and discounts at a relatively (i.e., relative to the volume of loans and investments) higher volume than the largest unit banks. As already explained, this is because the product, loan, and size mix of branch banks in many ways resembles that of smaller unit banks, a resemblance that reflects bank structure rather than size of bank. The high loan earnings in branch banks are further enhanced by their average miscellaneous earnings, which are also usually higher than those of the largest unit banks. These high earnings of branch banks are only partly compensated

by high unit costs.[5] The result is that branch bank net earnings
on loans and investments are generally higher than for the largest
unit banks.

With only a few exceptions, branch banks on the average earned
lower rates of return on loans and investments than the average
of unit banks. This was not owing primarily to the branch bank
earnings on securities although they were about the same or lower
for branch banks than for unit banks as a group. The different
earnings on loans and investments between branch banks and the
intermediate and smaller unit banks is largely explained by their
respective product mix and their comparative loan earnings. From
1938 through 1942, the branch banks typically had lower loan
ratios (loans/loans and investments) than any but the largest unit
banks. 1943 was a transition year, and between 1944–1950, the
branch banks usually had higher loan ratios than any of the unit
banks. During the entire period, however, the branch banks as a
group earned lower average interest rates on their loans than any
of the unit banks (except for the largest unit banks). The low
loan earnings were, of course, because of the particular product,
loan, and size mix in branch banks as compared to the medium-
size and smaller banks. Specifically, for the period as a whole,
branch banks had higher loan ratios than the unit banks. In many
ways, too, as a function of their bank structure, the loan and size
mix in branch banks resembles that in medium-size and small unit
banks. However, because of their great size, the branch banks' size
mix also contains huge loans which carry low interest rates. The
weight of these low-interest large loans was sufficient in dollar
volume to depress the average interest rate of branch banks below
that of the medium-size and small unit banks.[6]

The unit costs of branch banks were lower than any but those
of the largest unit banks, partly because of branch bank size mix,
partly because of the economies of specialization. Although the
large loans in branch bank portfolios help to reduce branch bank
unit costs, they hold down average interest rates, and the result
is lower net earnings on loans and investments by branch banks
than by most of the medium-size and small banks. Finally, branch
bank miscellaneous earnings were usually less per dollar of loan
and investment than in the medium and small unit banks.

---

[5] In absolute terms, branch bank unit costs are, of course, higher than those of the
largest unit banks.

[6] Significantly, this was least true of the large branch banks and most true of the
smaller branch banks.

In summary, there were diverse tendencies at work in determining the relation of unit and branch banks' earnings on loans and investments. The relatively greater importance of loans in the branch bank portfolios, and their generally lower costs[7] would, other things being equal, have made their earnings per dollar of loan and investment greater than for the average of unit banks. However, the branch banks' lower (or similar) rate of earnings on securities, their lower miscellaneous earnings, and their lower rate of earnings on loans worked in the opposite direction. As a result, branch bank net earnings on their loans and investments were lower, or about the same as unit bank net earnings for the study period as a whole.

NET EARNINGS ON ASSETS

UNIT BANKS

Table 30 shows the net earnings from current operations (before taxes) as a ratio of total assets for different size banks, both unit and branch. The table reveals no strong relationship between size of unit bank and earnings on assets except that the penultimate category almost always had the highest rate of earnings on assets. The largest category of unit banks had smaller earnings on assets than most of the other unit bank categories. Although there is no clear-cut pattern of earnings on assets by size of bank, a ranking of unit banks by earnings on assets is almost identical to the ranking of unit banks by net earnings on loans and investments. The main difference between them is owing to the blurring of the assets pattern as a result of the identity of earnings on assets of different size banks in various years. The highly similar ranking between earnings on assets and earnings on loans and investments suggests that the influence of the load factor is negligible. The load factor was, of course, randomly distributed by size of bank. However, the mean absolute difference in the range of the load factor among different size unit banks for the years under study amounted to 8.1 percentage points.[8] Despite these considerable differences, the assets pattern is basically unchanged from the pattern of earnings on loans and investments. It would appear, therefore, that the different load factors among different size unit banks are significantly less important than the pattern of net earnings on loans and investments in determining the pattern of net earnings on assets.

---

[7] However, cost differences were greatest in precisely those years when loans/loans and investments were least in the branch banks' favor, from an earning standpoint.

[8] Cf. p. 57.

TABLE 30

Net Earnings from Current Operations Before Taxes as a Percentage of Total Assets, by Size and Kind of Bank, California, 1938–1950

Unit banks [a] (by size)	1938	1939	1940	1941	1942	1943	1944	1945	1946	1947	1948	1949	1950
Smallest.........	2.07	1.08	1.02	0.83	0.8	0.7	0.6	0.5	0.6	0.3	0.88	0.53	1.06
2................	1.36	1.02	1.25	1.11	0.8	0.6	0.7	0.6	0.8	0.9	1.02	0.97	0.98
3................	1.25	1.26	0.89	1.26	1.2	0.7	0.7	0.7	0.8	0.9	0.95	1.0	1.06
4................	1.34	1.40	1.25	1.26	0.9	0.6	0.7	0.5	0.7	0.8	0.80	0.73	0.75
5................	1.27	1.17	0.97	1.00	0.8	0.8	0.8	0.7	1.0	1.1	1.13	1.08	1.20
6................	1.19	1.02	1.35	1.30	.....	0.63	0.53	0.53	0.53	0.47	0.60	0.50	0.63
7................	1.45	1.01	0.92	0.88	.....	.....	.....	.....	.....	.....	.....	.....	.....
8................	1.03	0.93	.....	.....	.....	.....	.....	.....	.....	.....	.....	.....	.....
Unit bank average......	1.30	1.18	1.11	1.13	0.95	0.65	0.68	0.61	0.77	0.84	0.94	0.88	0.98
Branch bank average...	1.00	0.82	0.97	1.06	0.8	0.8	0.7	0.7	0.7	0.8	0.90	1.20	1.05

For sources and notes to table, see Appendix.
[a] See notes to table 16.

BRANCH BANKS

The branch banks show no distinctive pattern in which net earnings on assets are related to size of branch bank. Like the unit banks, however, the ranking of branch banks by net returns on assets was practically identical to the ranking by net returns on loans and investments. This fact is less surprising for the branch banks than it was for the unit banks. Although the load factor of the branch banks tends to vary directly with size of branch bank, the mean of the absolute differences in the range was only about 5.4 percentage points among different size branch banks during the years under study.[9] Accordingly, any tendency for the load factor to impress a distinctive pattern on the ranking of banks by net returns on assets is again overcome by the effect of the net return on loans and investments.

BRANCH AND UNIT BANKS

In almost every year, the average net earnings on assets for all branch banks was higher than for the largest category of unit banks (table 30).[10] This pattern on assets follows from the fact that branch banks have higher average load factors and higher earnings on loans and investments than the largest unit banks.[11] The influence on the assets pattern of the high load factor among branch banks is clearly evident in the percentage differences between branch banks and largest unit banks on net earnings over loans and investments as compared with net earnings over assets. On the average, the branch banks earned 20 per cent more on their loans and investments than the largest unit banks. On the other hand, the branch banks earned 35 per cent more on their assets than the largest unit banks. In other words, the high load factor in branch banks almost doubled the mean percentage difference between the two categories of banks on net earnings on assets as compared with net earnings on loans and investments. These results are not surprising because the factors which influence the size of the load factor are related to the size of the bank and the type of its organization (i.e., branch or unit). Branch banks, because of their type of organization and of their size, have a load factor sufficiently greater than the largest unit banks to affect sig-

---

[9] Cf. p. 57.

[10] It is worth mentioning again, however, that the largest unit banks tended to have low ratios of net earnings on assets as compared with other size unit banks.

[11] Indeed, as stated earlier, even the branch banks with the lowest load factor among branch banks had a higher load factor than had the largest unit banks.

TABLE 31

Net Earnings from Current Operations Before Taxes as a Percentage of Total Capital Funds, by Size and Kind of Bank, California, 1938–1950

Unit banks[a] (by size)	1938	1939	1940	1941	1942	1943	1944	1945	1946	1947	1948	1949	1950
Smallest	11.6	6.3	7.8	6.4	8.4	8.2	10.0	8.2	10.5	5.4	12.8	8.5	13.0
2	9.6	8.3	10.6	10.6	7.9	8.9	12.5	14.0	17.6	19.1	18.2	16.0	15.2
3	9.4	9.7	9.8	11.2	9.3	9.7	13.0	14.4	18.7	18.7	17.3	16.2	16.3
4	11.8	10.8	10.8	12.2	10.9	9.9	13.3	12.0	16.0	16.5	15.6	13.7	13.6
5	11.4	10.4	8.3	10.9	10.9	13.2	15.6	17.2	25.3	24.8	24.9	21.8	23.4
6	10.3	10.2	13.7	13.2	....	16.0	13.4	14.3	13.5	10.8	11.9	11.8	12.3
7	15.0	13.3	12.0	12.8	....	....	....	....	....	....	....	....	....
8	11.0	10.4	....	....	....	....	....	....	....	....	....	....	....
Unit bank average	10.9	10.1	10.2	11.0	9.0	10.0	12.5	13.8	17.6	17.8	17.2	15.0	15.5
Branch bank average	13.2	12.1	11.0	12.1	10.9	13.2	14.4	14.6	15.8	16.6	18.9	20.0	19.6

For sources and notes to table, see Appendix.
[a] See notes to table 16.

nificantly the comparative net earnings on assets as compared to what they would be if the earnings/assets pattern were exclusively dominated by the earnings/loans and investments ratio.

For the period as a whole (1938–1950), the branch bank average ratio of net earnings on assets is neither distinctively higher nor distinctively lower than that for the average of unit banks; the branch bank average was sometimes above and sometimes below the unit bank average.[12] On their net earnings on loans and investments, however, branch banks were somewhat lower than the unit bank average in nine out of thirteen years. However, the average load factor in the branch banks was invariably higher than that in any of the unit banks. The influence of the load factor was sufficient, moreover, to raise the branch bank average earnings on assets to a level comparable to the average performance of the unit banks, although the branch banks earned somewhat less on their loans and investments than the average of unit banks. Again, so far as the load factor is related to branch organization and size of bank, these two factors are important in explaining the earnings/assets performance of branch as against unit banks.

NET EARNINGS ON CAPITAL

Table 31 shows net current operating earnings as a percentage of total capital funds for different size banks. As explained earlier, corporate income taxes are included in the "net" earnings. No doubt the level of taxes affects the entry and exit decisions of different size firms, and in this sense should not have been omitted. However, since tax burdens have varied significantly over the period in question, it seemed advisable to include taxes in net current earnings. Given the net returns on assets, the returns on capital are a function of the ratio of equity capital to borrowed funds (essentially deposits, time and demand). Since business and financial policy decisions affect this ratio, the resulting figure is partly arbitrary. Partly, however, the division between equity capital and borrowed capital is a function also of size of bank and of bank structure. Profitability on capital is particularly interesting so far as it reflects these other factors.

ALL BANKS

The unit banks reveal a rather mixed picture between size of bank and return on capital (table 31). There are only two definite

---

[12] Exact comparisons are difficult, because from 1942–1947, the Federal Reserve ratios for earnings on assets were rounded off to one decimal only, instead of the customary two decimals.

TABLE 32

Capital Funds as a Percentage of Total Deposits, by Size and Kind of Bank, California, 1938-1950

Unit banks [a] (by size)	1938	1939	1940	1941	1942	1943	1944	1945	1946	1947	1948	1949	1950
Smallest	21.8	30.4	18.4	16.6	11.3	8.8	6.3	6.9	7.5	10.0	7.7	8.8	9.5
2	19.5	17.7	14.7	13.5	11.6	7.3	6.1	4.8	5.0	5.5	6.1	6.7	7.7
3	17.5	17.2	16.1	14.2	10.5	7.9	5.9	5.3	4.9	5.5	6.1	6.9	7.1
4	15.6	15.9	13.6	12.6	9.4	7.1	5.5	4.7	4.7	5.1	5.5	5.6	5.9
5	14.4	13.7	15.8	10.5	7.4	6.2	5.0	4.1	4.2	4.9	5.2	5.6	5.8
6	11.9	11.8	11.3	11.1	....	5.3	4.9	4.4	4.8	5.4	5.3	5.7	5.7
7	11.2	11.4	8.0	7.4	....	....	....	....	....	....	....	....	....
8	9.6	9.5	....	....	....	....	....	....	....	....	....	....	....
Unit bank average	15.7	15.5	14.7	12.5	10.6	7.4	5.9	5.1	5.0	5.6	6.0	6.7	7.2
Branch bank average	9.3	9.2	10.3	9.9	8.8	6.6	5.7	5.1	4.6	4.9	5.1	5.5	5.7

For sources and notes to table, see Appendix.
[a] See notes to table 16.

threads in the total picture: In most years, the smallest size category of unit bank had the lowest returns. At the opposite extreme, the penultimate size category of banks had the highest returns on its capital in almost every year. All other size categories, however, reveal no clear-cut pattern. With the exceptions mentioned, any particular size category of unit bank may rank high in some years, low in others, and in an intermediate position in still other years.

By contrast with the unit banks, the large branch banks tend to earn higher rates of return on their capital than the smaller branch banks. The two largest branch banks shared top position almost evenly between themselves, with the largest branch bank having the edge on more years of highest returns, particularly in the postwar period, 1946–1950. The smallest branch bank earned considerably less on its capital than the most profitable branch bank. The average earnings of the branch banks are approximately the same as those of the largest category of unit banks, except for the postwar period (1946–1950) when the branch bank average pulled definitely ahead of the largest unit banks. Significantly, the branch banks as a group generally earned less than the penultimate size category of unit banks. In particular, the smallest of the branch banks had returns on capital which were usually on a par with those of the smallest category of unit banks, except for the postwar period. It should be stated in this connection that although the unit banks exhibited no pattern among themselves, the smallest category of unit banks usually had the lowest returns on capital. However, in all but two years, the branch banks as a group earned more per dollar of capital than the average of unit banks. Thus, the "profitability" of the branch banks as a group increases considerably when earnings on capital are substituted for earnings on loans and investments, or even earnings on assets.

Given the net earnings on assets of different categories of banks, the particular ratios of net current earnings on capital funds are a function of the ratio of capital funds to total assets, or, alternatively (although not strictly accurate mathematically) of capital funds to total deposits.

UNIT BANKS

Table 32 shows a pattern of inverse variation between size of unit bank and the ratio of capital to total deposits. This pattern is to be expected, because size of unit bank is related to the size of city in which the bank is situated. Smaller cities and towns are generally less wealthy and have smaller populations than larger cities and metropolitan areas. Hence, there is a limit to the amount of deposits which a bank can attract in such areas. Accordingly, the bank must rely relatively more heavily on its equity capital than on its deposits (both time and demand) in making loans than is true of the larger unit bank in larger cities and metropolitan centers. Notwithstanding the pattern of inverse variation between size of unit bank and its capital-deposit ratio, unit bank returns on capital show no striking pattern by size of bank except for the smallest size unit banks and the penultimate category. The former tends to have the lowest returns on capital in each year because the smallest banks have the highest ratio of capital to total deposits. Indeed, although the capital-deposit ratio varies inversely by size of bank, it is actually most strongly pronounced between the smallest category of banks and all larger unit banks. Despite the discernible pattern of variation, the ratio of capital/total deposits decreases less among other size categories than between the first and second smallest size categories in most instances. Thus, although there is no discernible pattern of variation by size of bank on net return on assets, the exceptionally high capital-deposit ratio of the smallest banks gives them a distinctively low ratio of net earnings on capital funds. On the other hand, the penultimate category of unit banks tends to have the highest returns on capital partly because its capital-deposit ratio is quite low, especially during the latter part of the period, and partly because its net earnings on assets ratio was generally highest of any of the unit banks. Among the intermediate size categories, size of bank tends to vary inversely with the capital-deposit ratio. In most years, however, the capital-deposit ratios are not strikingly dissimilar. Hence, earnings on capital are not clearly related to size of bank among the intermediate size bank categories.

BRANCH BANKS

Net earnings on capital vary widely among the different branch banks. The smallest branch bank, in particular, often earned much less on its capital than the larger branch banks. For the period as a whole, there was a distinct tendency for net earnings on capital funds to vary directly with size of branch bank. This variation could not have been owing to the earnings on assets of the various branch banks, since those earnings were not related to size of bank. The pattern of variation of earnings on capital was owing rather to the pattern on the capital-deposits ratio. With the exception of American Trust (which had the lowest capital-deposit ratio), branch bank size varied inversely with the size of the capital-deposit ratio. The smallest branch bank earned distinctively low returns on its capital because it had the highest capital-deposit ratio. The high capital-deposit ratio of the smallest branch bank was partly a result of deliberate policy. The management of Anglo Bank refused to accept and hold large deposits on which interest must be paid unless the bank received collateral advantages such as profitable commercial business.[13]

Although Anglo Bank's management followed a policy that resulted in a high capital-deposit ratio, an inverse variation of the capital-deposit ratio by size of branch bank might have been expected from a consideration of the other factors that affect that ratio. The capital-deposit ratio varied inversely with size of unit bank because size of unit bank tends to be related to size of city, and the objective potential volume of both demand and time deposits is conditioned by the size and wealth of the community in which a bank is located. Since large branch systems have many branch offices in smaller towns and rural areas, this fact alone should have resulted in a capital-deposit ratio which varied *directly* (rather than as it actually does, inversely) with size of branch bank.

For a variety of reasons, however, the capital-deposit ratio varies inversely with size of branch bank. First, the larger the branch bank, the greater its prestige in the area it serves. As a result, the deposits of wealthy individuals and of large corporations gravitate to such banks. Moreover, large banks in metropolitan centers often act as correspondents for country banks and carry the deposits of the latter. Thus, mere size of bank tends to lower the capital-deposit ratio. Second, the larger the area served by a branch bank, the greater are the possibilities for successful exploitation of the mobility of funds inherent in a branch type organization. This mobility of funds implies a reduced liquidity need of the very large branch bank as compared to smaller branch organizations. Correspondingly, the large branch bank can afford to maintain a lower ratio of cash to total deposits, which means a correspondingly greater expansion of its loans. The capital-deposit ratio in a bank depends not only on the volume of primary deposits (both time and demand) but also on derivative deposits. An increase in its loans because of fuller utilization of its resources results in a reduction of the capital-deposit ratio. Finally, the larger the branch

[13] In so doing, the management of the Bank was aware that "... this policy results in decreased deposit totals ..." Anglo Bank, *Annual Report,* January 1940, p. 6. Anglo Bank further discouraged savings accounts by eliminating the payment of interest on such accounts unless the amount on deposit exceeded $50.

bank, the more likely is it to enjoy flow-back deposits. Thus, with given resources, a branch organization can safely expand its loans still further (and, correspondingly, its derivative deposits) with a resulting further reduction in the capital-deposit ratio.

Other things being equal, the capital-deposit ratios in branch banks might be expected to vary inversely with size of bank for the reasons just given. In the American Trust Company, the unusually low capital-deposit ratio is no doubt partly a reflection of its aggressive loan policy[14] and the corresponding volume of its derivative deposits. Moreover, although American Trust is not the largest of the branch banks, the area it serves offers excellent opportunities for diversification and mobility of funds with a correspondingly reduced need for liquidity. Hence, it has a high loan ratio and a large volume of derivative deposits, with a correspondingly low capital-deposit ratio.

The capital-deposit ratio has no important effect on the pattern of net earnings on capital of unit banks. In branch banks, however, the pattern of capital-deposit ratios imposes a pattern on the earnings-capital ratio despite the fact that no pattern for the earnings-assets ratio can be found among the branch banks.

BRANCH AND UNIT BANKS

Branch banks as a group earned approximately the same returns on their capital as the largest category of unit banks, except for the postwar period (1946–1950) when the branch banks earned more than the largest unit banks. This is because branch banks earned more on their assets than the largest unit banks, especially in the postwar period. Moreover, the capital-deposit ratio of branch banks was somewhat higher than that of the largest unit banks in the early years and about the same in the postwar period. Thus the pattern of earnings on capital between the two groups is dominated by the earnings/assets ratios in the postwar period and by the high capital-deposit ratios of the branch banks in all other years. For the period as a whole, both factors were important. Although the factors mentioned earlier operate to lower the capital-deposit ratios of branch banks, the location of branch offices in many smaller towns and rural areas tends to raise the ratios. Compared to almost any category of the unit banks except the largest, the factors operating to lower the branch bank capital-deposit ratio will dominate. Compared to the category of largest unit banks which are in metropolitan areas and, hence, have access to a large

---
[14] Cf. p. 90.

potential volume of deposits, the fact that branches also operate in smaller towns dominates. Small town deposit volume is generally low. Moreover, the branch system must maintain certain minimum legal capital requirements to cover branches in small towns. Thus, the branch bank capital-deposit ratio is correspondingly raised relative to the largest unit banks.

The branch banks as a group earned more per dollar of capital than the average of unit banks in all but two years. The branch bank average earnings on assets were neither distinctively higher nor distinctively lower than the average of unit banks. However, the capital-deposit ratio of branch banks as a group was lower than the unit bank average. As a result, branch bank earnings on capital were higher than the unit bank average. In this case, the capital-deposit ratio is the dominating influence on the ratio of earnings on capital.

SUMMARY

This analysis of the "profitability" of unit banks, branch banks, and unit versus branch banks emphasizes the importance of distinguishing among alternative standards or measures in judging banking performance. Branch banks generally earned greater net returns on their capital than unit banks. By this measure, therefore, branch banks are the more profitable form of bank organization (whereas size of unit bank alone did not greatly affect profitability on capital). However, profitability on capital is greatly influenced by the relation of capital to total deposits, a relationship that is largely a function of size and banking organization, rather than of individual performance. When the influence of the capital-deposits ratio is excluded, as in the use of a net earnings/assets measure of profitability, branch bank earnings are less easily distinguished from unit bank earnings because they are lower in about 50 per cent of the cases, and higher in about 50 per cent.[15]

An assets measure of profitability is influenced in part by the load factor, which is primarily related to banking organization (rather than to individual bank performance). Earnings on loans and investments are independent of the load factor and thus reveal a different aspect of comparative profitability. When net earnings per dollar of loan and investment are compared for unit and branch banks, branch banks are generally less profitable than unit banks.

---

[15] Unit bank earnings are not significantly changed in ranking by size of bank when earnings are changed from a capital to an asset basis.

Specifically, branch banks earned less per dollar of loans and investments than unit banks in nine out of thirteen years, and in two of the four years in which they exceeded the unit banks, they were only slightly higher. In terms of earnings on loans and investments, branch banks cannot be considered on a par with unit banks, as they would if earnings on assets were the basic measure.[16] Therefore, both the load factor, and more importantly, the capital-deposit ratio heavily influence the comparative profitability on capital of unit and branch banking. For various reasons,[17] branch banks do not earn more than unit banks on their loans and investments, and are only of average profitability in terms of their earnings on assets. It is only when the leverage of a low capital-deposits ratio is admitted as an influence on profit figures that branch banks emerge as the more profitable form of organization.

From some points of view, average branch and unit bank figures are incomplete bases of comparison, irrespective of whether loans and investments, assets, or capital is the standard employed. For example, instead of comparing branch banks with all unit banks, it is preferable for certain purposes to compare branch banks with those unit banks of most nearly comparable size, i.e., the largest unit banks. This analysis has shown that branch banks are, on the whole, more profitable than the largest unit banks irrespective of whether a loan and investment, asset, or a capital measure is the criterion of profitability.[18] The basic superiority of branch bank earnings over those of the largest unit banks is established by their high earnings per dollar of loans and investments. Neither the load factor nor the capital-deposit ratio significantly alters the comparative profit relations[19] on assets and capital, respectively, from that established by earnings on loans and investments. The only exception concerns the early years of the study when the capital-deposit ratio was sufficiently important to reverse the relationship of branch and unit banks as measured by earnings on assets. It should be observed in this connection that the differences in the earnings on loans and investments between branch banks and the largest unit banks were quite small in the early part of

---

[16] Again, no significant changes in ranking among unit banks occur when profits are switched from an assets to a loans and investment measure.

[17] Cf. p. 180.

[18] In terms of earnings on capital, branch banks are strikingly superior only in the postwar period.

[19] However, the load factor does *increase* the basic profitability of branch banks by raising their earnings on assets higher than on loans and investments, compared with the largest unit banks. It does not, however, change their *relation* with the largest unit banks—branch banks are superior in either case.

the study period compared to the differences in the later part of the period. Generally, however, the pattern of earnings on loans and investments is sufficiently important by itself to stamp a similar pattern on the earnings per dollar of capital between the two categories of banks. Thus, the superior profitability of branch banks as compared with that of the largest unit banks must be traced back to the key operating factors which determine earnings on loans and investments—the average rate of interest on loans, the average return on securities, the product mix, size mix, loan mix, and unit costs.

In some contexts, the critical comparison between branch banks and unit banks does not involve all unit banks, nor even the largest, but only the most profitable category of unit banks. The penultimate size category is the most profitable unit bank measured by its earnings on loans and investments. In nine out of thirteen years, its earnings surpassed those of any other unit banks, often by a substantial margin. Its fundamentally superior earnings position is confirmed when earnings are measured on either an assets or a capital basis. It leads all other unit banks on an asset basis in eleven years; and on a capital basis it holds a commanding superiority in many of the eleven years during which it had the highest unit bank earnings. When compared to branch banks as a group, the penultimate size unit banks earned more per dollar of loans and investments in all years of the study period. On an asset basis, the penultimate size banks were more profitable in ten years and equally profitable in two more years. On a capital basis their earnings surpassed the earnings of branch banks in eleven years and matched them in two other years. Hence, there is definitely a size of unit bank that is more profitable than branch banks as a group, by all three measures of profitability. Both size and structure contain certain elements that enhance general profitability of a bank and others that reduce it. In the penultimate size category of unit banks, an optimal combination of profit-increasing factors is achieved as compared to branch banks as a group.

In short, profitability is not an unambiguous concept. In the first place, profitability of given banks varies, depending upon the particular measure of profitability employed. Second, even with a given measure of profitability, it is not possible to state precisely whether branch or unit banks are the more profitable. That question hinges on the choice of banks in each group. Although it is true that branch banks on the average are more profitable than unit banks on the average, the use of an average masks the heterogeneous performance of the component parts. In attempting to appraise the comparative profitability of branch and unit banking, the choice of the proper base as well as the relevant banks to be compared will depend upon the context in which the comparisons are made.

XI
Entry

"FREEDOM OF ENTRY into the commercial banking business . . . is an essential condition . . . (and) in most circumstances a sufficient condition of effective competition in it."[1] Since entry conditions are closely related to market structures and market performance of an industry, an examination of entry conditions in California banking is essential to this study. Free entry in particular is alleged to guarantee the absence of those monopoly features most generally held to be socially undesirable, viz., discrimination, excessive profits, inefficiency, malallocation of resources, and the like.

THE CONCEPT OF ENTRY

DEFINITION OF ENTRY

Free (ready, or easy) entry has been variously defined by different writers. Since definitions must be judged by pragmatic and heuristic criteria, the particular definition selected will vary, depending upon the context in which it is employed. At the outset, a succinct definition, like that provided by Robert Triffin, is most useful. Free entry exists "when competitors are able to arise and produce, at the same cost as firm i, a commodity economically homogeneous with the one produced by i. Both elements, of cost identity and product homogeneity, are necessary to the definition."[2] For the possibility of producing an identical good, but at a cost which may be superior, Triffin reserves the expression "homogeneous entry," whereas the freedom to produce imperfect substitutes is termed "heterogeneous entry."[3] Although the choice of name labels for concepts is hardly of prime importance, the great-

---

[1] Statement by Neil Jacoby, Transamerica Hearings, p. 8579.
[2] Robert Triffin, *Monopolistic Competition and General Equilibrium Theory* (Cambridge: Harvard University Press, 1941), p. 120.
[3] *Loc. cit.*

est possible precision in the concepts which the labels suggest is of critical importance. It is worth emphasizing, therefore, that the "freedom of entry" mentioned in the opening sentence of this chapter must be interpreted as "free entry" in Triffin's sense. As Triffin rightly points out, "many of the results traditionally associated with free entry are valid only when free entry is so defined."[4] It should also be noticed that if free entry is vaguely defined and could be satisfied retrospectively by little more than the fact that firms have entered a field, then there can be no *necessary* confidence in the competitive results which purportedly ensue from free entry.

ENTRY AND THE NUMBER OF ALTERNATIVE SOURCES

Entry into banking can take many different forms with differing impact on existing market situations. In unit bank entry, the matter is usually straightforward: a new bank is established in a community, and that is all there is to it. Branch bank entry exhibits many more possibilities. A branch bank can enter a community with a *de novo* branch, i.e., with a wholly new branch of the branch bank system. Or, the branch bank can acquire an existing unit bank and either convert the acquired bank into a branch or liquidate the acquired bank and transfer its assets and liabilities to an existing branch in the area. When the unit bank is liquidated and merged, there is a presumptive reduction in the number of banks in the community, and, hence, in the number of alternative sources of supply. On the other hand, during the 'thirties, many unit banks were acquired by branch banks in order to forestall the imminent bankruptcy of the former. In this case, the number of banks in the area is not different from what it would otherwise have been. If the acquired bank is converted into a new branch, the number of alternative sources of supply in the area might be increased, but not necessarily so. If, for example, the acquiring branch bank already has one or more branches in the community, and all branches in the system are operating under a common and centralized loan policy, the new branch would represent merely a spreading of the branch bank's existing facilities in the area. If reasonable autonomy is granted to the local branches and if they are in reasonable competition with each other, the new branch may constitute a net addition to the number of banks for certain borrowers but not necessarily for all borrowers. Branch bank policy on "large" loans almost uniformly requires that such loans be

---

[4] *Loc. cit.*

cleared through the head office. For large borrowers, therefore, the number of branch offices is indifferent in terms of alternative sources of supply. The position of the small borrowers cannot be deduced by analogy with those industrial corporations which may, as a matter of policy, foster competition among their subdivisions. A determination of the small borrowers' market position must be based on facts, not on deduction by analogy.[5]

BONA FIDE ENTRY

What constitutes a bona fide entry, i.e., an independent bank in the free entry sense? As specifically applied to this study, the foregoing question asks whether the respective branches of the Big Four branch systems in California are independent in loan policy? Can a borrower, especially a small borrower, secure a loan from one branch if another has turned him down? Can such a borrower shop for rates among the branches of a branch bank in his community? As mentioned earlier, independent surveys have already established the widespread tendency among different banks to refuse a loan to a borrower if some other bank has previously turned him down.[6] Furthermore, rates to small borrowers are characteristically rigid and uniform, especially away from metropolitan centers.[7]

Entry and large borrowers.—In this investigation, it is necessary to distinguish between business loans to large and to small borrowers, although there are no definite figures for each category which would hold under all circumstances.[8] Since "large" loans must be cleared with the head office, a large borrower who is turned down at one branch could not expect to get the same loan by applying to another branch of the same bank. Rates are a matter of negotiation between borrower and banker, but since rates, too, must be cleared with the head office, a large borrower cannot shop for rates among the different branches of the same bank. For the large borrower, therefore, the opening of even a *de novo* branch does not increase the total number of alternative sources of supply of business credit. This conclusion is hardly surprising but it seems worth stating because it has been alleged that the branches of a branch bank system compete with each other in a manner

---

[5] Cf. Jacoby's testimony in Transamerica Hearings, pp. 9363 and 8718 ff.

[6] Cf. pp. 23–24 above.

[7] To gain further information on this subject, interviews were held not only with senior loan officers at the head offices of the Big Four branch banks but also with the loan officers in some of the branches in Berkeley and surrounding communities.

[8] Cf. p. 41.

analogous to the various subdivisions of (say) General Motors. With respect to large borrowers, this is simply not true.

Entry and small borrowers.—The position of the small borrowers is slightly less definite. In interviews with the Big Four loan officers, all the bankers interviewed agreed that a small borrower who was turned down by another branch of the same bank would probably also be turned down by every other branch of that bank. Each bank operates under a common loan policy for its branches. This means that within the bounds of the innate heterogeneity of different loan applications, common standards of appraisal are applied.[9] On infrequent occasions, a loan refused by one branch might be granted by another branch if the latter has information about the loan application not available to the former. This fact would hardly justify the conclusion that in even these limited circumstances, a multiplication of branches in an area would increase the alternative sources *pari passu,* since the introduction of new facts also involves a different, and, therefore, new loan application.

In certain cases, two branches of a bank may, indeed, constitute two bona fide alternative sources of supply. Because of the inherent uniqueness of each loan application, the granting of a loan, even with head-office policy guides, involves banking judgment and interpretation. This element of banker discretion can make the loan acceptable in one branch and unacceptable in another. For example, one branch loan officer may be unfamiliar with a particular kind of loan and reject it, whereas some other branch, for the opposite reasons, might grant it. Again, one branch manager may be less ingenious than another in figuring out some way or combination of ways to make a borderline loan acceptable. The common characteristic in these cases is the human element—judgment, interpretation, and ingenuity.

In practice ("99 per cent of the times"), these exceptions are not important, and a refusal by one branch is a reasonably certain indication of refusal by the other branches of the bank. In principle, too, these exceptions are not significant. The high degree of uniformity in loan policy among the branches of a bank is more than a manifestation of some abstract idea of banking judgment, applied to an equally abstract idea of credit worthiness. Bank loan policies differ. Some banks are more conservative then others; they

---

[9] It should be mentioned, however, that no loan officer interviewed was aware of any explicit head-office policy that would preclude one branch granting a loan refused by some other branch.

vary in appraising loans to be refused under voluntary credit restraints; they may have different ideas about the desirability of loans with different kinds of collateral; they vary in the kinds of risks they are willing to assume in a loan, and so on. Thus the discretion for the branch of a particular bank is not a freely subjective appraisal of credit worthiness but is confined within the bounds of head-office loan policy (or guides) on a number of points.

In terms of availability of credit to small borrowers, it must be concluded that the existence of more than one branch of a bank in a given locality does not represent a corresponding number of alternative sources of supply. Moreover, there is not too much chance of a slip-up, i.e., of one branch not knowing of the action of another branch. This information is usually secured either directly or indirectly. Almost always it comes out in the credit check, and branches are not reluctant to request full information from some other branch concerning their experience with a particular loan applicant.

In the question of rates to small borrowers, the picture is similar to that of availability. All the bankers interviewed agreed that there was very little, if any, shopping for rates among the branches of a bank. Bankers disapprove of shopping for rates and try to discourage it. Nor would it profit the borrower to try, since each of the large branch banks operates under a "uniform rate policy." The head-office rate policy on different loans is well known by all branch loan officers. As a result, comparable loans are quoted similar rates in different branches of the same bank. Again, some very mild form of banker discretion may come into play, but within any given locality it is apparently unimportant, particularly since "rates in differerent communities are rather stable." Moreover, as a matter of policy there is *never* any attempt to solicit or steal business from other branches on the basis of rates; that is regarded as "suicidal." Intrabank "competition" by different branches of a bank usually means that one branch will be sympathetic with a disgruntled customer of another branch, and, if the alternative is losing the customer to some other bank, the branch will take him on as a customer. This always assumes, of course, that there is nothing intrinsically wrong with the customer and that the difficulty with the other branch was over "service," or a personality clash, or some similar reason.

Some branch officers take personal pride in their particular branch and tend to regard it as a unit bank. Although each would delight in the aggrandizement of his branch, he would not seek such aggrandizement at the expense of other branches of the same bank. That would "violate ethics," "endanger coöperation from the other branches," and would go counter to head-office policy.[10]

In view of the foregoing, it seems reasonable to conclude that the branches of a bank are independent only in the most limited sense. For all practical purposes, there is no effective interbranch competition in each of the California branch banks. In the free entry sense of affecting the objective number of alternative sources of supply in an area, bona fide entrants include unit bank entrants, and, for small borrowers only, branch bank entrants into a locality which does not already have an existing branch of the same bank.

CONDITIONS OF ENTRY

A convenient method of investigating the entry situation in California is to work through a full check list of the conventional conditions of free entry. In each case the criteria of entry are tested against the entry conditions actually found in California both for unit banks and branch banks.[11]

CAPITAL REQUIREMENTS

"The investment necessary to establish a firm is small enough that many potential entrants can obtain sufficient funds to establish a firm." Unlike most businesses, the capital requirements for entry into banking are primarily the legal requirements imposed by federal and state laws. Under federal law, capital requirements for national banks vary by size of community. The National Banking Act requires capital stock of $50,000 for unit banks in communities of 6,000 population and less; $100,000 in cities of 6,000–50,000 population; and $200,000 in cities of 50,000 population and more. California statutes impose the same capital requirements for unit state banks that are required for national banks, except that banks in cities with population of 200,000 and more must maintain a minimum capital of $300,000.

Capital requirements for branch banks are somewhat higher than for unit banks. The National Banking Act specified a minimum capital of $500,000 for banks which maintained branches outside the head-office city. The same capital requirement was reaffirmed in the Banking Act of 1935. Under California banking laws, no head-office capital requirements are set forth. However,

---

[10] One large branch system was currently conducting a campaign among its branches to secure new business, but an interbranch transfer of business accounts was not regarded by the head office as bona fide new business for the branch.

[11] The opening sentence (enclosed in quotation marks) of the different conditions of entry discussed in this section is quoted from Joe Bain, *Price Theory* (rev. ed., New York: Henry Holt and Company, 1952), p. 130 n.

intracity branches must have $50,000 capital, whereas branches outside the head-office city must maintain the same capital as that required for unit banks in the same localities.

It seems reasonable to conclude that existing legal capital requirements for unit banks would not compromise the existence of free entry if the other conditions of free entry were fully met. On the other hand, competent authorities have referred to the "unrealistic" and "onerous" capital requirements for the establishment of branches by national banks and state member banks.[12] The objection has been made because the capital requirements apply without reference to size of bank and the possibly limited functions of the branch.[13]

FEAR OF SPOILING THE MARKET PRICE

"The increment to industry output resulting from the entry of one additional firm is so small as to have no perceptible effect on industry price, and thus the potential entrant is not deterred by fear of changing the existing price situation." This point needs examination under various headings. If the entrant is a unit bank in a large city, the entrant need not be concerned about spoiling the market. If most of the dollar-volume of the unit bank's loans goes to large borrowers, the new supply of funds brought on the market by the entrant would be an insignificant part of the total. Large borrowers operate in a national credit market and no single bank is very impressive in that context. On the other hand, a unit bank entrant into a small town (where most of the dollar-volume of loans is assumed to be to small borrowers) might upset the market price—by *raising* that price![14] A raising of market price is not usually considered to "spoil" the market price, but since, *ceteris paribus*, the rise of market price is likely to be associated with a diminution of profits, a potential unit entrant might be deterred from entry into a small town. Indeed, the banking problem in many small towns in various parts of the country is caused by an exodus of unit banks.

A branch bank entrant into a large city need not be concerned about spoiling the market price, for reasons similar to those advanced for the unit bank entrant. Indeed, as far as the large borrowers are concerned, the statement would hold irrespective of the comparative costs of making large loans by branch banks as against

---

[12] Testimony of Chairman, Board of Governors, Federal Reserve System, Patman Report, Vol. I, p. 575.

[13] A limited power branch does not include military facilities, which are not considered branches.

[14] Cf. p. 33.

unit banks. Branch bank entry into a small town is a different matter. Since branch bank unit costs are probably lower than unit costs of small town banks, and because (quite independently of short run cost and profit considerations) the staying power of branch banks is far greater than that of their unit bank rivals, the branch bank need not worry about the possibility of spoiling the market price. Indeed, *at the time of entry,* there are instances in the past when a branch bank entrant has deliberately spoiled the market price by lowering that price.[15] Historically, when entry has been by acquisition, that has sometimes been the technique upon entry. For this particular type of branch bank entrant, free entry could exist quite consistently with spoiling the market price.[16] Usually, however, the present-day branch bank entrant into a small town does not attempt to compete upon a price basis, and simply accepts the going structure of rates in a town.[17] Indeed, even in those historical instances when a bona fide branch bank entry into a small town, which formerly had only unit banks, has resulted in an initial lowering of the *level* of rates on the smaller business loans, no further competition took place among banks.

In general, free entry into a small-town banking market is impossible, whether the entrant is a branch or unit bank. Small-town banking markets are usually either semimonopolistic or oligopolistic, and no single firm can help but affect the market price by its own action. Through a combination of credit rationing and oligopolistic price stabilization, small-town banks can usually prevent a "spoiling of market price" even under conditions of new entry.[18]

---

[15] Cf. chapter vii, n. 23.

[16] It is important to remember that there is nothing peculiar about banking per se which reverses the usual conditions of entry. The explanation lies rather in the innovational character of branch banking and, in particular, in its cost advantages vis-à-vis small unit banks. Although the innovator is, in fact, likely to secure a higher price for his product, he need not be deterred from entry by prospects of a low price, because of the cost-reducing characteristics of the innovation.

[17] At least one of the Big Four is very concerned about maintaining cordial relations with the unit banks in the general territory it serves and has deliberately refrained from even entering areas where profitable branches might have been established in line with its "live and let live" policy.

[18] The combination of credit rationing and oligopolistic price stabilization to prevent the small-town bank entrant from spoiling market price is abetted by the elements of product differentiation in banking. Since banking is a monopolistically competitive industry, unit bank entrants into small towns might plausibly expect to hold some customers even at lending rates which are mildly disadvantageous in view of existing alternatives. Thus there is a basis for at least some loans. Moreover, small-town banks always have an alternative to spoiling market price by unbridled price competition—they can turn to the government securities market for investment of otherwise "surplus" funds.

ACCESS TO MATERIALS AND RESOURCES

"All potential entrants have free access to all resources or factors needed for production, at competitive market prices, since there is no monopolization of resource ownership or control by established firms." The various factors and resources can be examined in turn. Most of the labor employed by a bank is unskilled, except perhaps in mechanical techniques which are quite readily acquired. Moreover, most bank labor is drawn from the general labor pool, and a small unit bank could secure needed personnel at this basic level at competitive rates. By and large, competitive markets also exist for minor executive personnel. However, the superior resources of a large bank enable it to attract more capable talent at top executive levels. To this extent, the small unit bank is at a disadvantage, but the disadvantage is not because of monopolization of top executive personnel by established firms. Indeed, for top executive personnel in any field, there is no competitive market, and, in many cases, no real market at all. Furthermore, this disadvantage is sometimes compensated by the preference of executive personnel to work in smaller banks to avoid the bureaucratic complications of large scale organization.

In purchasing materials and supplies, the large branch systems have an advantage in securing quantity discounts through bulk purchases. However, such quantity discounts do not imply branch bank control of materials markets, since the discounts may be based on bona fide cost economies to the manufacturer. Moreover, no single bank purchases supplies in such large quantities as to be able to extort monopsonistic or oligopsonistic concessions from suppliers, concessions that might otherwise work to the disadvantage of small unit banks.

In securing the bank premises and building, a small bank encounters no serious competitive disadvantage, if any, with the branch bank, since branch banks can not monopolize prospective bank sites or buildings. The disadvantage of the small unit banks is owing rather to the more elaborate premises they maintain, whereas even the humblest branch office shares the prestige of its parent bank.

The most important "raw material" is deposits, because deposits are the main source of bank loans and investments. Deposits are paid for either through interest on time deposits or, implicitly, through remission of service charges on checking accounts. Although the Big Four hold the greatest amount of deposits in California, basically, they have no controlling monopoly over deposits.

Probably the fundamental consideration with most depositors is the safety of their accounts. By comparison, conveniences of the bank are distinctly secondary. A large branch system would, other things being equal, probably command more confidence among prospective depositors than a small unit bank. However, the majority of small depositors rely for protection of their deposits on the guarantee of the Federal Deposit Insurance Corporation, and membership in the FDIC is open to all sound banks, irrespective of size, type of organization, or membership in the Federal Reserve System. Small depositors thus have nothing to choose between the large branch system and the small unit bank in terms of safety of deposits, and, hence, are not forced to deal with the large branch banks.

The large depositor is somewhat more restricted than the small depositor because FDIC protection is limited to $10,000 and, other things being equal, a large branch bank is presumably safer for large deposits than a small unit bank. The implicit element of control over such deposits by branch banks is somewhat reduced at the present time. Both large and small banks have invested heavily in government securities and that in itself is a significant guarantor of bank solvency. In one important respect, however, the branch systems do exercise significant control over large deposits. A large bank is the natural supplier of credit to large borrowers. So far as the large bank can and does demand that such borrowers maintain balances at the bank, the large banks effectively control these deposits, and the small bank has little chance of getting them. To this extent, the smaller unit banks are at a serious competitive disadvantage in securing a bank's most important raw material.

COMPARABILITY OF PRODUCT

"New entrants can produce outputs identical to those of established firms." Because of the overwhelming importance of the banker-customer relationship, especially to small borrowers, this condition of free entry can never be met in practice. It is not necessary to repeat in detail the earlier demonstration that the commercial banking field is characterized by a significant degree of product differentiation. Even some who contend that banking markets are "competitive" have conceded that every bank has a limited monopoly because of spatial factors and product differentiation.[19] For large borrowers, however, the problem of product differentiation is probably not serious.

---

[19] Cf., e.g., testimony of Neil Jacoby, Transamerica Hearings, p. 8471.

Large borrowers face a differentiated product in another sense, however. Bank loans, even if identical in other characteristics, are distinguished by size. To the extent that small banks cannot extend loans of the same size as large banks, they operate in noncompeting markets from the large banks. Nor can this separation of markets be overcome by assistance to small banks from metropolitan correspondents. It was a matter of note when the Chase National Bank of New York City recently set up a fund of $10,000,000 to aid its correspondent banks throughout the country in making loans in their local areas. However, this fund was established explicitly to enable such banks to compete for *loans to small business in their local areas.*[20] Furthermore, national banks are proscribed by law from lending more than 10 per cent of their capital and surplus to any one borrower. Thus small banks are effectively barred both as a practical matter and by legal restrictions from entry into the banking market for large loans.

OTHER ARTIFICAL IMPEDIMENTS TO ENTRY

Legal impediments.—"There are no other artificial impediments to entry." Banking is in fact characterized by numerous artificial impediments to entry, most of them legal. A bank entrant must secure a charter, either federal or state. Whether the chartering jurisdiction be the State of California or the federal government, both must satisfy themselves that a "need" exists for the new bank. "Need" can be a highly ambiguous concept, particularly if it is interpreted to mean that the status quo in an area must not be disturbed in a competitive sense. Indeed, the California Superintendent of Banks has stated that "When chartering banks, this department goes upon the theory that one strong bank in the community is much more desirable than two weak banks, and *competition is not a reasonable public necessity in the case of banking.*"[21]

A former Comptroller of the Currency of the federal government testified that in passing upon applications to establish branches, individual studies are made of the adequacy of the bank's management and, in effect, the soundness of the bank and its profitability. The Comptroller would also ask himself such questions as:

Will the proposed branch, by virtue of its location come into direct competition with existing banking facilities? If so, will the existing banking facilities be able to maintain themselves as profitable units

[20] *American Banker,* January 20, 1950, as quoted in Transamerica Hearings, p. 8736. (Italics mine.)
[21] Statement of Maurice C. Sparling, Patman Report, Vol. II, p. 995. (Italics mine.)

against the competition of the proposed new branch? In other words, will the proposed branch create an over-banked situation? *The rights of existing bank facilities to remain undisturbed and free from additional competition* are carefully weighed against the rights of the prospective branch to be permitted to enter the area as a competing unit.[22]

Although the statement was made about branch bank applications, there is no reason to suppose that the same criterion would not also apply to the charter applications of unit banks. All chartering jurisdictions are alive to the dangers inherent in an "over-banked" situation, and not without cause.[23] The reasons for this concern[24] are of less immediate interest than the fact that chartering officials openly admit the obstacles placed in the way of free entry—and *for the express purpose of preventing undue competition among banks.*

Not only are banks generally sheltered against undue competition from potential entrants, but, in federal law at least, branch banks are deliberately placed at a disadvantage with unit banks. This fact is manifest in the McFadden-Pepper Act, whose general purpose was ". . . to stifle the development of branch banking and to freeze it in its status quo; and . . . the national banks were *purposely* left at a disadvantage in respect to branch bank privileges."[25] At this point it is not necessary to debate the wisdom of these deliberate impediments to entry of branch banks; it is enough here to notice their existence. That at least some branch bank proponents felt the Act was "unduly severe" would seem to be suggested by their reference to "artificial, arbitrary, and inequitable restraints . . ."[26]

---

[22] Affidavit of Preston Delano, Comptroller of Currency; in the U. S. Court of Appeals for the Ninth Circuit Court; Board of Governors, Federal Reserve System vs. Transamerica Corporation and Bank of America; no. 12587, in Transamerica Hearings, Respondent's Exhibit no. 329. (Italics mine.)

[23] For example, President Earhart, Federal Reserve Bank of San Francisco, has testified that, "while competition among banking offices is highly desirable, it is not in the longer view of public interest to permit the establishment of a competing bank in an area where only one healthy banking facility can exist." C. E. Earhart, Patman Report, Vol. II, p. 778.

[24] "Due to the fact that banking is subject to a high degree of regulation and control, the area in which competition is permitted or is practicable is limited rather severely. The prevalence of full competition between two banks in the same town does not guarantee the existence of more adequate banking facilities. In fact, in towns where two banks are not economically justified, banking services would be improved, in all probability, by the elimination of one bank." R. R. Gilbert, Patman Report, Vol. II, pp. 777–778.

[25] R. B. Westerfield, *Branch Banking* (New York and London: Harper & Brothers, 1942), p. 108. (Italics mine.)

[26] *Ibid.*, p. 109.

Predatory practices.—Predatory practices can also be considered a deterrent to entry. The practice of local price cutting to drive out competitors characterized the historical development of various American industries. The possibility of a similar development in California banking was raised in the Transamerica case,[27] and was considered a deterrent to entry. Undoubtedly, predatory practices, if successful, could seriously deter potential entrants, especially unit bank entrants. A branch system could presumably engage in predatory price competition in local areas, since losses on any branch could be borne by the rest of the system.[28] Other things being equal, the advisability of this practice between two branch systems would depend upon their relative size and financial staying power.

The short-run success of predatory practices, whether conducted between branch banks or between a branch and a unit bank, is highly doubtful, for the "victimized" rival always has the option of placing its funds in open market investments rather than in customer loans, although at a considerable (and possibly crippling) sacrifice of earning power. In the long run, however, the ordinary commercial bank, especially a unit bank, is at a comparative disadvantage in making investments as compared with large insurance companies, or for that matter, with very large commercial banks. Whether at a comparative disadvantage or not, a so-called commercial bank, which almost literally places its full funds in investments, may indeed survive, but has been effectively knocked out as a rival. For public policy, the results may nevertheless be favorable, if society is primarily concerned with competitive results rather than the preservation of competitors. A large bank that engaged in predatory pricing practices might have to continue them indefinitely to suppress rivals, since potential entrants would always be waiting on the periphery if the large bank's price and output policy became oppressive toward its customers. Whether potential entrants could secure a charter at the appropriate time is not certain, but the possibility of entry might cause a large bank to pause and consider well the advisability of such unpopular action with such dubious prospects of success. Plaintiff in the Transamerica

[27] Cf. testimony of Oliver P. Wheeler, Transamerica Hearings, p. 2575.

[28] In 1939, for example, Bank of America reported that five of its four hundred ninety-five branches failed to show a net profit. Although they expected four of the branches to be put on a paying basis during the ensuing year, they thought that at least one of the branches could not be. There was, incidentally, no information as to why these branches were "unprofitable." Cf. Bank of America, *Annual Report, 1939,* p. 13.

case raised the question of predatory practices, but no instance of abuse was adduced. It seems reasonable to conclude that no such evidence existed, particularly in view of the known abhorrence and stated policy of all the Big Four banks to avoid price competition.

FREE EXIT

To the conditions of free entry already discussed, there should be added still another, viz., free exit. A condition of free exit may be said to exist when a firm can withdraw from the field upon comparatively short notice by liquidating its resources without serious loss. In a broad sense, free exit is an important condition of free entry, since a potential entrant may be deterred from entering a field if withdrawal is difficult and expensive. In most industries, the general condition for free exit is the absence of heavy fixed costs. Although heavy fixed costs are not a necessary feature of a commercial bank, easy exit is not likely, especially, as seems probable, if the attempted exit occurs during a general liquidation crisis. Unlike most small firms, the operations of a commercial bank which has become rooted in a locality ramify throughout the economic life of that community. Under conditions of orderly liquidation, none of the interested parties in the bank need suffer any losses. However, during a panic liquidation, when most liquidations in fact occur, not only stockholders, but depositors and bank customers are likely to be profoundly affected. Unlike most businesses, banks operate with a heavy proportion of borrowed capital (deposits). Thus, although an ordinary, comparatively small firm can go out of business with losses only to the owner, even a small bank can depress the entire area it serves if it tries unsuccessfully to liquidate under panic conditions. This consideration alone places commercial banking in a class apart from other businesses with respect to exit.

This need not be true of a branch, however, especially if the branch bank has other branches in the same vicinity. Under these conditions, an unprofitable branch can be closed, and its assets and liabilities simply transferred to a near-by branch.

FACTS OF ENTRY INTO CALIFORNIA BANKING

INTERPRETING THE DATA ON ENTRY

In interpreting data on entry, a distinction must be made between potential entry and actual entry. In a given situation, free entry in the potential sense can exist consistently with no actual entry.

Statistically, an absence of entrants per se provides no clue to the existence or lack of existence of potential free entry. On the other hand, actual entry (meaning that new firms have come into the field) is not per se automatically equated with free entry.

The distinction between actual entry and potential free entry must be stressed to avoid possibly misleading conclusions in interpreting data. In the Transamerica Hearings, for example, Jacoby agreed, in reply to a question by counsel for the defendant, that the allegedly large number of entrants in the five-state area (1941–1948) indicated freedom of entry.[29] It would seem, therefore, that Jacoby has interpreted the actual entry as indicating free entry. This leads to a curious result. As mentioned earlier, Jacoby also stated that freedom of entry is a necessary and usually sufficient condition of "effective competition." Yet Jacoby also testified that every bank has a limited monopoly because of spatial factors and product differentiation.[30] Thus, in Jacoby's terminology, freedom of entry leads to effective competition; and effective competition is consistent with limited monopoly. But freedom of entry is traditionally associated with pure, not effective, competition and pure competition is incompatible with monopoly elements.

The preceding discussion emphasizes once again the importance of seeking the greatest possible precision in use of terms, especially technical terms. It is clear that Jacoby was not thinking of free entry in the usually accepted technical sense. Indeed, in his testimony, he had the following to say about "freedom of entry": "I don't mean that entry into any market is completely costless, but rather that entry is not prohibited or restrained by law or by predatory practices of existing firms in the industry."[31] The absence of what Bain has termed "artificial impediments to entry" is certainly an important condition of free entry. However, by Bain's definition of free entry, this is only a single part of the definition. Again, in elaborating his testimony that there is freedom of entry into the commercial banking business today, Jacoby explained that "The National Bank Act and the various state banking laws generally permit new banking offices to be established without limit, provided that the specified minimum capital requirements are met and that the would-be entrants demonstrate a public need and demand for the services of the new banking office. *In the case of commercial banking, public policy does qualify freedom of entry to*

---

[29] Transamerica Hearings, pp. 8588 ff.
[30] Cf. p. 204.
[31] Transamerica Hearings, p. 8579.

this extent in the interest of protecting the safety of banking deposits."[32] The issue at this point is not with the social desirability of limiting bank entry, as Jacoby himself describes it to be limited. The point is simply that limited entry is not free entry; it is imperfect entry. Jacoby apparently believes that this qualification to free entry is not significant, because he further stated that "I know of no evidence which indicates that present laws have borne with undue severity upon freedom of entry into commercial banking. I presume if there were persuasive evidence of that kind it would be within the power of legislative bodies and the banking regulatory authorities to relax the conditions of entry."[33] As shown earlier in this chapter, Jacoby's evaluation of the legal restraints to entry in banking is not universally accepted.[34]

It is a truism of statistical theory that statistics can never "prove" anything; at best, they are consistent with a given hypothesis. Data pertaining to entry must be interpreted with extreme caution as the preceding paragraphs have shown. But an attitude of caution is not sufficient; relevant concepts must also be defined with meticulous care. Otherwise, the same set of figures can be used to support diametrically opposite conclusions. The introductory material in this section has been presented in the hope of obviating confusion and clarifying the bases for opposite conclusions by different investigators studying the same set of facts.

STATISTICAL RECORD OF ENTRY

Entry by the Big Four.—Defendant's presentation in the Transamerica Hearings left the clear impression that a large number of entrants have come into California banking during (say) the last twenty years. Table 33 shows the comparative entry of the Big Four branch banks. The period covered by the table (1932–1947) was one of very rapid growth of the California economy and of its population. Moreover, by the end of 1932, the Bank of America had already reached 80 per cent of its 1947 size in terms of numbers of banking offices. It is interesting to observe, therefore, how the other large branch systems fared in terms of entry in the face of the dominating size of Bank of America, and during a period of rapid economic expansion of the state.

Table 33 shows that the largest absolute growth in terms of *de novo* branches was overwhelmingly by the Bank of America.

---

[32] *Ibid.*, pp. 8582 and 8583. (Italics mine.)
[33] *Loc. cit.*
[34] Cf. p. 206.

The Security–First National Bank, American Trust Company, and Anglo-California Bank followed in that order. In absolute terms, the *de novo* entries by the latter banks during a fifteen-year period were small despite the rapid growth of the state. Furthermore, the *de novo* branches do not represent net entries by each bank during the period, because, during the same period, all the branch banks closed several offices. In every case, the number of closed branches far exceeded the number of *de novo* branches. During the same period, too, each of the Big Four acquired other banks, some of which were converted into branches whereas other banks

TABLE 33

DE NOVO ENTRIES BY THE BIG FOUR BRANCH BANKS,
1932–1947[a]

Bank of America	75
Security–First National Bank	14
American Trust	12
Anglo-California	5

[a] SOURCES: These figures were compiled for the author by the Research Department, Federal Reserve Bank of San Francisco.
The starting date of 1932 was selected because no significant mergers took place among any of the Big Four after that date.

were merged with existing branches. Hence, the present size of the Big Four is related to their bank acquisitions as well as to their *de novo* entries. With the exception of Bank of America, then, *de novo* entry by the other branch systems was certainly not impressive during this period.

Entry from the borrower's viewpoint.—The significance of even the limited amount of actual entry is reduced when considered from the viewpoint of a prospective borrower. Free entry is important to a borrower because it usually connotes an increase in the objective number of alternative sources of supply. No such presumption attaches to the *de novo* figures in table 33.[35] For a branch bank, the establishment of a wholly new branch is a *de novo* entry. For free entry, however, a mere multiplication of banking facilities *within the same market area* cannot be considered a bona fide entry. As shown earlier, the opening of a branch by a bank that already has an existing branch in the same market area repre-

[35] "Branch banking is more important in the twelfth district than in any other district. While the growth of branch banking has brought no decline, but has probably caused an increase, in the number and availability of banking facilities, it has undoubtedly resulted in a reduction in the number and availability of competing banking organizations." C. E. Earhart, Patman Report, Vol. II, p. 779.

sents merely an extension of existing banking facilities—not a new, independent source of supply.[36]

Table 34 shows the number of bona fide (as herein defined) *de novo* branches established by each of the Big Four banks for the same period as that shown in table 33. For the purposes of table 34, unit bank entries are defined analogously to branch bank entries. Specifically, when one unit bank is reconstituted as another unit bank, often on the same premises and with the same officers as the old bank, that is not considered an entry, since the

TABLE 34

NUMBER OF BONA FIDE DE NOVO BRANCHES OPENED IN
CALIFORNIA BY THE BIG FOUR BRANCH BANKS AND THE
UNIT BANKS, 1932–1947

Bank[a]	Number
Bank of America	53
Security–First National	8
American Trust	11
Anglo-California	3
Unit Banks	42

[a] SOURCE: *Rand McNally Bankers' Directory*, 1932–1947. A total of six banks or branches were opened in metropolitan areas.

net number of alternative sources is not affected. In a small number of cases, a branch system was assumed to have acquired a unit bank when the routing symbol of the branch differed from that of the unit bank, but most of the officer personnel of the unit bank were continued in the new branch. Under these circumstances, the new branch was not considered to constitute a net entry. Whatever discrepancies may have been introduced by the foregoing are insignificant, however, since the absolute numbers involved were very small. The only conspicuous omission from table 34 concerns military installations. Numerous military installations, especially by Bank of America, were opened during the Second World War. However, these installations were little more than checkeries and did not constitute a source of supply for business borrowers.[37] Finally, the category of "unit banks" includes a few "local" branch systems.

---

[36] The Federal Reserve Bank of San Francisco officially takes the same view: "In determining whether there were two or more competing banks in an area, branches of the same bank were not considered to be separate banks." Patman Report, Vol. II, p. 780.

[37] Cf., e.g., American Trust Company, *Annual Report,* 1943.

Table 33 shows that, except for Bank of America, *de novo* entries, as conventionally defined by the banks, were small in absolute terms for Security Bank, American Trust Company, and the Anglo-California Bank, and the figures are even smaller when *de novo* entry is more restrictively defined as in table 34. Even Bank of America's *de novo* figure in table 34 is reduced by almost one-third of the comparable figure in table 33. As for the unit banks, the number of unit bank entries in table 34 is smaller than the number of bona fide branches opened by Bank of America alone. It is significant, too, that a total of six banks or branches were opened in metropolitan areas where, presumably, they did not significantly affect the objective number of alternative sources of supply. Table 34 thus confirms and reinforces the impression derived from table 33, viz., with the exception of Bank of America, entry into California banking did not take place in impressive numbers by the branch banks during the period 1930 through 1947. Compared to the statistics on entry in many others businesses, the same conclusion would apply to the unit banks.

SUMMARY

The figures on entry can neither prove nor disprove the existence of free entry in California during the period in question. The figures do show that, contrary to the impression left in the Transamerica Hearings, and with the exception of Bank of America, entry in impressive numbers took place neither by branch systems nor by unit banks. Indeed, from the viewpoint of the borrower, even table 34 probably overstates the extent of bona fide *de novo* entry. This is owing to the difficulty of translating a theoretical definition of a banking market area into geographical terms. It has been convenient to assume that for small borrowers, the relevant market area is the city or town in which the borrower is located. However, where towns are in close proximity to each other, the relevant market area may encompass the banks in neighboring towns. If this is done, however, it might reduce the number of bona fide *de novo* entries listed in table 34, since any enlargement of the geographical boundaries of a market area is very likely to include existing branch facilities of the Big Four.

It might be argued that the dominating figures for Bank of America point to the conclusion that the existence of such a large institution has significantly impaired the willingness to enter of other branch systems and of unit banks. The same figures are as readily consistent with the contention that Bank of America is simply bolder and has more initiative in seeking out and exploiting profit-making opportunities.[38] As for evidence of interested parties, the Transamerica Hearings have amply shown that witnesses can readily be supplied on both sides of this question.

The earlier investigation of the conditions of entry has shown that entry into California banking is imperfect; it is certainly not free entry. Of course, the imperfect entry conditions for banks must be qualified with reference to potential nonbank suppliers of short-term business credit. So far as substitute suppliers can freely enter the market, the borrower's position is potentially improved, so far, that is, as these substitute suppliers are genuine substitutes for bank short-term commercial credit.[39]

To repeat, the statistics on entry neither prove nor disprove the existence of free entry. They do show, as a matter of record, that entry into California banking has not been impressive in the period under investigation, with the one exception of Bank of America. Neil Jacoby has testified that, "The mere fact that a comparatively few firms have entered into industry over a long period of time would not of itself demonstrate that entry was difficult or not free, because it may merely demonstrate or indicate that existing firms in the industry priced their products or services so low and improved the quality and quantity of their services that there were no attractive opportunities presented for entering firms in the industry."[40] If new entrants do not come into the market, it may indeed be because "no attractive opportunities" are presented to them. The main issue, however, is whether entry by banks is free.

---

[38] Cf., for example, the announced attitude of Anglo-California Bank on the subject of branch expansion. "Of the frankly branch systems, Anglo Bank has long followed a pattern somewhat different and distinct from that of its competitors. It has not sought a large number of offices in the area of the city of its domicile, nor has it sought either to establish or to acquire many offices throughout the State. Rather, the pattern of having complete and substantial offices in key cities and towns, generally not more than one to a city except in San Francisco, has been closely followed with the thought in mind that the best job of banking, both for shareholders and for depositors, could thus be accomplished. Our policy has been one of conservative branch development." Anglo Bank, *Annual Report,* 1949, p. 1.

By contrast, Security–First National Bank has a policy of expanding its facilities and services to keep pace with the growth of the area which the bank serves. Cf. Security Bank, *Annual Report,* 1948, p. 2. However, Security Bank will not necessarily open a branch in an area already being served by a unit bank, despite prospects of profitable operation of such a branch.

[39] The analysis of chapter ii disclosed that trade credit is the only important substitute for short-term bank business loans. However, trade credit is not a perfect substitute and is usually not a competitive alternative to bank business loans. Accordingly, the discussion of freedom of entry in this chapter has been limited to bank entry only.

[40] Transamerica Hearings, p. 8582.

This analysis has shown that it is not. In the absence of free entry, it is essential to point out that the small number of actual entrants does not *necessarily* imply that existing firms are charging low prices and giving good and adequate service.[41]

A likely explanation for a small number of entrants into a local market area (even assuming free entry) is the comparative ease with which banks (or branches) can expand to accommodate an increasing volume of business.[42] A comparable expansion would involve a manufacturing or industrial corporation in significant outlays and delays in time and might well induce new entrants in considerable numbers. In the case in point, actual entry has not occurred in impressive numbers. Although free entry is compatible with a small number of actual entrants, free entry at least in small-borrower markets is a logical impossibility.

Free entry and relatively easy entry.—This chapter has demonstrated that free entry in the strict sense does not characterize most banking markets. Free entry can only guarantee competitive results when all the conditions of free entry are met. The medium-size and small loan markets are oligopolistically organized. At best, these markets are characterized by *relatively* easy entry, where some of, but not all, the conditions of free entry are met. Where entry is only relatively easy but not free in the strict sense, there can be no necessary confidence in a reasonably competitive result. In small-town banking markets, for example, the banks typically operate under monopoly or oligopoly, with high prices and low output. A unit entrant into such a market would just share the market, at possibly higher rates, but also, conceivably, losses. This result is not peculiar to banking but would hold for other firms operating under analogous circumstances. First, small-town banking markets are restricted in scope. Second, the minimum feasible size of firm is such that the total number of firms that can profitably serve the market is incompatible with the fact that no one firm has a perceptible influence on market price, and, therefore, on its rivals. In short, banks in small-town markets are operating on the falling range of their cost curves even when market demand is reasonably met. As a result, the situation is ripe for oligopoly or monopoly practices.

---

[41] By the same token, good and adequate service is perfectly compatible with the absence of free entry conditions.

[42] Bank of America, for example, showed that although its deposits, loans, and number of customers more than doubled by 1947 from their prewar magnitudes, yet there was only a small increase in the number of branches. Admittedly, the resources were sometimes strained, but the feat was accomplished. Cf. Bank of America, *Annual Report*, 1947, p. 13.

A more nearly competitive result *might* be achieved under the conditions posited if the entrant is a branch bank. A new branch has no independent cost curve. To be profitable, a new branch bank need cover only its own marginal costs, whereas a new unit bank in the same town would eventually have to cover its full costs. The general overhead[43] of a branch system which contemplates the opening of a new branch is presumably already covered. Thus a branch system *could* enter a town characterized by oligopoly price and output conditions, lower its prices and still make a profit, whereas comparable rates for a unit bank might involve the latter in losses and even drive it into bankruptcy. The evidence in chapter vii indicates that a low-price policy has at times been historically pursued, but this is not a necessary result even for an otherwise "aggressive" branch bank. At the present time, moreover, even "aggressive" branch systems generally prefer to do nothing more about price than to "meet competition." In other words, they simply share the market at existing prices and reap the profits accordingly.

This discussion of entry illustrates the danger of employing technical terms in a loose manner. It is one thing to employ technical terms loosely as general descriptive terms, but it is quite different to employ technical terms loosely while positing consequences which are predicated upon a strict fulfillment of the conditions of the concept. Under the conditions described above, *relatively* easy entry may not guarantee "effective competition"— even when effective competition is not defined to be "pure" competition.

---

[43] For example, expenses of head office, advertising, research department, lawyers, higher administrative officers who do not administer any single branch, and so on.

XII

Banking Concentration and Monopoly

DURING THE LAST three decades, the total number of independent banks has decreased from about 30,000 in 1921 to less than 15,000 in 1952. This trend toward concentration of banking resources has not been less pronounced in California than in the rest of the country. Indeed, it has been greater. In 1920, California's four branch banks controlled less than 15 per cent of banking deposits in the state; by 1950, that figure had increased to about 65 per cent. The growing concentration of banking in California has meant an increase not only in the absolute size of the four branch bank systems but also a decline in the number of independently owned unit banks. In California, as in the country as a whole, the increase in concentration of banking resources has involved a wholesale elimination of *competitors*.

In the Transamerica Hearings, the Solicitor for the Board of Governors described a few instances in which unit banks in small towns had been acquired by Transamerica and indicated that the examples given could be "multiplied over and over again in communities of all sizes."[1] The Solicitor held that the cumulative effect of such acquisitions is to "substantially lessen *existing* competition" and that "present competition would . . . be 'substantially' increased" if the acquired institutions had remained in the field and the concentration of bank ownership had been accordingly reduced.[2] This study has shown, however, that mere numbers of independently owned banks do not tell the full banking story. The existence of many independent banks is no assurance of competitive behavior. Moreover, in at least some banking markets,

[1] Reply Brief of Counsel for the Board of Governors, Federal Reserve System, in the matter of Transamerica Corporation, November 9, 1951, pp. 22–23.
[2] *Loc. cit.*

[217]

increasing concentration of banking resources may not significantly alter the former market structures or behavior.

The analysis of the preceding chapters would not unqualifiedly support the contention of the Solicitor about the implied relationship between the objective number of competi*tors* and competitive behavior. Despite many loose assertions about the intensive degree of existing competition in unit banking markets, competitive behavior does not normally characterize such markets. As a result of price rigidities in many banking markets, rivalry is deflected from the price sphere. When bankers repeatedly allude— and no doubt sincerely—to the "keen competition" in banking, they are referring to competition along lines of product variation. In an industry like commercial banking, where entry is not blockaded, an existing oligopoly (or monopoly) position is no insurance of a self-perpetuating status quo. Potential entry is a standing threat to the position of the oligopolists taken as a group. Moreover, even oligopolists must be concerned with the maintenance of their market shares. Since competition is stultified on the price variable, rivalry is more intensively pushed on other fronts. In a service industry like banking, that rivalry has taken the form of greater efforts to be responsive to consumer demands. In this product competition, the California branch banks have taken a leading part in developing new forms of credit and new deposit-attracting devices.

Homogeneity characterizes neither the structure nor the behavior of banking generally. Banking markets show a wide range of market structures and a wide range of market behavior. This is because competition in banking is largely a function of alternative sources of supply available to prospective borrowers. More effective competition induces a lower level and a greater flexibility of the rate structure and presumably, too, greater credit availability. In large cities, there is generally no shortage of banks. An increase in the number of banks in large cities would not be likely to affect the rates, availability, or terms presently received by large borrowers. Small-size borrowers in large cities might benefit slightly by an increase in the number of banks, but, if present experience is any guide, not much more than slightly.

Although small cities do not offer numerous alternative sources, more effective competition will not result by increasing the number of banks. Inflexible, high-level rates characterize the oligopolistic (or monopolistic) customer loan markets in small towns. An increase in the number of banks in small towns would not break the oligopoly nor would it lower rates and ease availability of credit. In the first instance, new entrants would simply share the existing demand with the established banks, thereby driving each bank to a higher point on its cost curve with resulting *higher rates* for customers. If still more newcomers entered small towns, the oligopoly might eventually be broken, but only at the cost of numerous bankruptcies. The situation would revert to "normal" or might even be aggravated if the old marginal firms completely left the business.

The Comptroller of the Currency has taken official notice of the strong trend towards amalgamation and branch banking, "a trend which is away from the 'ideal' of giving all persons the opportunity of choosing between two or more competing banks."[3] But, in light of the above, it seems clear that the concentration of California banking in which branches of one of the four large branch systems replace formerly independent unit banks in small towns *would not significantly alter the existing market structure of those towns.* In other words, small borrowers would face the same kind of market situation before and after the growth of concentration. The very largest borrowers, who presumably borrow through banking offices in large cities, also would not be affected by the transition from a competitive market structure to an oligopolistic structure in large cities. Although local alternative sources of supply available to the large borrower would be reduced, his effective bargaining position would not be reduced, because the very large borrowers can secure funds anywhere in the country, and, in many cases, even on the open market. Accordingly, rates and terms offered to such borrowers would be approximately as competitive as the banks of the country could afford.

The contention of the Board's counsel that a reduction of independently owned banking offices would adversely affect existing competition might be true for the intermediate-size borrowers. In this study, intermediate-size borrowers are defined as those limited in their alternative sources of supply roughly to the banks within their own state boundaries. Although this delineation of relevant market boundaries is admittedly artificial, it suitably describes the situation facing a borrower neither so small as to be limited to one or two local banks nor so large as to have sources in many parts of the country. The reduction in the number of objective alternatives available to such a borrower following the growth of concentration in his area might also reduce his bargaining power in negotiating a loan. The emergence of oligopoly in

[3] Patman Report, Vol. II, p. 927.

an area formerly characterized by a relatively competitive market structure might quite conceivably worsen the market position of intermediate-size borrowers. Oligopoly markets quite often charge what the traffic will bear, and that is presumptively a higher price than the ruling price on competitive markets. The increase in concentration of banking resources might thus force this class of borrowers into a position more nearly resembling that of the small borrowers than of the large borrowers.

BRANCH BANKING AND MONOPOLY BEHAVIOR

Monopoly is generally condemned by the laws of the country and the mores of the people. As discussed in the introductory chapter, monopolies are generally charged with restricting output, charging high prices, and discriminating among customers in an attempt to extort excessive profits. The balance of this chapter examines the market performance of branch banks. In each case, the performance of branch banks is compared not to some theoretical ideal but rather to the performance of unit banking. To be useful for policy formulation, economic analysis cannot be conducted in a vacuum; ultimately, it must relate to realistic alternatives.

HIGH AND RIGID PRICES

For reasons well established in economic theory, concentrated markets are often characterized by high and rigid prices. Unfortunately it is not possible to measure directly the price performance of branch banks, nor of unit banks either. Individual interest rates are shrouded in secrecy. Perforce, resort must be had to indirect evidence. Under branch banking no less than under unit banking, the market is stratified by category of borrower. Interest rates for the largest borrowers are competitively determined. Since very large borrowers deal on a national credit market, branch bank rates to such borrowers are competitive with rates charged by unit bank rivals for the same business. Those rates are not high. Moreover, they are flexible and respond to changes in general credit conditions in the country. Rates on very large loans tend to respond to changes in open market rates. Since open market rates can be greatly influenced by the Federal Reserve System, the flexibility and level of rates to large borrowers are significantly conditioned by the monetary authorities.

The position of small borrowers is not worsened by the growth in over-all concentration of banking resources. They still face oligopolistic or monopolistic suppliers, and it makes little difference ratewise whether these are unit banks or branch banks. Small-borrower loan rates are comparatively rigid. Both under concentrated branch banking and under unit banking, small-borrower loan rates tend not to reflect changes in credit conditions as measured by open market rate changes. In extreme cases, the absence of price competition in small-loan markets is reflected in loan rates unchanged for two decades. This fact is suggestive for the alleged alternative sources to short-term business loans from banks. If the alleged alternative sources were effective competitors of the banks in small towns, the rates in small towns would perforce show a greater flexibility over time than is in fact the case. The rigidity of bank loan rates in small towns suggests, therefore, that such banks are not subjected to effective competition from other potential (nonbank) suppliers, even when the latter can be found in a particular town.

The position of the intermediate-size borrowers is the only category that is likely to be adversely affected by the growth of banking concentration. As explained earlier, such borrowers now face an oligopolistic market in California in lieu of the more nearly competitive markets which they faced before the increased concentration of banking resources. The statistical evidence is too crude to be conclusive, but the available evidence and the analysis in this study both raise the question whether for this class of borrowers, rates are not only somewhat higher but also more rigid than they would have been in less concentrated markets.

The basic explanation for the failure of bank concentration to affect customer loan rates adversely relative to unit bank rates is that (with the possible exception of the medium-size borrowers) the apparent growth of market concentration as conventionally measured is misleading and unrealistic. For example, when bank concentration statistics are computed on a state-wide basis, they are meaningless in terms of market structure and market performance. A possible exception, to repeat, is the case of the medium-size borrowers. But if bank concentration data on a state basis are meaningful in this latter case, it is quite accidental. It just happens that the market boundaries of medium-size borrowers in California happen to be roughly coterminous with state boundaries. In other words, conventional methods of computing bank concentration on a state basis might just happen to be pertinent for one particular class of borrowers, i.e., for one particular market. Conventional measures of banking concentration are misleading as indications of market concentration for two reasons. Bank concen-

tration is usually computed on a legal or political-jurisdiction base
rather than an economic base. Moreover, it has been too glibly
assumed that the entire customer loan market is directly a part
of a national credit market. There has been a widespread failure
to recognize the heterogeneity of banking markets and the implications of this heterogeneity for a market structure analysis. Once
the appropriate economic stratification of banking markets is admitted into the analysis as a dominating feature of banking markets, the entire question of the effects of concentrated banking
resources on market concentration assumes a different perspective.

LOW OUTPUT

Availability of credit to local borrowers.—A common charge
against concentrated industries is that they restrict output to secure
high prices, and presumably, therefore, high profits. All banks are
multiproduct firms, but loans are the most characteristic product
of commercial banks as such. Hence, one aspect of this charge concerns the availability of loan credit to business borrowers. Credit
rationing in some degree is, of course, an inevitable feature of bank
credit because bank credit is not available in unlimited quantities.
The two major forms of bank credit are loans and investments. Investments are made impersonally in national markets and primarily
in securities of the United States government, whereas loans are
made primarily in local borrower markets. Hence, the relevant
question is whether branch banks devote a smaller percentage of
their resources to local borrowers than do unit banks.

As a group, branch banks usually had higher ratios of loans
to total assets than unit banks as a group. Moreover, on this same
basis, branch banks usually outperformed the unit banks most
nearly comparable in size, viz., the largest unit banks. Compared
with the average performance of unit banks or with the largest
unit banks, branch banks cannot be charged with restriction of
output. The average performance of both branch and unit banks
masks considerable heterogeneity in the performance of individual banks. For example, in nine out of thirteen years, branch bank
loan output (relatively to assets) was either matched or surpassed
by at least one and sometimes by more than one category of unit
banks. Similarly, at least some unit banks regularly produced relatively more loans than individual branch banks. By the same token,
however, at least some of the individual branch banks made a much
higher percentage of loans than did any of the unit banks. As
explained in chapter v, it is impossible to know whether concen-

tration of banking resources in California has *on balance* restricted
the total level of loan output. However, if restriction of output
is judged by the average performance of branch and unit banks,
the answer is unambiguous. Bank concentration has not meant
restriction of total loan output.

Growth and development.—On another level, the fear has been
expressed that monopolistic banking houses could "so restrict
credit as to hamper growth and development" of an area.[4] The
possibility of this development can be assessed in terms of credit
availability to different categories of borrowers, for the "growth
and development" of an area presumably refers to projects initi-
ated by private borrowers. Even a state-wide monopoly could not
seriously hamper large-scale development projects. Large-scale
projects are usually undertaken by large and important borrowers
who do not need to depend exclusively on local banking resources
for funds.

If the "growth and development of an area" refers to projects
undertaken by medium-size and small borrowers, a state-wide
banking monopoly could temporarily hamper such projects by
withholding capital, since medium-size and small borrowers are
limited to the state and local areas, respectively. Unless capital is
being withheld for sound business reasons, however, such credit
blocks cannot be indefinitely maintained. Given the conditions of
entry as they exist today, evidence of withholding credit to hamper
the development of an area would constitute abundant proof of
the "need" for a new bank. Under existing banking markets, entry
would be almost inevitable. The mere fact that entry, though imperfect, is not blockaded offers sufficient assurance against the kind
of restrictive practice described above. It is worth stating, moreover, that the possibility of such credit blocks in local areas would
be no different under a hypothetical state-wide monopoly from
what it is under existing conditions of unit banking.

Finally, one must wonder why any bank, even a monopoly bank,
would desire to hamper the growth and development of the area
it serves. The bank's own welfare is, after all, directly related to
the economic health and vitality of the business community it
serves. If the charge is just another way of expressing the fear of
general monopoly restriction to enhance profits, then the charge
has been already examined in the analysis of the preceding section,
and will be examined again in a later section on profitability.

[4] Statement of Solicitor for the Board of Governors, Transamerica Hearings.

DISCRIMINATION

Price discrimination.—Monopolies are alleged to discriminate among buyers or, at least, to have the power to discriminate. Whether discrimination has occurred under the conditions of heavy concentration of banking resources in California partly depends upon how discrimination is defined. Discrimination can take many forms. Price discrimination, for example, occurs when a product is sold to different consumers at different prices. That is probably the most common meaning of price discrimination, and in this sense it undoubtedly occurs in California banking. From the bankers' viewpoint, price discrimination to different size borrowers is based upon a complex of factors. The most important considerations are the borrowers' previous borrowing history, the size of the average balance maintained, the value to the bank of the borrower's business, and the costs and risks involved in extending him credit. There can be no doubt that all these factors are of legitimate concern to the banker. The real question, however, is whether all these factors actively *force* price discrimination or whether, realistically, they are intended to *justify* it.

Rates charged borrowers are a result of many considerations; no unique determinant can be identified. But that is not to suggest that all factors carry equal weight. In the complex of factors that affect rates, a most important determinant is the relative bargaining power of different borrowers. Bargaining power in turn is closely related to size of borrower, because size of borrower is highly correlated with the number of effective alternative sources of supply available to a borrower. As a result of their different bargaining strength, rates paid by different size borrowers in California may vary by 100 per cent or more. The fact that loan agreements are individually and secretly negotiated facilitates this kind of extreme price discrimination. The point to remember, however, is that price discrimination of this sort did not develop with the increasing concentration of California banking. Price discrimination antedates the rise of concentration of the past three decades and is a characteristic feature of unit-banking markets as well. In short, this kind of price discrimination would not automatically pass away with the dissolution of existing aggregations of banking power in the form of large branch banks.

Price discrimination based on alleged cost differences merits special attention. For public policy, it is relevant whether or not price differences are based on compensating cost differences. The question in banking is whether price discrimination is *fully* covered by equivalent cost differences. Because of joint costs in the production of bank credit, this question cannot be answered with precision. Reasonable presumptions are not without interest, however.

As discussed in chapter vii, price discrimination cannot be wholly based on cost differences, because (1) banks do not compute direct costs for different size loans; (2) bank costs are not constant, but small loan rates often are; (3) small borrowers face the same loan rates from branch banks and unit banks even though the former (appear to) have a cost advantage over the latter. It would appear, therefore, that price discrimination allegedly based on costs is not in fact always met by equivalent cost differences. To be sure, in certain phases of the cycle, costs may be less than adequately met by price.

The major burden of justifying price differences by cost differences must thus fall upon the differences in risk. Costs may be affected by the risk factor if the actuarial risk of default can be imputed as an effective increase in the cost of making the loan to all loans in a particular category. Statistically, however, the record of losses is not great enough to support the wide differences in prices charged to different size borrowers. As a matter of record, those losses have been slight for many years on *all* loans, and, a fortiori, on small loans as well. To be sure, risks do fluctuate cyclically, but there is no evidence that risk premiums also fluctuate with the cycle. Furthermore, small-loan rates are uniform among banks despite different policies about risk assumption in different banks.[5] It would seem, therefore, that risk differences could not fully account for rate differences. However, this conclusion applies to unit banks as well as to branch banks.

Again, there is very strong indirect evidence that among unit banks at least, price discrimination in rates to small borrowers more than compensates for the higher costs involved in small loans. The evidence cannot be regarded as conclusive because bank costs are not exclusively loan costs, and publicly available figures provide no basis for distinguishing between loan-connected costs and other bank costs. With this proviso, the comparative earnings of different size unit banks is highly suggestive. Net earnings on loans and investments are a good clue to the profit markup in different

[5] C. S. Young of the Seventh Federal Reserve District has noted that "The question of whether a firm is large or small does not of itself have much influence on decisions as to the risk involved in granting a bank loan." Patman Report, Vol. II, p. 810.

banks. The largest unit banks generally earned the lowest net returns on their loans and investments. The size mix of the largest unit banks contains predominantly large loans which are low cost per dollar of loan and which carry low rates because of the strong bargaining position of large borrowers. Presumably, therefore, the markup on large loans is a competitive markup. By contrast, the size mix of small unit banks contains mostly small loans which are high cost per dollar of loan and which carry high rates. Since small unit banks generally earn more than the largest unit banks on their loans and investments, there is a strong presumption that the high rates on small loans more than compensates for the higher costs of small loans and contains monopolylike rents. In other words, it is reasonable to conclude that price discrimination between large and small loans is not fully compensated by differences in cost but is rather a reflection of the great differences in bargaining power of large and small borrowers.

This conclusion accords with a statement of the Comptroller of the Currency that ". . . in some situations, the availability of credit could be broadened, and its cost to American business reduced if a feasible means could be devised for achieving effective banking competition in all communities and areas."[6] This last analysis of price discrimination has dealt exclusively with the small-borrower markets served by unit banks. There is a strong presumption that the same conclusions would hold for branch banks as for unit banks. The matter is impossible of conclusive proof, however, because it is not possible to deduce with absolute certainty how branch bank costs on different size loans compare with those of unit banks.

Discrimination in availability of credit.—Banker discrimination to borrowers may take place not only on a price basis but also in terms of credit availability. The most important role of the commercial banking system as such is allocation of resources through the credit mechanism. Credit is a limited resource, and the granting of credit to some borrowers necessarily implies the withholding of credit from others. The fact of unsatisfied credit demand is not, therefore, presumptive evidence of discrimination in availability of credit. The existence of discrimination must be judged in terms of the criteria by which credit allocation is determined. The granting of a bank loan requires business and financial judgment by the banker. Hence, discrimination is not necessarily implied when credit resources are not fully expended even when there are unsat-

---

[6] Statement of Comptroller of Currency, Patman Report, Vol. II, p. 928.

isfied seekers of funds. The banking decision to withhold funds may be in error, but if so, it is an impersonal error, an error of judgment—not discrimination based on arbitrary considerations.

The kind of discrimination which particularly concerns a market structure study is sinister discrimination by monopolistic (or oligopolistic) suppliers. It has been alleged that the concentration of banking resources in an area could lead to this kind of sinister discrimination, i.e., discrimination intended to injure particular enterprises independently of the business or financial soundness of those enterprises. Large borrowers could not be effectively victimized by this kind of discrimination in an area with concentrated banking resources, because large borrowers have direct access to a national credit market, and no single supplier holds a monopolistic or even an oligopolistic position in that market. However, even borrowers without direct access to a national credit market could not be subjected to other than sporadic sinister discrimination by large and powerful credit suppliers. For reasons detailed in the chapter on entry, sustained and large-scale sinister discrimination is precluded by the conditions of entry not only into California banking, but in banking generally throughout the country. Even in a completely monopolized banking market, such discrimination could occur only if entry were effectively blockaded. Entry conditions into banking are certainly imperfect, but imperfect entry is not blockaded entry.

It would require very detailed information of the operations of each of the Big Four branch banks to know whether any one was guilty of *sporadic* sinister discrimination either through outright refusal of credit, or, alternatively, through outrageous rates. This writer does not have that kind of first-hand knowledge. It is worth mentioning, however, that with all the investigative resources available to the Board of Governors, their legal staff presented no single instance of sinister discrimination with regard to availability of credit in the Transamerica Hearings. This fact is particularly significant because the Transamerica suit involved the Bank of America. If serious abuse through discrimination were possible, Bank of America's enormous size makes it most likely able to exercise that kind of discrimination.

HIGH PROFITS

A serious charge leveled against firms in concentrated industries is that they can and often do exploit their strong market position vis-à-vis their customers to extract monopolistic profits from their operations. The excessive profits charge is integrally related to the charge of high prices and curtailed output which was analyzed earlier. Excess profits in the sense of profits above a competitive norm need not be present even when monopolistic restriction of output and a high price policy are followed. On the other hand, the presence of excessive profits without extenuating circumstances (such as innovations or transitional periods during movements toward new equilibrium positions) is presumptive confirmation of monopolistic price and output policies.

Although the theoretical issues are clear enough, it is far from simple to identify the empirical counterparts of theoretical components. The most obvious difficulty is to establish the competitive norm for profits against which the performance of branch banks can be gauged. This analysis has shown, however, that banking markets generally are not characterized by competition, with the sole exception of the market for prime loans. There are, however, no banks in the entire country which deal exclusively with prime loans. In a very real sense, therefore, there is no bank or category of banks that might serve as a profits criterion for the performance of other banks. Under the circumstances, it is necessary to resort to approximations to the theoretical ideal. The closest empirical counterpart to the theoretical ideal of a bank operating exclusively in competitive banking markets is the category of the largest unit banks. The largest unit banks, because of their size and location in metropolitan areas, deal primarily with large business borrowers. Accordingly, their operating performance is closet to the theoretical equivalent of a bank operating in a competitive market.

The statistical record reveals that the Big Four branch banks were generally more profitable than the largest unit banks, irrespective of whether the measure of profitability was based on loans and investments, on assets, or on capital. Superficially, therefore, the charge that banking concentration leads to monopolistic exploitation and excessive profits would seem to be established. Unfortunately, however, the summary performance of branch banks, which is here compared with that of the largest unit banks, encompasses the net result of branch bank operations in all three of the broad categories of banking markets, i.e., of operations in the competitive loan markets as well as in those which are decidedly not competitive. Thus these figures are consistent with the interpretation that excessive profits have been extracted in the imperfectly competitive markets but not in the competitive loan markets. However, a breakdown of the specific performance of branch banks in each of the several loan markets is simply not available. Moreover, a legitimate difference of opinion can exist on whether the profitability of branch banking should be compared with the largest unit banks only, or with all unit banks as a group. Thus, whether concentrated branch banking results in a monopolistic extraction of excessive profits must remain a matter of interpretation.

As has just been suggested, it might be argued that the most realistic way to examine the "excess profits" charge is not to compare branch banking with some approximation to a theoretical ideal of competition in banking. The comparison might rather be made between branch banking and the only realistic alternative, viz., unit banking. If this line of argument is followed, no single category of unit banks can be isolated for comparison with branch bank performance; the comparison must deal with all the unit banks. This comparison reveals uneven results. Branch banks on the average were less profitable on loans and investments than the unit bank average; branch banks were about equally profitable with unit banks on an assets basis; and branch banks were definitely more profitable than unit banks when earnings are measured on a capital basis.

Of the three measures of profitability—earnings on loans and investments, assets, and capital—the most relevant one for appraising the monopoly charge of excessive profits is the comparative performance of branch banks and unit banks on a loans and investments basis. This latter measure is a clue to the amount of the markup over costs. If branch banks extract monopoly profits, it should show up most clearly in the earnings on loans and investments, because the assets measure of profitability is also a result of high branch bank load factors whereas the capital measure of profitability depends, in addition, on the low capital-deposit ratio of branch banks. But neither the high load factor nor the low capital-deposit ratios of branch banks is owing to monopolistic activity by the branch banks. On the basis of loans and investments, however, branch banks as a group are less profitable than unit banks as a group. Thus, this statistical test is consistent with the interpretation that branch banks have not extracted monopoly profits from their customers because of their concentrated position in California banking markets.

The acceptability of this view, too, must depend upon individual interpretation. It could be argued that the lesser profitability of branch banks on earnings on loans and investments is primarily because branch banks, owing to their enormous size, automatically are involved at least in part in the operations of competitive banking markets, with a resultant net reduction in their profitability on loans and investments. By contrast, the majority of unit banks are considerably smaller than the branch banks and operate, therefore, in smaller loan markets which this analysis has shown are imperfectly competitive. Hence, the question is again raised whether the proper basis for comparing branch and unit bank performance is in terms of specific kinds of output or on over-all performance. Again, the answer to this question is necessarily subjective.

The problem of noncomparability of portfolios between branch banks and the largest unit banks or between branch banks and unit banks as a group can be very crudely overcome by comparing branch banks with the penultimate category of unit banks. The penultimate category of unit banks is, like the branch banks, large enough to operate in the competitive large loan markets, and is also small enough to have significant contact with the imperfectly competitive smaller loan markets, again like branch banks. In a very rough sort of way, the business loan portfolios of the penultimate size unit banks is an approximate microcosm of the branch bank portfolios. This comparison reveals that branch banks are less profitable than the penultimate size unit banks by all three measures of profitability. This conclusion suggests, therefore, that branch banks have not exploited their concentrated position to extract greater profits than the nearest "comparable" unit bank; indeed, they earned less profits.

The results of this comparison, too, are subject to individual interpretation of different investigators. Even if the obvious imperfections in alleging comparable portfolios between branch banks and the penultimate size unit banks be ignored, it is legitimate to wonder whether the penultimate size unit bank is most nearly "comparable" to the branch banks. Even if the size mix of its portfolio structure be most similar to that of the branch banks, the largest unit banks are more nearly comparable to the branch banks in terms of size—and size is an important determinant of price, cost, and profit variables. In short, in appraising the excess profits monopoly charge, is portfolio similarity or size similarity the more important consideration in selecting the most nearly comparable unit bank?

The preceding discussion has shown that it is impossible to answer uniquely the monopoly charge of excess profits leveled

against concentrated banking markets. In part, the difficulty is owing to inadequacies of the data. More important, however, a unique
answer could not be given even if the data were perfect in every
respect. Statistics can only describe facts, but a decision on the
monopoly charge also involves an inescapable element of human
judgment. The most important area of discretion is the selection
of the basis of comparison. In this latter connection, the preceding discussion has concentrated on the difficulties of selecting the
unit bank or banks on which to base the comparison. However,
the branch banks themselves are not homogeneous in all critical
aspects. The question must thus be faced whether some particular
unit bank or all unit banks should be selected as a base to gauge
the performance of branch banks as a group or of some individual
branch bank.

For all these reasons, the element of human judgment is unavoidable, and, to this extent, an evaluation of the excessive profits
monopoly charge must remain a matter of individual interpretation. In any particular policy decision, the particular context of
the problem may help to narrow the alternatives but it is unlikely
that the relevant alternatives could be narrowed until only one
remained. Ultimately, the resolution of this question must involve
an arbitrary decision.

The subjective nature of the decision on the excessive profits
charge has been stressed. It is important to stress, too, that the
interpretive problems concern only the limited and narrow question of excessive profits per se. The ambiguity on this point is
not communicated—certainly not to the same degree—to the more
general question of the market structure of different banking markets. Profits performance can be a clue to market structures and
market performance, even if it is sometimes a fallible clue. However, the determination of the kinds of market structures in different banking markets can be made without reference to profits
performance. The discussion of the pricing chapters and the examination of the relevant institutional characteristics of different
banking markets leave little room for uncertainty as to the general
character of those markets.

SUMMARY

The concentration of banking resources in California under branch
banking has been amply documented. To those with a bias against
economic concentration in any form and independently of other
considerations, the policy prescription would call for the dissolu-

tion of existing aggregations of financial power. To the economist *qua* economist, however, normative prescription is of less legitimate concern than the more pedestrian tracings of economic analysis. Cause and effect relationships are par excellence the mechanism of economic investigation.

In strictly economic terms, the concentration of banking resources has been long feared and fought because it is widely believed to undermine "competitive" unit banking structures. This analysis has revealed the very limited extent of price competition in unit banking markets. This analysis has also shown that, except for the intermediate-size borrowers, the *effective* concentration in different banking markets in California is no greater under branch banking than it is under unit banking. As long as the separation of customer loan markets is taken into account, this result is likely in any other area where concentration develops in the form of large branch banks.

As far as the consumer of bank lending services is concerned, the growth of branch banking in California has not been deleterious as compared to unit banking, with the possible exception of the medium-size borrowers. At the present time, price performance is similar in branch and unit banks. As a result of their superior lending power in local markets, branch banks have produced a larger volume of loans per dollar of assets than unit banks as a group. As a function of their structure, branch banks have also been able to make banking facilities available in areas where unit banks could not survive. Finally, branch banks have demonstrable economies of scale and of structure which are not available to unit banks generally.

The price society must pay for the various efficiencies and other advantages of branch banking is an unavoidable concentration of financial power. Whether society wishes to pay this price cannot be determined by economic considerations alone. Efficiency, for example, is a major economic criterion of performance. In a democratic society, however, efficiency is sometimes deliberately sacrificed to broader political and social goals, as in the separation of powers in the structure of the federal government. It is beyond the scope of the present study to speculate on these broader aspects of banking organization. The major attempt in this investigation has been to reveal the nature and consequences of concentrating banking resources in the form of branch banking, and to provide an economic base for policy decisions involving banking concentration.

APPENDIX

APPENDIX

The following comments are pertinent for tables 16, 17, 21–24, 26, 29–32, and all tables in this Appendix except tables L and M.

(1) All figures in these tables are based on data published by the Federal Reserve Bank of San Francisco, *Operating Ratios of Member Banks, Twelfth Federal Reserve District,* 1938–1950.

(2) Federal Reserve figures are arithmetic averages of individual bank operating ratios, not ratios obtained from dollar totals for all banks. The operations of each bank, irrespective of its size, have equal weight in the determination of the average.

(3) In the Federal Reserve Operating Ratios of Member Banks, ratios for the Big Four branch banks are not listed separately, but are included in the appropriate size category with other banks. In this study, the Federal Reserve figures have been adjusted to exclude ratios for the Big Four branch banks. The latter are presented separately because of their special interest in this study. (The only exception concerns 1938 and 1939; see n. 4, below.) Since the branch banks always fell in the largest category, the adjusted figures for the largest unit banks are fully comparable with the figures for other size categories.

(4) The branch bank average has been computed similarly to the ratios for unit banks in any given size category. Specifically, the branch bank average is an arithmetic average of individual branch bank ratios, with each bank thus receiving equal weight. In 1938 and 1939, however, the branch bank average does not include Anglo-California Bank. For 1938 and 1939, the author was unable to obtain separate figures for Anglo Bank. Therefore, Anglo Bank is included in the largest category of unit banks in those years.

(5) Federal Reserve size groupings of banks changed considerably during the study period. For example, the smallest category of banks in 1938 was described as "Under $250,000," but in 1950 the smallest category was "Under $2,000,000." Hence, in this study, absolute size groupings were ignored, and banks were ranked by size from smallest to largest in each year. Accordingly, the tables can only be read vertically, but not horizontally. Table L in this Appendix shows the actual size groupings of unit banks, classified by dollar-volume of deposits for the years included in the study.

(6) The unit bank average was computed by weighting the figures in each size category by the number of banks in that category in each year, respectively. Table M in this Appendix shows the number of unit banks in different size categories for the years studied.

The preceding general comments apply to all the tables listed above. All tables are based on the Federal Reserve Operating Ratios (cf. n. 1, above). However, certain ratios employed in this study were not directly available in the desired form in the published statements of the Federal Reserve. The figures in the tables listed below were derived by simple algebraic computations. For the branch banks, there is no bias because the individual branch bank figures were made available to the author. For the unit banks, bias presents no serious problem because of the homogeneity of banks within each size category.

For convenience in discussing the tables, the following symbols are used.

W&S—wages and salaries
L&I—loans and investments
TE—total earnings
TA—total assets
ITD—interest on time deposits
MX—all other (miscellaneous) expenses
NE—net earnings from current operations before taxes
TX—total expenses (does not include income taxes)
ME—all other (miscellaneous) earnings
L—loans
T_1D—time deposits
T_oD—total deposits
S—total securities
C—capital

Table 21. $TX/L\&I = TX/TE \, (TE/TA \div L\&I/TA)$
Table 22. $W\&S/L\&I = W\&S/TE \, (TE/TA \div L\&I/TA)$
Table 23. $ITD/L\&I = ITD/TE \, (TE/TA \div L\&I/TA)$
Table 24. $MX/L\&I = MX/TE \, (TE/TA \div L\&I/TA)$
Table 29. $NE/L\&I = NE/TA \div L\&I/TA$

Table 30. For the years 1938–1941, net earnings were adjusted for taxes by multiplying NE/TE by TE/TA. Federal Reserve figures were employed directly for all other years.

Table 31. For the years 1938–1941, net earnings were adjusted for taxes. The Federal Reserve figures gave net earnings after taxes as a percentage of capital. These figures were made comparable with later years by multiplying them by the ratio of net earnings before taxes to net earnings after taxes. Federal Reserve figures were employed directly for all others years.

Table C. $W\&S/TX = W\&S/TE \div TX/TE$
Table D. $ITD/TX = ITD/TE \div TX/TE$
Table E. $MX/TX = MX/TE \div TX/TE$
Table G. $C/TA \div C/T_oD = T_oD/TA$
    $T_oD/TA \div L\&I/TA = T_oD/L\&I$
    $T_1D/L\&I = (T_oD/L\&I) \, (T_1D/T_oD)$
Table H. $L/L\&I = L/TA \div L\&I/TA$
Table J. $S/L\&I = S/TA \div L\&I/TA$
Table K. $ME/L\&I = ME/TA \div L\&I/TA$

TABLE A

Time Deposits as a Percentage of Total Deposits by Size and Kind of Bank, California, 1938–1950

Unit banks (by size)	1938	1939	1940	1941	1942	1943	1944	1945	1946	1947	1948	1949	1950
Smallest	48.5	43.5	42.9	41.4	40.2	34.7	35.6	30.1	27.6	25.6	24.4	29.8	25.4
2	43.5	45.0	53.6	49.9	37.1	31.0	28.4	31.7	32.4	34.5	35.9	37.5	37.5
3	51.1	52.1	44.6	42.4	44.1	29.4	36.7	35.7	35.8	39.2	40.0	40.8	41.6
4	45.8	46.0	52.7	51.3	43.7	38.9	32.8	32.6	36.8	40.8	42.2	42.8	42.2
5	56.3	54.7	51.6	52.0	29.7	35.5	31.5	33.5	34.5	39.2	39.6	38.5	41.0
6	53.9	53.4	55.5	49.9	....	23.9	23.4	23.4	25.5	29.9	30.0	30.5	29.4
7	56.3	55.5	37.5	34.7	....	....	....	....	....	....	....	....	....
8	43.4	41.5	....	....	....	....	....	....	....	....	....	....	....
Unit bank average	49.7	49.9	49.1	46.8	39.8	32.6	32.2	32.5	33.6	35.9	37.1	38.1	38.0
Branch bank average	57.6	55.4	50.2	47.0	41.8	34.2	33.7	34.9	36.8	41.2	41.7	43.0	43.0

TABLE B

TOTAL SECURITIES (A), U. S. GOVERNMENT SECURITIES (B), OTHER SECURITIES (C), AS A PERCENTAGE OF TOTAL ASSETS, BY SIZE AND KIND OF BANK, CALIFORNIA, 1938–1950

Unit banks (by size)	A													B									C								
	1938	1939	1940	1941	1942	1943	1944	1945	1946	1947	1948	1949	1950	1942	1943	1944	1945	1946	1947	1948	1949	1950	1942	1943	1944	1945	1946	1947	1948	1949	1950
Smallest	19.1	19.4	18.9	21.0	28.9	43.3	54.5	55.3	59.0	49.0	44.6	41.9	35.0	18.4	33.8	47.6	51.6	55.5	46.2	43.3	39.7	33.3	10.5	9.5	6.9	3.7	3.5	2.8	1.3	2.2	1.7
2	26.7	21.0	27.1	24.2	30.8	41.9	57.7	61.5	60.0	55.3	48.3	46.2	45.8	20.1	34.7	52.2	56.8	56.3	51.4	44.0	41.8	41.3	10.7	7.2	5.5	4.7	3.7	3.9	4.3	4.4	4.5
3	29.5	27.0	24.6	22.0	31.3	48.0	58.1	63.2	62.9	58.6	54.0	51.5	47.6	21.2	40.0	52.5	58.7	58.9	53.7	48.8	46.4	42.8	10.1	8.0	5.6	4.5	4.0	4.9	5.2	5.1	4.8
4	24.1	24.3	22.2	20.6	25.7	46.6	57.6	59.4	59.2	51.7	48.2	46.7	46.5	19.2	40.1	54.5	56.9	55.7	49.0	44.6	42.5	40.7	6.5	6.5	3.1	2.5	3.5	2.7	3.6	4.2	5.8
5	32.6	27.4	31.5	35.7	42.0	49.4	56.6	60.9	58.2	49.4	45.1	47.4	45.5	38.1	45.0	51.6	56.8	53.6	44.4	40.1	41.4	40.2	3.9	4.4	5.0	4.1	4.6	5.0	5.0	6.0	5.3
6	30.3	27.7	21.8	19.3	…	57.3	62.9	66.8	66.0	58.6	54.0	54.9	57.0	…	54.5	60.9	65.2	64.6	56.7	51.9	52.7	53.8	3.9	2.8	2.0	1.6	1.4	1.9	2.1	2.2	3.2
7	27.7	26.9	41.0	40.6	…	…	…	…	…	…	…	…	…	…	…	…	…	…	…	…	…	…	…	…	…	…	…	…	…	…	…
8	38.5	41.4	…	…	…	…	…	…	…	…	…	…	…	…	…	…	…	…	…	…	…	…	…	…	…	…	…	…	…	…	…
Unit bank average	28.5	26.6	25.2	23.9	30.9	46.2	57.6	61.5	61.1	55.6	50.1	47.8	46.0	21.3	39.2	52.2	57.4	57.4	51.6	45.8	43.8	41.6	9.6	7.0	5.4	4.1	3.7	4.0	4.3	4.0	4.4
Branch bank average	34.6	35.1	35.0	33.3	37.1	51.8	59.8	63.6	62.2	51.6	43.7	42.8	45.1	27.9	45.2	54.6	59.2	57.8	47.0	39.4	37.9	39.1	9.2	6.6	5.2	4.4	4.4	4.6	4.3	4.9	6.0

TABLE C

Wages and Salaries as a Percentage of Total Expenses by Size and Kind of Bank, California, 1938–1950

Unit banks (by size)	1938	1939	1940	1941	1942	1943	1944	1945	1946	1947	1948	1949	1950
Smallest	51	47	52	53	47	51	47	50	53	50	53	50	53
2	50	51	44	45	47	48	48	49	49	50	49	49	49
3	46	45	46	49	45	50	48	46	47	50	47	48	48
4	46	46	45	46	41	46	43	43	46	45	45	45	45
5	44	44	46	46	46	45	43	42	46	45	46	47	48
6	46	45	39	43	..	50	49	49	52	51	52	53	52
7	39	38	46	47	..	..	..	..	..	..	..	..	..
8	44	44	..	..	..	..	..	..	..	..	..	..	..
Unit bank average	46	45	46	47	46	48	46	47	48	49	48	47	49
Branch bank average	44	43	44	47	46	47	47	46	49	49	47	48	47

TABLE D

Interest on Time Deposits as a Percentage of Total Expenses by Size and Kind of Bank, California, 1938–1950

Unit banks (by size)	1938	1939	1940	1941	1942	1943	1944	1945	1946	1947	1948	1949	1950
Smallest	20	17	19	19	20	16	22	18	13	9	9	10	9
2	18	19	29	27	21	20	18	22	20	20	21	21	20
3	29	28	26	25	24	17	21	23	22	22	23	24	23
4	25	26	29	27	24	22	21	23	23	23	25	23	22
5	33	30	30	30	21	23	24	25	24	24	25	21	22
6	32	31	31	27	..	16	18	18	17	17	15	15	15
7	33	29	25	22	..	..	..	..	..	..	..	..	..
8	29	27	..	..	..	..	..	..	..	..	..	..	..
Unit bank average	27	27	27	26	22	19	20	22	21	21	21	21	20
Branch bank average	33	30	30	27	23	19	18	23	22	22	22	22	25

TABLE E

All Other Expenses as a Percentage of Total Expenses by Size and Kind of Bank, California, 1938–1950

Unit banks (by size)	1938	1939	1940	1941	1942	1943	1944	1945	1946	1947	1948	1949	1950
Smallest	29	34	27	28	33	32	31	33	34	41	38	39	38
2	32	27	24	30	33	32	34	31	30	31	29	30	30
3	25	25	25	24	31	33	30	32	31	29	29	28	29
4	29	26	24	27	35	32	36	30	31	31	30	32	33
5	22	23	21	24	35	31	34	33	30	31	29	32	30
6	22	21	26	30	..	34	34	33	30	32	29	32	33
7	28	28	26	30	..	..	..	..	..	..	..	..	..
8	28	26	..	..	..	..	..	..	..	..	..	..	..
Unit bank average	27	25	25	27	33	32	32	32	31	31	30	31	31
Branch bank average	23	23	24	27	32	34	32	31	30	30	31	30	28

TABLE F

Interest on Time Deposits as a Percentage of Time Deposits by Size and Kind of Bank, California, 1938–1950

Unit banks (by size)	1938	1939	1940	1941	1942	1943	1944	1945	1946	1947	1948	1949	1950
Smallest	2.0	2.2	1.7	1.7	1.4	1.2	0.9	0.8	0.7	0.9	0.9	1.0	1.0
2	1.7	1.8	1.7	1.6	1.4	1.0	0.8	0.8	0.8	0.8	1.0	1.2	1.2
3	1.7	1.7	1.5	1.5	1.4	0.9	0.9	0.8	0.8	0.9	1.0	1.1	1.2
4	1.7	1.7	1.6	1.5	1.3	1.0	0.9	0.9	0.9	0.9	1.1	1.1	1.2
5	1.7	1.6	1.6	1.4	1.0	1.0	1.0	0.9	0.9	0.9	1.1	1.1	1.2
6	1.8	1.7	1.6	1.4	...	0.8	0.8	0.8	0.8	0.7	0.7	0.8	0.9
7	1.7	1.5	1.2	1.3	...	...	...	...	...	...	...	...	...
8	1.5	1.4	...	...	...	...	...	...	...	...	...	...	...
Unit bank average	1.7	1.7	1.6	1.5	1.4	1.0	0.9	0.8	0.8	0.8	1.0	1.1	1.2
Branch bank average	1.5	1.5	1.4	1.3	1.2	0.8	0.8	0.8	0.8	0.9	0.9	1.0	1.2

TABLE G

TIME DEPOSITS AS A PERCENTAGE OF LOANS AND INVESTMENTS, BY SIZE AND KIND OF BANK, CALIFORNIA, 1939–1950

Unit banks (by size)	1939	1940	1943	1944	1945	1946	1947	1948	1949	1950
Smallest	56.3	88.5	50.3	49.9	41.1	35.8	32.8	32.3	40.2	33.4
2	86.4	91.9	46.8	37.6	42.1	40.9	42.4	44.7	45.9	45.2
3	84.2	92.0	41.2	46.6	44.2	43.8	47.0	47.2	48.2	49.1
4	76.0	102.1	53.8	42.0	41.1	45.1	50.6	52.1	52.8	51.8
5	99.1	102.6	45.8	40.0	42.0	41.4	46.5	47.8	45.5	46.6
6	92.8	101.4	31.2	29.4	29.9	38.4	37.3	38.6	38.8	35.8
7	94.6	76.2	....	....	....	....	....	....	....	....
8	75.2	....	....	....	....	....	....	....	....	....
Unit bank average	85.3	94.1	46.2	42.3	41.2	42.1	45.3	45.4	46.5	45.7
Branch bank average	81.5	80.2	42.0	40.4	40.6	43.6	49.5	50.4	51.3	49.8

TABLE H

Loans as a Percentage of Loans and Investments, by Size and Kind of Bank, California, 1938–1950

Unit banks (by size)	1938	1939	1940	1941	1942	1943	1944	1945	1946	1947	1948	1949	1950
Smallest	72.6	73.5	69.5	66.1	48.9	30.9	18.4	19.6	16.9	29.4	36.0	37.8	48.5
2	61.7	68.0	61.0	62.5	49.7	32.1	18.3	14.8	19.5	26.8	35.7	38.8	39.3
3	58.6	61.9	62.7	64.4	50.8	26.2	20.8	17.0	19.7	26.3	31.8	34.4	39.6
4	64.9	65.2	66.8	68.1	58.8	30.8	22.0	19.9	22.5	32.0	37.0	39.0	38.7
5	55.5	60.2	51.5	45.5	37.6	31.6	24.1	21.7	26.7	37.5	42.1	39.6	44.4
6	57.1	59.7	67.8	70.3	....	20.7	15.9	13.4	14.5	22.4	27.3	27.4	26.4
7	60.1	61.6	39.5	39.5	....	....	....	....	....	....	....	....	....
8	45.3	41.3	....	....	....	....	....	....	....	....	....	....	....
Unit bank average	59.6	61.8	62.2	61.8	49.9	29.3	19.5	16.7	19.8	27.7	34.5	36.7	39.7
Branch bank average	55.0	54.0	51.8	54.0	48.9	31.4	24.4	20.9	22.7	34.6	43.5	45.7	44.2

TABLE I

Returns on Total Securities as a Percentage of Total Securities (A); Interest on U. S. Government Securities as a Percentage of Total U. S. Government Securities (B); Interest and Dividends on Other Securities as a Percentage of Total Other Securities (C), by Size and Kind of Bank, California, 1938–1950

Unit banks (by size)	A													B						C					
	1938	1939	1940	1941	1942	1943	1944	1945	1946	1947	1948	1949	1950	1945	1946	1947	1948	1949	1950	1945	1946	1947	1948	1949	1950
Smallest	4.2	10.8	4.5	4.2	2.5	1.8	1.6	1.5	1.3	1.6	1.3	1.6	1.5	1.5	1.3	1.6	1.3	1.6	1.5	3.1	3.3	2.2	2.0	3.6	3.7
2	4.3	6.5	3.7	4.0	2.3	1.5	1.4	1.3	1.4	1.5	1.5	1.6	1.6	1.3	1.4	1.5	1.5	1.6	1.6	3.5	3.4	3.0	3.0	2.9	2.8
3	4.9	4.2	5.5	5.3	2.4	1.6	1.4	1.3	1.4	1.5	1.5	1.6	1.6	1.3	1.4	1.5	1.5	1.6	1.6	3.0	3.3	3.0	3.0	3.0	2.7
4	4.3	4.4	3.8	3.4	2.1	1.6	1.4	1.3	1.4	1.4	1.4	1.5	1.5	1.3	1.4	1.4	1.4	1.5	1.5	2.7	2.8	2.8	2.3	2.3	1.9
5	3.5	4.0	3.4	3.2	2.3	1.3	1.4	1.2	1.3	1.4	1.6	1.5	1.5	1.2	1.3	1.4	1.6	1.5	1.5	4.4	3.6	3.8	3.7	3.8	3.3
6	3.7	3.8	4.0	3.0	…	1.7	1.6	1.5	1.5	1.6	1.7	1.8	1.7	1.5	1.5	1.6	1.7	1.8	1.7	3.8	3.8	4.7	3.9	2.8	2.0
7	4.0	3.7	2.8	2.7	…	…	…	…	…	…	…	…	…	…	…	…	…	…	…	…	…	…	…	…	…
8	3.1	3.3	…	…	…	…	…	…	…	…	…	…	…	…	…	…	…	…	…	…	…	…	…	…	…
Unit bank average	4.2	4.5	4.1	3.9	2.3	1.6	1.4	1.3	1.4	1.5	1.5	1.6	1.6	1.3	1.4	1.5	1.5	1.6	1.6	3.3	3.3	3.0	2.9	2.9	2.7
Branch bank average	3.4	3.3	2.8	2.7	1.9	1.5	1.4	1.2	1.3	1.4	1.4	1.5	1.5	1.2	1.3	1.4	1.4	1.5	1.5	2.8	2.6	2.4	2.4	2.5	2.3

TABLE J

Total Securities (A), U. S. Government Securities (B), Other Securities (C), as a Percentage of Loans and Investments, by Size and Kind of Bank, California, 1938–1950

Unit banks (by size)	A													B									C								
	1938	1939	1940	1941	1942	1943	1944	1945	1946	1947	1948	1949	1950	1942	1943	1944	1945	1946	1947	1948	1949	1950	1942	1943	1944	1945	1946	1947	1948	1949	1950
Smallest	27.3	26.5	30.5	33.8	32.0	53.9	71.3	75.0	78.2	66.6	62.1	58.9	49.0	32.0	53.9	71.3	75.0	78.2	66.6	62.1	58.9	49.0	18.6	15.6	10.3	5.3	4.9	4.0	1.9	3.2	2.5
2	38.3	32.0	39.0	37.5	32.8	56.2	73.9	78.7	68.1	68.1	58.6	55.3	54.8	32.8	56.2	73.9	78.7	68.1	68.1	58.6	55.3	54.8	17.5	11.6	7.8	6.5	4.9	5.1	5.7	5.8	5.8
3	41.4	38.1	38.9	35.6	33.3	61.5	71.5	77.1	75.2	67.5	61.6	59.1	54.3	33.3	61.5	71.5	77.1	75.2	67.5	61.6	59.1	54.3	15.9	12.3	7.6	5.9	5.1	6.1	6.6	6.5	6.1
4	35.1	34.7	33.2	31.9	30.8	59.5	73.8	76.7	72.9	64.6	58.3	55.5	53.6	30.8	59.5	73.8	76.7	72.9	64.6	58.3	55.5	53.6	10.4	9.6	4.2	3.7	4.6	3.6	4.7	5.5	7.6
5	44.5	39.8	48.5	54.5	56.3	62.3	69.2	73.0	67.5	56.1	51.3	52.7	49.1	56.3	62.3	69.2	73.0	67.5	56.1	51.3	52.7	49.1	5.9	6.0	6.7	5.3	5.8	6.3	6.4	7.6	6.5
6	42.9	40.3	32.2	29.7	…	75.4	81.1	84.2	83.6	74.8	69.9	69.5	69.3	…	75.4	81.1	84.2	83.6	74.8	69.9	69.5	69.3	…	4.0	2.8	2.0	1.8	2.6	2.9	3.0	4.2
7	39.9	38.4	60.5	60.6	…	…	…	…	…	…	…	…	…	…	…	…	…	…	…	…	…	…	…	…	…	…	…	…	…	…	…
8	54.7	58.8	…	…	…	…	…	…	…	…	…	…	…	…	…	…	…	…	…	…	…	…	…	…	…	…	…	…	…	…	…
Unit bank average	40.1	38.2	38.1	37.2	34.2	59.8	73.0	77.7	71.5	67.2	60.1	57.6	54.5	34.2	59.8	73.0	77.7	71.5	67.2	60.1	57.6	54.5	15.8	10.9	7.5	5.2	4.8	5.2	5.5	5.6	5.8
Branch bank averages	45.1	45.9	47.9	45.8	38.4	59.6	69.1	74.0	71.8	59.5	50.7	48.2	48.5	38.4	59.6	69.1	74.0	71.8	59.5	50.7	48.2	48.5	12.7	8.7	6.5	5.5	5.5	5.8	5.6	6.2	7.4

TABLE K

Other Current Earnings as a Percentage of Loans and Investments, by Size and Kind of Bank, California, 1938–1950

Unit banks (by size)	1938	1939	1940	1941	1942	1943	1944	1945	1946	1947	1948	1949	1950
Smallest	1.83	0.86	1.26	1.18	0.45	0.93	0.56	0.49	0.75	0.92	1.57	1.35	1.53
2	0.99	1.12	0.84	1.12	0.75	0.81	0.52	0.44	0.47	0.54	0.61	0.61	0.68
3	0.83	0.85	0.85	0.92	0.84	0.66	0.56	0.45	0.41	0.45	0.53	0.57	0.61
4	0.88	0.79	0.92	0.97	0.91	0.65	0.52	0.46	0.49	0.51	0.58	0.64	0.74
5	0.86	0.84	1.01	0.91	0.61	0.61	0.48	0.44	0.46	0.53	0.55	0.64	0.63
6	1.09	1.01	1.22	1.11	....	0.40	0.36	0.31	0.37	0.45	0.50	0.54	0.52
7	1.36	1.27	0.66	0.62	....	....	....	....	....	....	....	....	....
8	0.75	0.61	....	....	....	....	....	....	....	....	....	....	....
Unit bank average	0.94	0.88	1.00	1.00	0.72	0.70	0.53	0.44	0.46	0.52	0.63	0.67	0.73
Branch bank average	0.81	0.78	0.68	0.67	0.56	0.46	0.41	0.39	0.38	0.45	0.50	0.53	0.54

TABLE L

Size of Unit Banks Classified by Deposits, California, 1938–1950
(Federal Reserve Bank Classification)

Deposits (in thousands of dollars)[a]	1938	1939	1940	1941	1942	1943	1944	1945	1946	1947	1948	1949	1950
Under 250	1[a]	1[a]											
250–500	2	2											
Under 500			1[a]	1[a]									
500–1,000	3	3	2	2									
Under 1,000					1[a]	1[a]							
1,000–2,000	4	4	3	3	2	2							
Under 2,000							1[a]	1[a]	1[a]	1[a]	1[a]	1[a]	1[a]
2,000–5,000	5	5	4	4		3	2	2	2	2	2	2	2
2,000–10,000					3								
5,000–10,000	6	6	5	5									
5,000–15,000							3	3	3	3	3	3	3
5,000–25,000						4							
10,000–50,000	7	7	6	6	4								
15,000–50,000							4	4	4	4	4	4	4
25,000–100,000						5							
Over 50,000	8	8	7	7	5								
50,000–130,000							5						
50,000–150,000								5	5	5	5	5	5
Over 200,000						6	6						
Over 250,000								6	6				
Over 270,000										6	6		
Over 275,000												6	6

[a] Indicates *smallest* size category of bank for each year, respectively.

TABLE M

Number of Unit Banks in Different Size Categories, California, 1938–1950

Size of bank	1938	1939	1940	1941	1942	1943	1944	1945	1946	1947	1948	1949	1950
Smallest	3	3	14	11	24	9	17	9	5	5	7	11	10
2	14	13	26	26	28	28	37	40	41	43	41	39	40
3	36	33	24	25	38	32	31	33	36	36	35	34	36
4	24	21	21	21	9	26	9	12	14	14	14	14	13
5	14	18	8	7	7	6	4	5	5	5	5	4	6
6	8	8	8	10	..	6	6	6	6	6	6	6	6
7	7	7	6	6	..	..	..	..	..	..	..	..	..
8	5	6	..	..	..	..	..	..	..	..	..	..	..

INDEX

Adelman, M. A., 25 n.

American Trust Company. *See* Big Four branch banks

Anglo-California Bank. *See* Big Four branch banks

Bank of America. *See* Big Four branch banks

Bankers Trust Company, 114

Banks: role of, 9–12; and size of cities, 44; number of, by cities, 46, 51; offices of Big Four, 47–48; in metropolitan areas, 49; "giant," 92–93; operating ratios of (12th district), 235. *See also* Branch banks; Unit banks

Beckhart, Benjamin H., 133 n., 143 n.

Big Four branch banks: defined, 38; in national markets, 40–41; concentration of, 42–44; and large borrowers, 46–47; and intermediate-size borrowers, 48; number of competitors, 49–50; load factor of, 57, 60, 65–66; investments of, 63–64; loans of, 67–74; unit costs of, 87–88; wage costs of, 88–90; location of branches, 91; interest costs of, 93–95; miscellaneous costs of, 95; interest rates of, 109–111; interest rate policy of, 111–127; entry by, 210–213. *See also* Branch banks

Borrower, size of: and sources of funds, 22–24, 35–36, 38–39; and interest rates, 36–37, 113–125; defined, 41; and entry, 197–200; and concentration, 219–221. *See also* Concentration

Borrowing by banks: profit theory of, 153–154, 163; tradition against, 155–156; need theory of, 156–158; need theory vs. profit theory, 159–160; reasons for not, 168

Branch banks: defined for California, 38; concentration of, 39–54; load factors of, 57–58; investments of, 62–64; and loan output, 66–76; costs of, 87–95; costs of, compared to unit banks, 96–107; interest rate policy of, 111–127; interest rates of, 127–128; earnings on loans and investments, 177–181; earnings on assets, 183–185; earnings on capital, 188–194; entry of, 201–202, 216; and monopoly behavior, 221–232

Burgess, Randolph W., 132 n., 134, 135 n., 136 n., 143 n., 146 n.

Capacity. *See* Load factor

Capital funds: and earnings, 30, 184–191; and deposits, 186; and entry, 200–201

Cartinhour, Gaines T., 31 n.

Chamberlin, Edward H., 8, 33 n., 83, 149

Chandler, L. V., 20, 21 n.

Chapman, John M., 26 n., 33 n.

Chase National Bank, 94 n., 95, 114, 205

Chemical Bank, 114

Clark, Lawrence E., 156 n.

Clearinghouse agreements, 25–26

Competition: from non-bank suppliers, 12–20; legal restraints on, 24–25, 205–206; and independent action, 25–26; between open market and customer loan market, 141 ff.; and discount rates, 169; and entry, 195, 209, 215–216; among branches of a bank, 199–200. *See also* Concentration; Customer loan market; Size of borrower

Concentration: measuring problems, 39–40; in large borrower markets, 40–41; in intermediate-size borrower markets, 41–44; comparison of California and U.S., 43 ff., 51–52; in small-borrower markets, 44–46; in California, 47–52; and loan production, 66–74; and monopoly behavior. *See also* Monopoly

Costs: and size of city, 29–31; of unit banks, 77–87; of branch banks, 87–95; compared for branch and unit banks, 96–107; and rate differences, 119–120; and discount rate, 168–170; and net earnings, 177–179; and time deposits, 240, 242. *See also* Expenses

Credit, availability of: and size of borrower, 23–24; and open market, 148; and prime rate changes, 149; and central bank, 160; and number of branches, 199; and market structure, 218–219; to local borrowers, 222–223; and discrimination, 226–227. *See also* Loans

Credit, non-bank suppliers of: private individuals, 12–13; Federal Reserve banks, 13; Reconstruction Finance Corporation, 13–14; trade credit, 14–15, 19; finance companies, 15–19

Currie, Lauchlin, 159, 160, 167, 168

Customer loan markets: characteristics of, 22–25; in small towns, 31–33; in large cities, 33–37; and open market competition, 141 ff.; and discount rate,